NOTES ON
BLOOD MERIDIAN

Southwestern Writers Collection Series
Connie Todd, EDITOR

The Southwestern Writers Collection Series originates from the Southwestern Writers Collection, an archive and literary center established at Texas State University–San Marcos to celebrate the region's writers and literary heritage.

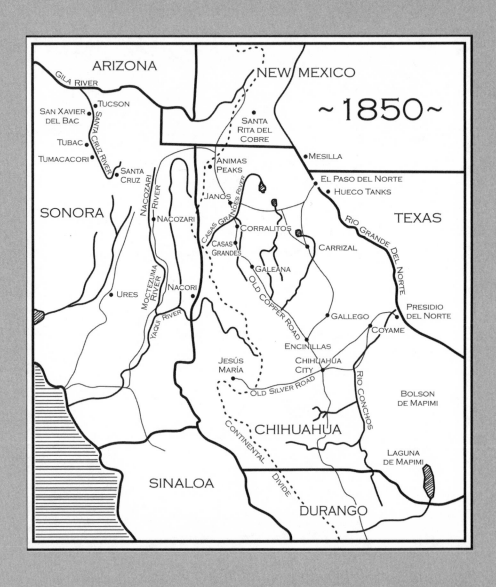

NOTES ON
BLOOD MERIDIAN

REVISED AND EXPANDED EDITION

John Sepich

Foreword by Edwin T. Arnold

UNIVERSITY OF TEXAS PRESS AUSTIN

The essay "Tarot and Divination" appeared, in slightly different form, as "The Dance of History in Cormac McCarthy's *Blood Meridian*," *Southern Literary Journal* 24, no. 1 (Fall 1991): 16–31. A group of selected items appeared as "'What kind of indians was them?' Some Historical Sources in Cormac McCarthy's *Blood Meridian*," *Southern Quarterly* 30, no. 4 (Summer 1992): 93–110. The essay "Judge Holden's Gunpowder" and selected other notes appeared as "A 'bloody dark pastryman': Cormac McCarthy's Recipe for Gunpowder and Historical Fiction in *Blood Meridian*," *Mississippi Quarterly* 46, no. 4 (Fall 1993): 547–563.

Requests for permission to reproduce material from this work should be sent to:
    Permissions
    University of Texas Press
    P.O. Box 7819
    Austin, TX 78713-7819
    www.utexas.edu/utpress/about/bpermission.html

∞ The paper used in this book meets the minimum requirements
of ANSI/NISO Z39.48-1992 (R1997) (Permanence of Paper).

Library of Congress Cataloging-in-Publication Data

Sepich, John, 1951–
  Notes on blood meridian : revised and expanded edition / John Sepich ; foreword by
Edwin T. Arnold. — 1st University of Texas Press ed.
    p.   cm. — (Southwestern writers collection series)
  Includes bibliographical references and index.
    ISBN 978-0-292-71820-3 (cloth : alk. paper) — ISBN 978-0-292-71821-0 (pbk. : alk. paper)
  1. McCarthy, Cormac, 1933– Blood meridian. 2. West (U.S.)—In literature.
  3. Massacres in literature. 4. Indians in literature. 5. Outlaws in literature. I. Title.
  PS3563.C337B437 2008
  813'.54—dc22

                                                              2008023297

For Cormac McCarthy

Contents

Foreword

Edwin T. Arnold

We should start with the title: *Notes on* Blood Meridian. Like the title of the novel it studies, *Blood Meridian, or The Evening Redness in the West,* one of the most allusive and elusive in Cormac McCarthy's canon, John Sepich's description packs a lot into a few words. We might first look at his choice of "notes" as identifier rather than "annotations" or "explications" or "reflections," all of which at times apply to his approach but none of which adequately contains the scope of his intent. The much more serviceable and plainly spoken "notes" allows this author to follow his bent, to combine his historical research with his literary, to explore his penchant for the mystical as well as the philosophical, to weave his own voice into McCarthy's dialogue along with those of the other novelists, dramatists, memoirists, reporters and recorders, biblical scribes, poets, scientists, and historians whose work informs every page of this astonishing book *Blood Meridian.* "Notes" deflects expectation, but it also allows free range, a chance to follow at will each source or impression or, at times, perhaps, apparition.

The rest of the title seems clear enough but does require explanation nonetheless. At the time of its publication, in 1985, *Blood Meridian* received mixed reviews, but as was the case with McCarthy's previous novels, a strong core of readers and critics recognized its enormous accomplishment. Still, this was a mystifying book. It was McCarthy's first "western": his previous four novels had all been set either in Tennessee or in some mysterious approximation of the South (the world of *Outer Dark* [1968] has few identifiable landmarks, quite unlike the other books that offer specific locales, place names, times and dates. It may, in fact, be McCarthy's first fictional trip toward the West: its descriptions of swamps, the "dull lowing of an alligator" [12], and dark bandits on the road suggest something like the Natchez Trace).[1] It was also his first historical novel, set in the mid-nineteenth century and peopled by both real and fictional characters. And it was his most violent. The earlier novels, certainly, had been brutal affairs on occasion, and *Child of God* had especially challenged its readers with its horrifying and yet strangely sympathetic portrait of the killer-necrophile Lester Ballard. But nothing had prepared for the

---

1. Two possible influences on *Outer Dark*, apart from the obvious spirit of Flannery O'Connor, are Eudora Welty's *Robber Bridegroom* (1946) and Madison Jones's *Forest of the Night* (1960).

unremitting slaughter of this book, and for many, it was simply too much. Some of his southern readers soon yearned in print for him to return home to the hills and towns of twentieth-century Tennessee as quickly as possible. He had "Gone to Texas," as had so many of his fellow Tennesseeans, but along the way he seemed to have lost his bearings.[2]

What so many of us did not realize at the time was exactly what John Sepich was to discover: that this latest book, while a work of the imagination, was also one grounded in the history of the West. Just as McCarthy had researched his southern works, through reading and listening and exploring and, to a yet-unknown degree, experiencing the worlds he described, so had he also made himself a student of this western world. After exploratory visits, he had moved to El Paso in the 1970s, "as far west as I could go and still be in the South," as he sometimes said. But this time his research was more systematic, his reading more directed and intentional. He knew the South intimately because he had grown up there; the West required more intensive study.

As Sepich convincingly illustrates, the work that most likely gave McCarthy his focus for this story is Samuel Chamberlain's memoir, *My Confession: Recollections of a Rogue*. Excerpts from Chamberlain's work, a mixture of fact and fiction illustrated by sketches and watercolors done by the author, first appeared as a series of three articles in *Life* magazine in the summer of 1956. That same year Roger Butterfield edited a more complete version for book publication by Harper's, but the full, unexpurgated text did not appear until William H. Goetzmann produced the fine edition published by the Texas State Historical Association in 1996. When McCarthy first encountered Chamberlain's *Confession* is uncertain, but its introduction of Judge Holden, and less direct similarities between the young Sam Chamberlain and "the kid" of the novel, offer strong evidence of this work's importance in the development of McCarthy's book.[3] However, as Sepich further shows, McCarthy's research extended far beyond Chamberlain's exuberant reconstruction of his youthful adventures. Sources such as Bancroft's *History of Texas and the North Mexican States* (1890), Hall's *Sketches of History, Life, and Manners, in the West* (1835), Ruxton's *Adventures in Mexico and the Rocky Mountains* (1861), Reid's *The Scalp-Hunters: Or, Romantic Adventures in Northern Mexico* (1852), and many others figure in the making of this novel. McCarthy, it is clear, went to school in the writings of nineteenth- and twentieth-century western authors and historians such as Frederick Ober, Ralph A. Smith, and Joseph Allen Stout. It is along this path that Sepich carefully follows.

2. The southern critic Hal Crowther, for example, worried that McCarthy had "been seduced and in some way misled by the desert Southwest." He suggested that the author "should pay a visit home to Tennessee, where stoic cowboys and desert oracles don't much signify, where even the best readers resent untranslated Spanish dialogue." See "The Tennessee Stud," 36, 37.

3. Goetzmann notes, "The contemporary novelist Cormac McCarthy, in his savage novel *Blood Meridian*, based on an edited version of Sam's tale, was probably the first person to see that the young Sam was dancing with the devils as he rode with the Sonoran scalp-hunters. McCarthy has plumbed the depths of this horrible experience in a way that makes Sam Peckinpah's *The Wild Bunch* seem tame" (4).

This, then, is one virtue of Sepich's *Notes*. It provides us with historical footing. That figures like John Joel Glanton, Marcus Webster, the Reverend Green, Sarah Borginnis, Mangas Colorado, black John Jackson, Albert Speyer, and others, both major and minor, actually existed, and that remarkable scenes such as Holden's lifting of the meteorite anvil, the hazardous journey to the silver mines of Jesús María, and even the Yuma-ferry massacre that ends the Glanton gang have historical analogues, inform us of McCarthy's care in getting the details right. The more we learn of McCarthy's methods as a writer—and we still know very little—the more we come to appreciate his predilection for building his works of fiction on locales in the real world (McCarthy traveled by auto and on horseback through much of the territory described in the book, following the trail of Glanton's gang as best he could). The kind of attention to the historical and geographical that Sepich illustrates here can also be found in works like *Suttree* or the Border Trilogy, and even in the seemingly less ambitious noir thriller *No Country for Old Men* or the bleak, dead futuristic landscape of *The Road*.[4]

Blood Meridian is, however, primarily a work of fiction. Sepich makes a strong case that it is, in fact, a romance, in the sense that it gives us wild settings, extravagant characters and deeds, and suggestions of the uncanny, especially in the mortal and moral slipperiness of Judge Holden but also in its persistent epistemological considerations.[5] One might argue that the work, for all its care for accuracy and detail, is, finally, a recognition of the limits of history, and this book cannot be adequately explained by historical annotations alone. Holden, for example, certainly the most fascinating character in the novel, has no historical source other than Chamberlain's engaging but factually unreliable *Confession*. *Blood Meridian*'s narrator tweaks us on this point: "Whatever his antecedents he was something wholly other than their sum, nor was there system by which to divide him back into his origins for he would not go" (309). Something similar is true of the kid, whose moniker in the novel is both a blatant cliché, lifted from western dime novels and B-movie oaters, and yet strangely resonant in its nods toward innocence and youth. But even a figure in the book such as John Joel Glanton, whose life and deeds are well documented, is finally an imaginative construction, derived from fact but given additional dimension and depth by the author's art.

Indeed, the narrator in *Blood Meridian* (whose role Sepich thoughtfully critiques) constantly acknowledges the odds inherent in history. What is unseen or unrecorded or

---

4. The scholar who has done the most with this aspect of McCarthy's southern work is Wesley G. Morgan, a professor of psychology at the University of Tennessee–Knoxville. Morgan's investigation of these backgrounds stands as an effective companion to Sepich's study of *Blood Meridian*. See, for example, "'A season of death and epidemic violence': Knoxville Rogues in *Suttree*," *Cormac McCarthy Journal* 5, no. 1 (Spring 2005): 195–209; and "Red Callahan in *Suttree*: The Actual and the Fictitious," *Cormac McCarthy Journal* 5, no. 1: 210–219. See also Morgan's Web site "Searching for Suttree," http://web.utk.edu/~wmorgan/Suttree/suttree.htm

5. Sepich discusses this definition of the novel with McCarthy in "Conversations with McCarthy," 2.

forgotten must be lost to following generations. "The desert wind would salt their ruins and there would be nothing, nor ghost nor scribe, to tell to any pilgrim in his passing how it was that people had lived in this place and in this place died," we are told after one bloodletting (174), and Holden argues that the role of the "witness" constitutes "the prime" factor, "for what could be said to occur unobserved?" (153). History as we have it, then, is at best haphazard, and the confirmations that have come down to us can only suggest the multitude of things lost. Sepich's work recognizes this truth. Historical research can take us only so far in the study of this book. Thus, Sepich broadens his scope, bringing in such esoteric topics as the importance of the tarot and the role of divination and the implications of the supernatural in the book. In this context, he makes a strong argument that McCarthy employs the Faust legend, among others, in his development of the kid's relationship with the judge, and in doing so offers a convincing explanation of what happens to the kid in the jakes at the end of the book, and why. The wide-ranging, and sometimes idiosyncratic, nature of Sepich's study is further illustrated by the concordances he offers, ranging from "Wolves" and "Apes" and "Smiles and Laughter" to such less specific ideas as "Hallucinatory Void" and "Chance, Fortune, and Deception." These thematic patterns, carefully noted throughout the text, reveal structure in what has sometimes been unfairly criticized as a shapeless book, one dominated by movement but lacking development.

There are few works that encourage or can bear the kind of devotion that John Sepich has shown to *Blood Meridian*. For him, it seems to be a magical, revelatory text in the sense that it contains secrets that go beyond the sorts of things discussed above. One gets the sense in reading *Notes on* Blood Meridian that Sepich is searching for some urtext, a cabala hidden in the guise of this western novel. He may be right. Certainly the book has taken a mysterious grip on many of its readers. But something similar has occurred with Sepich's own work, which began as a University of North Carolina–Chapel Hill masters thesis, "Notes Toward an Explication of Cormac McCarthy's *Blood Meridian*," in 1989. He had decided on this subject after reading Vereen Bell's groundbreaking study *The Achievement of Cormac McCarthy*, published the year before. Bell had concentrated on McCarthy's "southern" novels, and these chapters made up the bulk of the book, but he had added a chapter, almost an addendum, on *Blood Meridian*, which had so suddenly changed the landscape of McCarthy's writings. Sepich felt that "Bell had read a different book than I had,"[6] and he wanted to know why. His subsequent research convinced Sepich that Bell, in failing to recognize the rich historical context of *Blood Meridian*, had missed the "bigger world–referencing novel McCarthy had written."[7] His thesis, then, was a first attempt at pointing out some of these references and differences.

6. Telephone interview with Sepich, June 3, 2007.
7. "Conversations with McCarthy," 4.

Over the next few years, Sepich added to the work he had done in his thesis, expanding his original study with "More Notes on Cormac McCarthy's *Blood Meridian* and an Explication," in a privately printed and circulated but unpublished collection that he considered a work in progress. Sepich made contact with other scholars in the now-growing field of McCarthy studies, sharing his discoveries with them while exploring the directions of their own research.

In 1990, my colleague Dianne Luce and I had proposed to Stephen Flinn Young, the editor of the *Southern Quarterly*, a special issue devoted to Cormac McCarthy. Young had never heard of McCarthy—*Blood Meridian* was five years in the past and had had only a small readership, and *All the Pretty Horses*, the book that would finally bring McCarthy the attention and the popularity he deserved, was still two years in the future— but he was intrigued and, after discussing it with other southern scholars, gave us the go-ahead. He wondered, however, if we would be able to fill an entire issue, and, frankly, so did we. Our call for essays, however, elicited a remarkable amount of interest and a number of proposals, and one of these was from John Sepich, who sent us a comb-bound copy of his work. We both soon realized how little we knew about *Blood Meridian* and how important John's research would be to this special issue, the first of its kind on this still little-known writer. By the time our issue appeared in 1992, John had already published his examination of the tarot as "The Dance of History in Cormac McCarthy's *Blood Meridian*" in the *Southern Literary Journal*. For us, he contributed "'What kind of indians was them?' Some Historical Sources in Cormac McCarthy's *Blood Meridian*"; and the following year he published a third excerpt from his work as "A 'bloody dark pastryman': Cormac McCarthy's Recipe for Gunpowder and Historical Fiction in *Blood Meridian*" in the *Mississippi Quarterly*.

During this time, Sepich made contact with McCarthy himself, and they exchanged letters and telephone calls discussing Sepich's work, which McCarthy read and encouraged. Sepich also responded to calls from Rick Wallach, an independent scholar who was in the early stages of finding out more about McCarthy and his books. In 1992, Sepich sent Wallach copies of his writings on *Blood Meridian*, and Wallach grew more intrigued, eventually suggesting that they might all be edited into a publishable volume. With this in mind, Wallach and Sepich corresponded and then met in both New York and Chapel Hill during the winter and spring of 1993.

At approximately this same time, Wallach, in conversation with Jay McGowan, whom he had known at Fordham University and who had recently been named president of Bellarmine College in Louisville, Kentucky, came up with the idea of holding a conference devoted to McCarthy's work. Wade Hall, the head of the Bellarmine English Department, had long admired McCarthy and seconded the idea. With the help of Wallach's friend Alan Shapiro, Wallach, Hall, and McGowan coordinated "Cormac McCarthy: The First Conference" (the title indicating their confidence that more would follow), which took place in October 1993. The Cormac McCarthy Society, another of Wallach's concepts, was also established at this gathering.

Alan Shapiro suggested that in connection with the conference, Bellarmine College consider publication of the Sepich manuscript, which Sepich, with Wallach's editorial advice, had now developed into a publishable text. McGowan offered the resources of the college, and *Notes on* Blood Meridian was produced by the newly established Bellarmine College Press in a run of approximately 700 copies. The paperback book was given to each attendee of the conference, and some fifty additional copies were sold. After that, sales lagged. Two years later, Bellarmine contacted Wallach, offering to sell him the remaining books at $1.25 each, plus shipping costs, and Wallach, on behalf of the society, accepted. For the next few years, a copy was given gratis to each newly enrolled member of the McCarthy Society until the run was exhausted.[8]

Meanwhile, *Blood Meridian*'s readership continued to grow, as did academic interest in the book and its author. Harold Bloom's proclamation in 2000 that *Blood Meridian* was "the authentic American apocalyptic novel" and that "Cormac McCarthy is the worthy disciple both of Melville and of Faulkner" was the imprimatur that finally ushered the book into the realm of the modern classics.[9] As the value of first-edition copies of McCarthy's novel increased (a recent search priced an unsigned first edition at $3,500), so too did that of Sepich's book, which, now out of print and hard to find, had garnered its own mythology. In the summer of 2007, a used copy of *Notes* could be bought for prices ranging from $500 to $1,000.

The proposal to reprint Sepich's study came from the Southwestern Writers Collection at Texas State University–San Marcos, which now houses the premiere McCarthy archives. This resulting publication by the University of Texas Press of the new *Notes on "Blood Meridian": Revised and Expanded Edition* makes Sepich's work again available to the general public. In addition to the basic research he began almost twenty years ago, in this new edition the author continues his thoughtful, persistent engagement with both the novel and its characters. The addition of two new essays, "Knitting the Winds" and "Why Believe the Judge?" provides material aplenty for further conversations about and reconsiderations of what many feel to be McCarthy's masterpiece, as do the extended concordances. But most essential is the impulse that initially drove Sepich, the sense that *Blood Meridian* is more than a history, more than a story: the sense that, in its genesis, its development, and its final presentation, it is a great book that defines us as a time and as a people. The southern novelist and historian Shelby Foote wrote of Sepich that his "constructive scholarship" enabled readers to see more clearly what a "wonderment" McCarthy's novel was.[10] Borrowing from Mr. Foote, I would extend this sense of singular-

---

8. Information taken from e-mail correspondence with Rick Wallach, May 20, 2007.

9. Harold Bloom, introduction to *Cormac McCarthy: Modern Critical Views*, 1.

10. Prefatory material included in *Notes on* Blood Meridian.

ity to Mr. Sepich's work as well. It is an achievement that defies simple definition, one that studiously, doggedly follows the path of its own inspired interests and invites us to follow if we will.

Works Cited

Bloom, Harold, ed. Introduction to *Modern Critical Views: Cormac McCarthy* (Philadelphia: Chelsea House, 2002). The material originally appeared in Bloom, *How to Read and Why* (New York: Scribner, 2000).

Crowther, Hal. "The Tennessee Stud." In *Cathedrals of Kudzu: A Personal Landscape of the South*. Baton Rouge: Louisiana State University Press, 2000.

Goetzmann, William H. Introduction to Samuel Chamberlain, *My Confession: Recollections of a Rogue*. Austin: Texas State Historical Association, 1996.

McCarthy, Cormac. *Blood Meridian, or The Evening Redness in the West*. New York: Random House, 1985.

———. *Outer Dark*. New York: Random House, 1968.

Sepich, John. "Conversations with McCarthy." Unpublished typescript.

———. *Notes on "Blood Meridian."* Louisville, Ky.: Bellarmine College Press, 1993.

Preface

You've been stunned by *Blood Meridian.*

Now you're here and wonder what's ahead. At its best, *Notes* gives you what Cormac McCarthy saw in the Southwest's mid-nineteenth-century journals, narratives, diaries. A good deal of what he read is here. This *Notes* is not a definitive compendium with every scholarly remark of the last twenty years. *Notes* gives a sense of the scale, number, quality, variety, sheer multiplicity of nineteenth-century sources McCarthy had available as he worked toward writing *Blood Meridian,* and though he may say Ruxton was the best writer of the bunch, McCarthy's storytelling talent makes all their eyewitness items his own. His own? He absolutely pales them in the bargain.

Yes, *Notes* has parentheses and footnotes, and they all look so impenetrable. The parentheses are markers for the few who want to go on. If you don't need them, in five pages they will disappear from consciousness. The footnotes are a way for me to reflect on a presentation, and are in fact meant, often as not, as light diversions.

None of this has to be memorized. Poke around. Use the index a little. Imagine I have a relentless sense of humor. Go back and read the novel: it remains undiminished.

In the fall of 1988, I wrote a letter introducing myself and my notes to McCarthy. I had found Chamberlain and Ruxton and Wislizenus. In early summer 1989 came a letter from McCarthy, writing that he had, indeed, read hundreds of books to make his *Blood Meridian.* By that time I had put together most all of what is here in Introductions, Biographies, Settings and Sources and had identified items for the concordances. I wrote him again. I believe he liked the idea of the project. He called, and we talked for twenty minutes or so, and he called every few months from mid-1990 through mid-1994. We would talk about house building, books, probably horses, any number of things, but always he would ask a question about my little searches. I sent him a copy of the book as published by Bellarmine, and he called saying nothing but heartening things.

Dedicating this book to Cormac McCarthy is in admiration of his novel, but make no mistake, it marks his supportive presence in my spirit.

I have for this edition checked all earlier material against all original documents, and rectified dozens of virtually invisible problems. I have retained idiosyncratic spelling and punctuation in extracts and quotations.

The essays "Knitting the Winds" and "Why Believe the Judge?" which end my notes, are new. In "Knitting," I now find myself analyzing Chamberlain's *My Confession* (please, read it yourself) as text in terms of McCarthy's book, adding weight to conclusions I had reached a half dozen years ago. "Knitting" is meant to stand on its own, but also acts as a bridge between earlier work and "Why Believe."

Acknowledgments

With thanks to Bellarmine College for a first edition and to Rick Wallach for his support in so many ways.

I am grateful to my wife, Kathy, and also thank Roald Tweet, Christopher Forbis, Peter Josyph, Kip Keller, Paulo Faria, Steven G. Kellman, and Janet Sepich for this edition, and, equally, Jake Mills, Ralph A. Smith, Don Jarrell, Alejandra Garcia Quintanilla del Reyes, William Wallace, Kevin Hutt, Clint Shaffer, Cormac McCarthy, Philippe Garnier, Dianne Luce, Gilbert Joseph, Caesar Caballero, Roger Lotchin, Mark Wasserman, Oscar Martinez, Evelyn Hu–DeHart, Thomas Burdett, Michael Hunt, Linda Hall, Leo Daugherty, Edward Montgomery, George B. Daniel, Mark Weinburd, Chip Arnold, Shelby Foote, Rick Woodward, Carol Keller, Terry Harn, Charles Waldrup, Deb and Kip Shelby, and Tom Klise for their contributions—sometimes unwitting, nevertheless genuinely appreciated—to the directions this research has taken.

Assistance provided by the Arizona Historical Society, by Becky Brezeale and the Interlibrary Borrowing division of the Humanities Reference Desk of the Walter Royal Davis Library, and by Celia D. Pratt and the Maps Collection at the libraries of the University of North Carolina at Chapel Hill has been indispensable.

With deepest regards to the Southwestern Writers Collection, Texas State University–San Marcos; to Connie Todd for her determination that a revised reprint could work; to Steve Davis for his support; and to the collection's angels, Bill and Sally Wittliff. With thanks to Theresa May and the design and production staff at the University of Texas Press for their steadiness when steadiness counted.

CHAPTER 1

Introductions

The Problem of Information

In *Blood Meridian* are historically verifiable characters, places, and events, though few of these correspondences are immediately apparent to the novel's reader.[1] After sifting a fair number of documents treating its settings, characters, and themes, I have assembled these notes as a step toward insights into McCarthy's novel. Without an overview of the mid-nineteenth-century Southwest that includes, for example, the significance of the Leonid meteor shower of 1833 or Fort Griffin, Texas, *Blood Meridian* looks like three hundred pages of grotesque evidence, derived from McCarthy's imagination, to support Judge Holden's claim that war and violence dominate men's lives.

Though the novel is presented as a life of McCarthy's otherwise nameless "kid," historical accounts of the Glanton gang are the backbone of the book. Decorated Union Army general Samuel Chamberlain's narrative *My Confession* provides McCarthy with his core Glanton tales and the historical basis for his essential character, Judge Holden. It also supplies one analogue to the kid, since the youthful Chamberlain joins Glanton in midadventure, is occasionally sympathetic to the gang's Indian victims, is linked in an attraction-repulsion relationship with Holden, and might have been a filibusterer. Sam Chamberlain's contact with the gang may have suggested McCarthy's use of an "outsider" to contrast with the gang.[2] As a result of this contrast, McCarthy's Holden can reasonably declare that the kid "sat in judgement" during his time with the gang (307; see also 173) and so was not really a member.

Yuma-ferry massacre survivor William Carr's deposition and newspaper correspondent Theodoro Goodman's letter provide a historical source for the novel's ferry-massacre

---

1. The hardcover dust jacket includes these statements: "Certain events that took place in the southwestern United States and northern Mexico in 1849 and 1850 provide the framework of Cormac McCarthy's fifth book." Glanton, Holden, "and a number of their followers, including the ex-priest Tobin, actually existed, and various accounts of their exploits can be found in chronicles of the period."

2. Recruits and recruiting almost invisibly shape the novel (30, 32, 37–39, 49, 98, 218, 223, 232, 237, 239, 241–242, 251–252, 269–270).

scene. *Blood Meridian* is built upon the "facts" presented by these men, though eyewitness accounts by others also contribute details to McCarthy's tale.

One of the greatest delights of the historical novel is the reader's comparison of traditional versions of an event with the author's personalized version (Butterfield 27, 80; see also Manzoni 70–71), yet most readers have not apprehended the degree to which *Blood Meridian* is historical. For example, Edwin T. Arnold's review of *Blood Meridian* notes that both Glanton and Holden are "apparently historical figures" (*Appalachian* 103). Jerry Leath Mills writes that in the novel "all but a handful of the named characters are historical figures" (10), and Mark Royden Winchell proposes that "*Blood Meridian* is loosely based on history" (308). Arnold's review links "the Pilgrims . . . Vietnam, [and] Nicaragua" in his understanding of the novel's import (104). It is nevertheless probably true, given Arnold's temporal sequencing, that he refers to the American interest in Nicaragua during the 1980s and not to William Walker's interest of the 1850s, which is discussed in Chapter 2 in the Captain White section.

The initial critical confusion about the genre of *Blood Meridian* (its scenes were called, among other things, "wonders of the imagination") illustrates the uniqueness of McCarthy's artifice (Bell, *Achievement* 124). It is as if McCarthy has taken Manzoni's critical challenge at face value and has made *Blood Meridian* so particular in its references that "people of that time" would have found the people and places so "probable" that "the novel [might have] been written for them" (Manzoni 125).[3] Readers attempting to identify its genre confront the tension McCarthy creates between the eyewitness testimony ("bare historical facts")[4] underpinning *Blood Meridian* and the dimension of historical romance that he adds to unify them.[5]

McCarthy does not simplify this problem of information with omniscient introductions of characters, places, events.[6] The kid, McCarthy's protagonist, wouldn't know who

3. McCarthy's detailed chapter headings emulate a nineteenth-century book format.

4. Dust jacket, *Blood Meridian*.

5. Thomas D. Young, Jr., presents good historical information about Glanton in Appendix C of his dissertation (234–265).

6. Jeremiah Clemens's 1858 novel *Mustang Gray* presents characters, in a novel declared to be historical, in a manner quite similar to McCarthy's. Chapter 12 of *Mustang Gray* begins: "Fifteen or twenty adventurers were easily recruited in Western Texas for any service, by a leader so well known and so highly esteemed as Mustang Gray" (220). But there is no expanded, individuating introduction of recruits as they enter and exit. "Ben" appears, with no trivia attached, seven pages into the chapter. "Smith" is named two pages later. "Mason" and "John" surface in another eight, though "John" might have been either "Allison" or "Cameron." Other men are named. "Burton" enters with no ceremony thirty-two pages after the opening of Chapter 12. And it is fourteen pages after this point that he is identified as "Dare-devil Will."

McCarthy introduces "Glanton" (79). More than fifty pages later, in Tobin's story of the judge, he is "Captain Glanton" (133). Only at the moment of his death is he "John Joel Glanton" (275). Marcus "Long" Webster's name is given in sections: "Webster" (140), "Marcus" (141), "Long Webster" (264). And, re-

Albert Speyer is, since the kid didn't ride with the Rangers during the Mexican War. And it would be the rare reader who would easily connect *Blood Meridian*'s account of Speyer's involvement in the sale of guns to Glanton in Chihuahua City with James Hobbs's eyewitness accounts of the historical Speyer selling guns to scalp-hunting James Kirker in the mid-1840s. Nor would a reader likely be aware of other accounts of Speyer racing to Chihuahua City ahead of Doniphan's American expedition for the purpose of selling guns to the enemy during the Mexican War.

It is of course still possible to appreciate *Blood Meridian* as a work of pure fiction. However, an underinformed reading of this novel is comparable to the kid's question to Sproule, just after their filibustering expedition to Sonora has been devastated by an Indian attack: "What kind of indians was them?" (56). The assailant's name hardly matters. But readers of historical novels expect to know such names, to know background information and relationships.[7] *Blood Meridian*'s reader would intuitively accept John Bourke's firsthand wonder at the early western settlers' translations of cold geographic "facts" into folk history, since the "unduly excitable brain" of the newcomer to the historical Southwest encountered the:

impossibility of learning exactly how many miles it was to a given point. It wasn't "fifty miles," or "sixty miles," or "just a trifle beyond the Cienaga, and that's twenty-five miles," but rather, "Jes' on th' rise of the mesa as you git to th' place whar Samaniego's train stood off th' Apaches;" or, "A little yan way from whar they took in Colonel Stone's stage;" or "Jes' whar th' big 'killin' tuk place on th' long mesa," and much more of the same sort. (64)

A modern traveler, lulled by the regularities of jet and interstate travel, would find the computation of distance and time on an abacus of historical record overwhelming. *Blood Meridian* poses to the pilgrim reader a need to recognize underlying layers of information, from the geography of its setting to the biographies of its many historical characters. McCarthy's craft can better be appreciated when his reader can distinguish the nineteenth-century backgrounds within the imaginative synthesis of his novel. A review of source texts displays both McCarthy's devotion to historical authenticity and the audacity with which he tailors sources to his own ends.

Beyond the contribution to an understanding of *Blood Meridian* that the assessment

---

markably, the judge calls Toadvine "Louis" (282) two hundred seventy-four pages after his first appearance in *Blood Meridian*.

7. When Glanton asks a new recruit named Sloat about "the commodore" of the same name (204), Sloat's uninformed response to Glanton indicates his insulated condition. Commodore Sloat took California for the United States upon his arrival at Monterey during the Mexican War (Hughes 86; Sherman 81, 96). McCarthy, simply by using the name Sloat, introduces a biographically verifiable character into the novel. Glanton's question to the recruit can be seen, too, as associating Glanton with the Army of the West in California.

of sources and analogues can supply, the book challenges its readers with webs of arcane reference. As Samuel Chamberlain's account of the man Judge Holden yields insights into McCarthy's character Holden, so, too, for instance, an examination of the tarot symbolism associated with Holden is necessary to appreciate the mythic dimension with which McCarthy endows him. What is presented here is, then, an examination of McCarthy's novel in light of scholarship significantly wider afield than has so far been applied.

Three Sections

Blood Meridian divides into three sections. The first begins with the birth of the kid and ends with his membership in Glanton's gang. This section includes the kid's home life, travels in Texas, experiences with the filibustering expedition, and imprisonment in Chihuahua City. The first section of *Blood Meridian*, though "historical" in its events and experiences, exists as a vehicle designed to introduce the world of the late 1840s and the Glanton gang. The information about scalp hunting, below, and the Leonids (Chapter 3) provides the reader of *Blood Meridian* with a perspective on McCarthy's treatment of the period. The filibustering expedition appears to be the novelist's conflation of later and verifiable filibusters.

The second section spans the period of the gang's scalp-hunting, ending with their arrival at the Yuma ferry. It includes the gang's three expeditions out of Chihuahua, their contact with the gypsy family, their stop at the Santa Rita del Cobre mines, the knifing of Grimley at Nacori, the fight at Jesús María, the brush with Elías, and ends with the scenes in and around Tucson, which involve Mangas Colorado. The second section of the novel (and a majority of the third) is often based on information derived from historical sources on the Glanton gang.

The third section of the novel covers the time between the arrival of the gang at the Pima villages until the death of the protagonist some twenty-eight years later. It includes the skirmish with the Yumas, two trips to San Diego for provisions, the massacre, the escape of the survivors and their trip west to San Diego, the accelerated presentation of the kid's years from 1850 until 1878, the reappearance of the judge, and the murder of the kid (then known in the novel as "the man") by the judge. The third section's key events are, generally, historically verifiable. Information about the Yuma-ferry massacre and the flight of the survivors is presented in several sections, based on historians' documents, in the next chapter, but particularly in the sections on Glanton and Holden and in Carr's deposition. The final chapter of the novel appears to be largely of McCarthy's dramatic design. The Fort Griffin section, along with the essays, provides clues that mark Griffin as an appropriate place for the novel's end.

Scalp Hunting and the Glanton Gang

The identity of these regions [between El Paso and Chihuahua City] with the names of certain stormy characters supports the law of the survival of the fittest. Among the hardiest of these persons were certain Apache chiefs and scalp hunters like Captain Santiago Kirker, Captain John Joel Glanton, Major Michael H. Chevallié, Major J. S. Gillett, Colonel Joaquín Terrazas, and Captain Juan de Mata Órtiz. (Smith, "Indians" 38)

Cormac McCarthy's gang leader is a historical figure. His name punctuates any number of histories of the mid-nineteenth-century Southwest. He appears, for example, as a character in Jeremiah Clemens's 1856 romance *Bernard Lile*. As recently as 1956 he was featured in *Life* magazine as a character in the serialization of Samuel Chamberlain's long-lost personal narrative of the late 1840s, *My Confession*. The story of John Glanton, though, is an unsettling one. He has been seen as a misfit since word of his adventures first spread.

But Captain Glanton did what the state of Chihuahua hired him to do, and his life story, as well as the conditions of the time in which he lived, is presented in McCarthy's novel with remarkable fidelity. The conflicts existing in and among the states of Texas, Chihuahua, New Mexico, and Arizona in 1849 and 1850 involved many peoples: Mexicans, both peon and military; United States Army troops; Texans, both Ranger and civilian; Comanches and Apaches; and Anglo gold-rush travellers on the Gila Trail.

The Comanches had moved eastward into what would be north-central Texas at least a hundred years before the Anglos began their settlements. They had come for the buffalo and for the area's convenient access to trails southward into north-central Mexico (Smith, "Comanche Invasion" 4–8).[8] John Hughes described them as "uncompromising enemies" (131). Annual trips into Chihuahua, and as far south as Zacatecas, provided the Comanches with Mexican horses, livestock, and slaves, all of which could be traded to more northern Indian tribes and to Anglo traders on the Arkansas River:

For [the] decade [of the 1840s] columns in gazettes of north Mexican states overflowed with pitiful tales about Indians sweeping away unfortunate persons and confirm what one historian of the Comanches (Rupert N. Richardson) has described as "the most horrendous holocaust ever enacted against a civilized people in the Western World." In exchange for their staples of trade, they received from the civilized people cloth, paints, rifles, powder, lead, knives, guns, and iron from which to make arrow and lance points. Eastern tribes moved by the United States government to the Indian Territory sold many of their government-issued rifles to Comanches for five dollars each. Mexican authorities complained about American traffic with these Indians and also saw the Yankee image behind Apache raids. (Smith, "Indians" 41)

8. Much of the supporting documentation for this section is based on the works of historian Ralph A. Smith. His are the only articles routinely based on both Mexican and United States documents of the period. His attention to the Mexican perspective, when taken with some evidence that McCarthy had seen at least one of Smith's bibliographies, makes him the authority of choice here.

During the time in which *Blood Meridian* is set the Comanches were following an established economic pattern of raids based in part on the productivity of the Mexicans, but also in part fuelled by what Ralph A. Smith calls "a taste for European manufactures" ("Mexican" 103). The Indians at this time also found swelling numbers of westward-bound caravans of gold seekers: "As the Forty-niners swarmed across the vast vacancies of west Texas, there were hardly enough warriors to go around, but the Indians did the best they could" (Sonnichsen, *Pass* 130).

The decade of the forties saw the northern Mexican state of Chihuahua, in its attempt to break the cycle of Indian incursions, hire Anglo aliens to kill the raiders. James (don Santiago) Kirker, in particular, brought hundreds of "proofs" of the deaths of Indians and thousands of head of livestock to Chihuahua City during the first half of the decade.[9] "Proofs": that is, the scalps of Indians, or "receipts." James Hobbs, a professional Indian hunter with James Kirker's gang in the 1840s, apparently held to the practice. Decades later and still scalping, but then in the company of gentler folk, he writes: "some of the party said it looked barbarous; but I kept on scalping, saying that business men always took receipts, and I wanted something to show our success" (409).[10] Ralph Smith quotes the historical Marcus Webster: "For those of posterity who considered scalping a 'grewsome business . . . it was a war necessity'" ("'Long' Webster" 106; see also Sack 92–93).

Evidence of an Indian's death depended on a hunter producing a scalp. And an Indian's scalp was dearer to him than is immediately obvious. Of the "two ways in which the Indian soul can be prevented from reaching [its] paradise:"

The first is by scalping the head of the dead body. Scalping is annihilation; the soul ceases to exist. This accounts for . . . the care they take to avoid being themselves scalped.

Let the scalp be torn off, and the body becomes mere carrion, not even worthy of burial.

The other method by which an Indian can be cut off from the Happy Hunting Grounds is by strangulation.

Should death ensue by strangulation, the soul can never escape, but must always remain with, or hovering near the remains, even after complete decomposition. (Dodge 101–103)

9. McGaw's is the only book-length biography of Kirker; Smith (in "The 'King of New Mexico' and the Doniphan Expedition") and Brandes provide article-length information.

10. McCarthy certainly uses Hobbs's "receipts" for Glanton's "Get that receipt for us" (98). Historically, General Elías's troops had nine pairs of ears tacked to their cannon trucks when they met Colonel Jack Hays in 1849 (Greer 243). The tradition of "trophies and verifications" continues into the present day: "Once bagged, [the Viet Cong] were statistics fed into Westmoreland's computer, with their severed ears on occasion tied to the antenna of a troop carrier as trophies and verifications of the body count" (Drinnon 451; cf. Falk, Kolko, and Lifton 25). Also see Davis on Indians beheading for identification (170), and McWhiney and Jamieson on Southern troops beheading enemy dead during the Civil War (182).

The scalp is both proof of an Indian's capture, given the stipulation that the scalp must show the crown of the hair (and in some cases, for further specificity, the ears), and proof of the Indian's death, given the lengths to which an Indian would go to protect his body from this disfigurement (Smith, "Comanche Sun" 39). Chamberlain, travelling with Wild Tom Hitchcock to meet Glanton's gang, recounts the Indian's desire, even over life, to keep his scalp:

The wounded warrior presented a ghastly sight, he tried to call his pony to him, but the affrightened animal stood at a distance, snorting in terror. The savage then gave a wild startling yell, and by his hands alone, dragged himself to the brink of the deep barranca, then singing his death chant and waving his hand in defiance towards us he plunged into the awful abyss.
"Cincuenta pesos gone to h——l, muchacho," cried Tom. "The doggone mean red nigger done that thar, to cheat us out of his har!" (263–264)

Chihuahua paid scalp bounties not only to licensed alien parties, but also to peon guerilla bands, who found that the governmental payment for a single scalp exceeded the amount that a peon who became a gang member "could earn by hard labor in a year" (Smith, "Scalp Hunt" 125). Even for Anglos, the money was attractive. Pay in the United States Army at about that time ran between seven and fifteen dollars a month when bonuses were included (Chamberlain 239; Nevin 24). A group of fifty Indian hunters paid two hundred dollars a scalp would have to bring only four scalps a month into Chihuahua City in order to exceed the army's rate of pay, and for work not much more hazardous than the army's. Kirker's group was known to have killed as many as two hundred Indians on a single trip, bringing in one hundred and eighty two scalps. This approach yielded sixty times what the men would have earned in other employment. At one point, Chihuahua owed James Kirker $30,000 (Smith, "King" 30). Chihuahua was desperate to have the Comanche invasions stopped. So aliens and peons—even some Indians—were paid by the scalp for their contribution to Chihuahua's protection (Richardson 202).[11]

As the *New York Daily Tribune* noted on its front page for August 1, 1849:

The Government of Chihuahua has made a bloody contract with an individual named Chevallie, stipulating to give him a bounty of so much per head for every Indian, dead or alive, whom he may secure. The terms of this atrocious bargain are published in the Mexican papers, which, to their credit be it said, denounce them as inhuman and revolting. The Chihuahuans themselves are disgusted with the treaty.

11. "Many of the most intelligent backed [the payment-for-scalps] scheme for dealing with the Indians, but others looked upon it with horror. The national government never sanctioned it. In this it followed a course similar to that of the government of the United States, which never bought Indian scalps; although many American states, counties, and cities did" (Smith, "Mexican" 102). British general Henry Hamilton, the "Hair-Buyer," hired tribes to murder settlers in Illinois as late as 1778 (Eifert 9). Bourke

Michael Chevallié had been a Texas Ranger and a volunteer in the Mexican War.[12] Clarence Wharton writes that he was on his way to California for the gold when, out of money, he took a scalp contract with Chihuahua on May 27, 1849 (34–37). The "inhuman" aspects of the job apparently didn't deter him or John Glanton, who applied for a license on June 27 of the same year (Smith, "Poor Mexico" 90–91).

The scalp hunters' problem, though, arose in late 1849 and early 1850 as the scalp business peaked (Smith, "Scalp Hunter" 20). A "depletion" of the number of Indians venturing into Mexico occurred, in part because of Chihuahua's willingness to pay for the scalps of women and children, though at a rate below that for warriors (Smith, "Scalp Hunter" 21; "Comanche Sun" 44).[13] The response to Chihuahua's desire to end Indian incursions, signalled to all by the fabulous amounts of money involved, exceeded the state's ability to determine the origins of scalps. Besides a large Indian population antedating Spanish settlement, Chihuahua was inhabited by mestizos, whose hair was similar to the Indians' in color and texture. The hair of fighting and farming Indians looked about the same. And Glanton's scalpers found this "problem" of identification to be a boon, enriching their coffers with the surreptitious murder of Mexican citizens until their deceptions were discovered by the authorities.

Indian Haters

Glanton fought Mexicans during the Mexican War, and later killed Indians and Mexicans for profit. Chamberlain writes that Glanton's seventeen-year-old fiancée had been taken and killed by Indians in Texas: "From this tragic scene Glanton returned a changed man. . . . He drank deeply and sought the companionship of the most hardened desperados of the frontier; in all Indian fights he was the devil incarnate" (269).[14] The reader of *Blood Meridian* recognizes McCarthy's Glanton in these details: the drinking, the desperados, the Indian fights. Jeremiah Clemens, in *Mustang Gray*, touches on the question

---

notes an instance from the 1870s in which Indians found it necessary to carry the heads of slain criminals to General Crook for identification (220).

12. Michael Chevallié's name (and, later, Bennet Riddell's name) is spelled in various ways by different authors. The spellings used in quoted sources have been left, without comment, as they originally appeared.

13. In *Blood Meridian*, Glanton must deal with an absence of raiding Indians (148).

14. In *Blood Meridian*, Glanton is married. Chamberlain's mention of Glanton's fiancée refers to another, earlier woman in Glanton's life. In 1832, Hall told the story of Monson, an Indian hater (*Legends*, 261–262). Hall's *Sketches* (1835) retells this earlier story and is the source of Melville's Indian-hating Colonel Moredock in *The Confidence-Man* (74–82). Melville's story is told by a man recounting "judge" [*sic*] Hall's telling of Moredock's life story. Hall on Indian hating in *Legends* is remarkably similar to Clemens on hating Mexicans, below.

of Texans' regard for Mexicans during the period of the Mexican War, and the aftermath of that war, when he writes that Texans:

remembered only the retaliation. To be just, we must judge of actions in connection with the causes from which they flow. No wonder that a man whose house had been burned down, his property pillaged, and his fields laid waste, should seek to spoil the spoiler in his turn. No wonder that a man whose brother had been murdered, should long to smite the murderer. No wonder that a man whose wife had been violated, and then her body mangled with wounds, should be deaf to the cry of mercy when the ravisher is at his feet. To all this, and more, the Texans had been subjected. They felt it like men—like men they avenged it. He who would have done less, can claim little kindred with humanity. (269)

The brutal crimes attributed to the Indians in the death of Glanton's fiancée are also present in Clemens, yet are laid at the feet of Mexicans. Glanton's Texan background can be thought to predispose him, in general terms, when taken with the profit motive, to his murders of Mexicans.

Early in Chamberlain's narrative, in a scene that precedes his running away from home, he fist-fights with a "rough" after the other fellow used "profane language on the Holy Sabbath": "'I consciously believed,'" Chamberlain defends himself before a Church committee, "'that I had acted as a good Christian should act, and for the interest of the Church!' My good friends appeared for me and I was cleared of all sinful intention in this wholesome rebuke to a sinner" (8). Fighting the "good fight" was an apparently literal injunction for Chamberlain and, possibly, Glanton: Chamberlain writes, "Nothing remarkable distinguished Glanton in his youth from the other young men of the settlement [except] a deep *religious* feeling and a strict moral conduct" (268; original emphasis). McCarthy would have seen this detail. As noted in the next chapter in the Holden section, Glanton also had "recollections of the Bible teaching his young mind had undergone" (Chamberlain 276). The reader wonders if Chamberlain's "church" is not somehow also Glanton's, though Chamberlain was not trained in Glanton's hard Texas Ranger environment. Neither man has a moral compunction against hunting Indians for their scalps, though Chamberlain shows some sympathy for "harmless" Indians (264), whereas McCarthy's Glanton does not (97–98).

The Anglos' hatred of Indians was a concomitant of the westward expansion of the United States. From this perspective, "the white man's burden of Winning the West was . . . global folly," for:

The West was quite literally nowhere—or everywhere, which was to say the same thing. For Homer's Greeks and North American tribal peoples alike, the West was the land beyond. Spiritland, the land of mystery, of death and of life eternal. It was not a Dark and Bloody Ground to be "won." But for Anglo-Americans it was exactly that, the latest conquest. Yet how could they conclusively "win" it? If the West was at bottom a form of society, as Turner contended, then on our round earth, Winning the West amounted to no less than winning the world. It could be finally and decisively "won" only by rationalizing (Americanizing, Westernizing, modernizing) the world, and that meant conquering the land beyond, banishing mystery, and negating or extirpating other peoples, so the whole would be subject to the regimented reason of one settlement culture with its professedly self-evident middle-class values. (Drinnon 465)

Toadvine, late in the novel, runs "plumb out of country" (285). The judge declares in favor of zoos and an end to the thought of mystery (199, 252). His intellect demands Drinnon's "regimented reason," even though his murder of children seems at odds with this demand.[15]

But the gang is also a group of businessmen, in this novel of businessmen (examined in the Speyer and Riddells sections, Chapter 2). The morality of scalp hunting is not problematic for them. Scalpers are licensed to do a job for the benefit of the state. The conflicting Indian and Mexican cultures in Chihuahua in the mid-nineteenth century, as Ralph Smith has documented, often came to bloodshed. The imposition of a third culture, the Texas American, brought a state of equilibrium, but only after fifty years of warfare, and that equilibrium came, in large part, only as a result of the extinction of the southern buffalo herd. Glanton's Indian and Mexican scalping, then, is both of individualized (his fiancée murdered) and of culturally widespread, generalized origins.

James Hall's Indian hater would kill any Indian he found (*Legends* 259–260). Yet Glanton rode with Indians in his gang and rode with Mexicans (*Blood Meridian* 86, 98; Smith, "John Joel Glanton" 9). Robert Eccleston reports that Glanton's party consisted of "27 Americans, 30 Mexicans, & 1 Apache who had proven traitor to his nation" (232).

McCarthy's John Glanton is less rigidly an Indian hater than Hall's model would suggest. He is also less compulsively a hater of Mexicans than is Clemens's Mabry "Mustang" Gray. The absolutely predatory nature of bigotry in the sources that McCarthy may have used is paradoxically softened in the novel. When Black Jackson killed white John Jackson at the gang's campfire, "Glanton rose" (107).[16] He said and did nothing else. Glanton's acceptance of his gang member's murder in this scene is a careful demonstration by McCarthy of Glanton's unqualified acceptance of both John Jacksons as equals. This scene's group dynamic is similar to that described by Clemens, presented in the Cham-

---

15. Drinnon's "middle-class values" may be thought of, in his terms, as embodied in the "overseas outrider of . . . empire" whose "twin metaphysics" were to nation-build as he native-hated. "But was there no terminus," Drinnon continues, "no ultimately remote West beyond which the metaphysics lost their power to uproot and destroy? Not if one accepted Turner's definition in 'The Problem of the West': 'The West, at bottom, is a form of society, rather than an area'" (464); "At bottom . . . [their] . . . hate rested on the collective refusal to conceive of Native Americans as persons, a refusal Turner shared in full measure. No less than the judge [James Hall] did he glorify Indian-killers as pathfinders of 'civilization,' glorify their mastery over every dusky tribe, and throw sheaves of patriotic rhetoric over the real human bodies left behind" (463).

berlain section in Chapter 3. Only if the men had found Black Jackson's act abhorrent might Glanton have confronted the killer. Glanton's loyalties seem not to favor Anglos over Indians, or Anglos over Mexicans, but gang members over outsiders.

Indeed, Richard Drinnon's words on Herman Melville and James Hall might with few changes apply to McCarthy on the "terrain of racial hatred" in *Blood Meridian*:

Melville knew his Hall. By the 1850s the collective moral confusion was so dumbfoundingly pervasive that Melville's surrealism was in truth the harshest realism, just the means for ripping off false fronts and exposing sham and deception, floating identities, the true patriotism of empty rhetoric. "The Metaphysics of Indian-Hating" gave the reader the best single overview to date of the terrain of racial hatred. It was an acute progress report on the state of the animosity after only two and a half centuries of growth. (214)

---

16. Tobin tells the kid, once the kid has removed an arrow from David Brown's leg, that the kid has done this at the risk of his own life (163; cf. "The dead would take the living with them if they could": McCarthy, *Suttree* 13; Chamberlain 36). The bondings within the gang are not to be viewed without some qualification.

CHAPTER 2

Biographies

The Reverend Green

The Reverend Green is the first verifiable historical character named in *Blood Meridian*. The biography of R. G. Green poses interesting questions if the reader takes the judge's allegations of Green's moral character (6, 7) as purely malicious. After demolishing Green's revival meeting, Holden says: "I never laid eyes on the man before today. Never even heard of him" (8). Are his allegations against Green's character only mischief-making lies? Do the judge's charges project his own sexual peculiarities? Are all men simply gullible? Indeed, might the judge have knowledge of Green that has not come to him through ordinary eyes or ears?

This is, it must be remembered, the judge who would know that the kid had left Shelby alive, who knew that the kid had "abandoned" Tate (331). The judge knows things he reasonably cannot know. A look at Green's biography tends to confirm the judge's omniscience. J. S. Newman, in his *History of the Primitive Baptists in Texas, Oklahoma, and Indian Territory*, discovers that "Elder R. G. Green joined [the Baptist church on the outskirts of Nacogdoches] by letter in December, 1838, and was excluded for drunkenness in February, 1840" (quoted in J. M. Carroll 125; see also Barnes 92).[1] In the novel, Green's tent meeting outside of Nacogdoches occurs nine years after this dismissal.[2]

The judge was not entirely amiss in his attack on Green, then, though his particular charges appear to be exaggerated. Apparently, McCarthy's scene is meant to emphasize the credulity of the church members as well as the judge's "intuitive" understanding of Green. Carroll includes in a note on Green: "he affiliated almost exclusively with the anti-missionaries, but before very long he appears to have become a moral wreck, resulting, it was said, from some sort of domestic trouble" (113). The suggestion that Green's behavior troubled his home life confirms in principle the judge's allegations of Green's misconduct. To evaluate the judge's allegations solely as the projection of his own psyche, then, would be to discount Green's moral turpitude.

---

1. An examination of microfilm copies of the *Nacogdoches Times* for the period January–July 1849, though not containing every number, does not mention a tent meeting or a Reverend Green.

2. Glanton in the novel drinks excessively. Mangas Colorado likes his drink, though he is practical about it (Baen 56). This note of Green's predilection puts him in select company.

Of the several possible motivations for the judge's disruption of the tent meeting, none emerges as definitive. It is certainly possible that the judge was simply being malicious. That he might have been mocking the credulity of the tent-meeting crowd, whose "order in creation" is "that which [they] have put there," is just as likely (245).[3]

Judge Holden

While McCarthy's character John Glanton is mentioned with some consistency in many stories of the Southwest, Judge Holden's named historical existence rests solely on information provided by Samuel Chamberlain in *My Confession*, the only personal narrative written by a member of Glanton's gang, although Smith suggests otherwise ("Poor Mexico" 103).[4] McCarthy's choice of the name "Holden" for a character is comparable, in its historical validation, to his choice of the names "John Jackson" and "James Miller," whose names enter history only in the closing paragraphs of Carr's deposition and in the contemporary newspaper accounts of the massacre at the Yuma ferry. Hubert Howe Bancroft and Arthur Woodward quote from these sources and cite the names, but references to Holden begin with the publication of Chamberlain in 1956. Little of Chamberlain's historical Holden will surprise McCarthy's reader:

3. Holden also derides the credulity of the gang members; see 116, 251–252. In *The Crossing*, McCarthy writes, "there is no order in the world save that which death has put there" (45).

4. In "Poor Mexico," Smith writes:

> The half dozen or so survivors [of the Yuma-ferry massacre] reached California, the destination of Kirker and scores of other scalp hunters. Space does not permit listing their names, nor chronicling their activities on the West Coast and elsewhere. But evidence that they were a strenuous breed comes not only from their past but from their future as well. In their horoscope was a *Union Army General, three authors* of books that describe life in the scalp country, *a scientist* of no mean repute, *two doctors, a professor of medicine* at Willamette Medical College, Portland, Oregon, the first *Mayor of Whitesboro*, Texas, a *deputy sheriff* of Los Angeles, a *county commissioner*, a *stage driver*, and other useful citizens—and some not so useful (103, my emphasis).

Professor Smith responded to my inquiry regarding the identities of these men with the explanation, used by permission, that

> the paragraph that you asked about has been an embarrassment to me. I made a real grammatical blunder in it. The way that it appears, "their" clearly refers back to "half dozen." That is not at all what I meant, but did not realize what I had done until too late. I meant to be referring to the scalp hunters in general. In this latter case or the broadest sense the persons that you point to were Union General—Samuel E. Chamberlain; three authors about scalp hunting who finally got to California were Michael James Box, Chamberlain, and James Hobbs; scientist John Allen Veatch; two doctors—"Doc" Holden [sic], and Veatch; Prof. of Medicine—Veatch; first Mayor of Whitesboro—Marcus L. Webster; David Brown—Deputy Sheriff; County Commissioner—Gabriel Allen; and stage driver—John Dusenberry. (letter, November 27, 1989)

The second in command, now left in charge of the camp, was a man of gigantic size called "Judge" Holden of Texas. Who or what he was no one knew but a cooler blooded villain never went unhung; he stood six feet six in his moccasins, had a large fleshy frame, a dull tallow colored face destitute of hair and all expression. His desires was blood and women, and terrible stories were circulated in camp of horrid crimes committed by him when bearing another name, in the Cherokee nation and Texas; and before we left Frontreras a little girl of ten years was found in the chapperal, foully violated and murdered. The mark of a huge hand on her little throat pointed him out as the ravisher as no other man had such a hand, but though all suspected, no one charged him with the crime. (271)

In Chamberlain, Holden has a "face destitute of hair," a detail McCarthy's Holden retains, a detail generalized by McCarthy into Holden's total infant-like baldness.[5] Chamberlain's Holden's "face destitute . . . of all expression" does not continue in McCarthy's character. Chamberlain's Holden is "six feet six" (in his moccasins), and for McCarthy "close on to seven feet" (apparently in boots) (6). The "large fleshy frame" is matched in McCarthy's detail of the judge as twenty-four stone, i.e., three hundred thirty-six pounds (128).

Of note as Chamberlain introduces the judge is that "terrible stories were circulated in camp of horrid crimes committed by him when bearing another name, in the Cherokee nation and Texas." "When bearing another name" seems an apt point of departure for McCarthy's enhancement of the historical figure who was Judge Holden. In McCarthy's novel, Holden's ability to appear, disappear, and reappear—an ability first suggested in Chamberlain's mention of the judge's routine change of name—bears on questions of Holden's origins and self-proclaimed immortality. Chamberlain here also presents Holden as a suspected child murderer when a "foully violated" young girl was found dead, and, in fact, Chamberlain later writes that Holden caught up a Pima Indian girl and was "proceeding to take gross liberties with her person" when drawn guns shied him from his "prey" (287).[6] Nevertheless, and though McCarthy's Holden is several times associated with dead children (118–119, 164, 239, 333), there is not a single hint of sexuality in these events.

Chamberlain continues his introduction of Holden:

Holden was by far the best educated man in northern Mexico; he conversed with all in their own language, spoke in several Indian lingos, at a fandango would take the Harp or Guitar from the hands of the musicians and charm all with his wonderful performance, and

---

5. Chamberlain's illustration "Lecture on Geology, by Judge Holden" appears in Goetzmann's edition of *My Confession* (312). In it, Holden has head hair worn long, dark eyebrows, and no moustache or beard. Also, of this picture's portraits of eight men, Holden is remarkably fair complexioned.

6. Chamberlain's closing thought, in this story, that Holden appeases his adversaries in Spanish, is analogous to McCarthy's scene of the judge convincing Sergeant Aguilar, in Spanish, that the sale of guns from Speyer to the gang is not to be disturbed (84–85).

out-waltz any poblana of the ball. He was "plum centre" with rifle or revolver, a daring horseman, acquainted with the nature of all the strange plants and their botanical names, great in Geology and Mineralogy, in short another Admirable Crichton, and with all an arrant coward. Not but that he possessed enough courage to fight Indians and Mexicans or anyone where he had the advantage in strength, skill and weapons, but where the combat would be equal, he would avoid it if possible. I hated him at first sight, and he knew it, yet nothing could be more gentle and kind than his deportment towards me; he would often seek conversation with me and speak of Massachusetts and to my astonishment I found he knew more about Boston than I did. (271–272)

McCarthy's Holden's education, musical talent, and marksmanship (116, 123, 134, 335, etc.) are derived from Chamberlain. This characterization ends with Chamberlain's "I hated him at first sight, and he knew it, yet nothing could be more gentle and kind than his deportment towards me"—as if it were some undefined antagonism. The cowardice Chamberlain attributes to Holden does not characterize McCarthy's Holden, though *Blood Meridian*'s sustained thematic interest in "deceptions," if viewed as nonconfrontational winning, may in fact be related to "cowardice."

The next mention of Holden in *My Confession* seems to inform several incidents in the novel:

Glanton proved that he was well fitted to be the master spirit of the fiendish band. Drinking deeply, he swore with the most fearful oaths that we were all sinners bound to eternal Perdition, that it was his mission to save us. He then knelt down and in well chosen words prayed with all the fervor of a hard shell Baptist for the salvation of all. Suddenly he sprang up and drawing his revolver opened fire on us right and left. One of the Canadians received a shot in the leg, as a gentle reminder to flee from the wrath to come. Judge Holden seized the madman in his powerful arms, laid him down and soothed him as a mother would a fretful child, and Glanton soon sank into a drunken sleep. (274)

In *Blood Meridian*, at Jesús María, Glanton "in his drunkenness was taken with a kind of fit and he lurched crazed and disheveled into the little courtyard and began to open fire with his pistols. In the afternoon he lay bound to his bed like a madman while the judge sat with him and cooled his brow with rags of water and spoke to him in a low voice. . . . After a while Glanton slept and the judge rose and went out" (191). A second scene in the novel quite possibly shaped by these Chamberlain sentences occurs as James Robert nearly drowns at the Yuma crossing. There, the judge "stepped into the river and seized up the drowning idiot, snatching it aloft by the heels like a great midwife and slapping it on the back to let the water out. A birth scene or a baptism or some other ritual not yet inaugurated into any canon. He twisted the water from its hair and he gath-

7. Unless otherwise noted, all page-cited material is from the *Harper* Chamberlain.

ered the naked and sobbing fool into his arms and carried it up into the camp and restored it among its fellows" (259).

When the novel's gang rides past the "sandstone cities in the dusk" (113) on their way
to the mines of Santa Rita del Cobre, Chamberlain's influence may again be discerned.
Riding with the gang in search of Cibola, the "golden mirage" of El Dorado, which "for
three hundred years haunted the misty frontiers of Spanish America" (Lister and Lister
133), Chamberlain found, to Holden's "mocking laughter" (275), "only walls of marl with
yuccas and cactus growing behind them" (276). Almost at once, Chamberlain writes that
Holden presented a "scientific lecture on Geology," which "no doubt was very learned,
but hardly true, for one statement he made was 'that *millions* of years had witnessed the
operation producing the result around us,'" which Glanton with recollections of the Bible
teaching his young mind had undergone said "was a d——d lie" (276).[8] In Chamberlain's words are prefigured the sequence of events, and the types of responses to the events,
that occur in McCarthy's novel. The "sandstone cities in the dusk" in McCarthy almost
immediately precede the judge's disquisition on "geological evidence" (108, 113, 116). And
in both stories his remarks are rejected on scriptural grounds. McCarthy's "a few would
quote him scripture" (116) turns out to be, as this source is examined, a refutation orig-
inating with John Glanton, history's erstwhile blackguard.

Another Chamberlain observation on the judge appears to contribute to *Blood Meridian*'s "geological evidence" section, when he writes of Holden:

He also was fluent regarding the ancient races of Indians that at a remote period covered
the desert with fields of corn, wheat, barley and melons, and built large cities with canals
bringing water from rivers hundreds of miles distant. To my question "how he knew all
this," this encyclopaedian Scalp Hunter replied, "Nature, these rocks, this little broken
piece of clay (holding up a little fragment of painted pottery such are found all over the
desert), the ruins scattered all over the land, tell me the story of the past." (283–284)

The judge's statement that "Books lie," but that God's "words" are spoken "in stones
and trees, the bones of things" (116), echoes Chamberlain's story.

The final pages of Chamberlain's narrative describe the escape of the survivors from
the Yuma-ferry massacre and depict Holden as both ubiquitous and unstoppable. The
scene opens with Tobin, Webster, Hitchcock, and Chamberlain already on the desert
heading west after the massacre. Tobin points out a distant interplay behind them, perhaps Indians and a white man. They ride back and discover Judge Holden—using an

---

8. The judge's "*millions* of years," with Chamberlain's emphasis, gives the reader an appreciation of
the judge's uncommonly advanced education; for example, Sir Charles Lyell's revolutionary *Principles of
Geology* was published in England in 1833, but Lyell's work did not become current in North America until
his visits there in the 1840s.

empty rifle as a club—circled by Yumas with clubs, but who scatter as the four riders near. Chamberlain tramples a Yuma, who is then killed by Holden's blow to his head. Holden offers his handshake in thanks, and Chamerlain refuses.[9]

Rescued, Holden travels west with the four but steals Chamberlain's horse, rides ahead a little way, stops, and calls back to them, "You cursed robbers and murderers, I go to denounce you in the settlements! You shall hang in California!" This portion of the narrative suggests the kid's otherwise inexplicable imprisonment in San Diego (305). This passage prefigures both Tobin's desire to have the judge dead in the desert (285) and Holden's charge that the kid was "responsible" for the Yuma massacre (306). But the horse stumbles, throwing Holden, and the four are on him before he can escape. As Chamberlain guards Holden, Tobin, Hitchcock, and Webster, decide to—and do—leave Holden bound and helpless there in the desert.

These men ride on for "several miles" before Chamberlain decides to go back and cut Holden free, does so, and turns back to rejoin his companions. When he reaches the spot where he had parted from his friends, he sees them "some six miles away" (Chamberlain must have ridden three miles east to Holden, three miles back), and "was surprised to see Holden, not over a mile in my rear," having made almost as good time on foot as Chamberlain on horseback (293–294).

As Chamberlain travels west and now alone, his horse fails for lack of water. He leaves it, going on, himself almost gone, and probably dead but for the "Digger" Indian men who find him and bring him to their camp farther west, where Chamberlain's three companions have already found sustenance. Chamberlain is delighted to meet them. No mention is made of Holden, no one wonders about him. But two mornings later, there is the judge, sitting and eating breakfast at these survivors' fire. Chamberlain's Holden seems hardly down and never out: only a few tense minutes pass before the five are sharing jokes. So ends Chamberlain's *Confession*.

Another historical figure, equal in some ways to Chamberlain's Holden, and one who may have influenced McCarthy's rendering of Holden, is the Englishman "Self" presented in James Greer's biography *Colonel Jack Hays* (1952). Self is "huge, fat," though his height is not given. He is a master of the violin. And like Chamberlain's Holden, Self is a coward in both of the Greer episodes in which he appears: "A huge, fat Englishman named Self was encamped near San Antonio. He bragged continuously about how he would conduct himself in a fight with the Indians. Even the patient Hays became wearied from listening to the braggart, who could, to give him his due, play the violin. In a

---

9. Chamberlain, in Goetzmann's "unexpurgated" *My Confession*, here remembers the "finger marks" on the dead girl at "Frontreras," and will not touch Holden (327). An illustration in the *Harper's My Confession* shows Chamberlain dismounted after Holden has killed the Indian (293).

benevolent mood one day Hays invited him to bring his violin and spend several days with the Rangers. The boys enjoyed his fiddling, but detested his bragging" (59; cf. 174). Chamberlain's introduction of the judge as having borne "another name" in other territories brings the reader of the Hays biography to question whether McCarthy found in Self an echo of the judge's resort to an alias when desirable.

Early in his narrative, John Russell Bartlett writes that he met a man who had been a prisoner of the Mexicans in 1836 during the secession of Texas from Mexico, "a gentleman, Judge H., . . . whose singular escape may be worth relating" (1:28):

The gentleman above referred to was in the second division, and owes his escape to the most wonderful presence of mind. As his division was marching out, he heard the report of the muskets, which were fired upon the preceding division. Instantly the truth flashed upon his mind, and his course of action was decided. As he saw the lips of the Mexican officer move to give the order for the soldiers to fire, now fell upon his face as if dead. The soldiers stood within six feet of the prisoners, and fired with fixed bayonets. As soon as they had fired, they rushed upon the victims with their bayonets to complete the slaughter. Judge H. was pierced through the shoulder, bearing the wound without showing signs of life. After the execution, the scavengers and camp followers came to rob the dead. A Mexican, in cutting away his hunting shirt to get at his coat which was beneath, wounded him in the neck, at which he let escape some expression of pain; whereupon the Mexican, finding him still alive, beat him upon the head with the butt of his escopetto until he supposed life extinct, and then went on with his robbery. All this time the Judge retained a consciousness of his situation; and when all had left the bloody scene, he crawled, as well as his remaining strength would allow, to some concealment near the river, and at dark made his escape. After wandering three days without food, he obtained assistance from some kindhearted Mexicans, and finally reached the coast in safety. (1: 29)

Chamberlain's account of Judge Holden's nearly miraculous power to survive corresponds to Bartlett's description of "Judge H." One wonders if this could be one and the same man. Chamberlain's assertion of Holden's "cowardice" may be interpretable as practical good sense in Bartlett's "Judge H."[10]

The correlations between Self, Judge H., and Chamberlain's Holden, especially concerning their uncanny talent for survival, brings the reader's understanding of McCarthy's Holden's claims of living forever into a historically less ironic sort of a statement than is otherwise possible to defend. The excess of the judge's claim of immortality is softened if the judge is seen as elemental, informing several stories rather than only Chamberlain.

10. John J. Linn's *Reminiscences* contains an account of Judge W. L. Hunter's "extraordinary escape from the 'Fannin Massacre'" (190–191), partly answering these conjectures regarding the identity of the "Judge H." of Bartlett's pages.

Captain White

The existence of Captain White's filibustering expedition into Sonora in the spring of 1849 is not verifiable. A nonmilitary and presumably illegally constituted troop of free-booters that was attacked and virtually wiped out by Indians in the desolate eastern Chihuahua country would leave few traces in the record.[11] Although there are references to U.S. involvement in the Mexican War as an instance of filibustering, histories of private Anglo filibustering tend to begin with William Walker's expedition into Sonora in 1853. However, Ralph Smith's article on Mexican defense needs in 1845 mentions Mexican soldiers "who were needed to watch filibusters and Texas and United States armies about to descend upon their borders, [who yet] stayed busy trailing Indians in the interior," clearly stating that operations of the type designated filibusters took place on the Mexican border several years before Walker's Sonora incident ("Indians" 60). It is possible that small-scale low-profile expeditions took place during the late 1840s. The time seems to have been ripe.

The names of the men involved in White's expedition (Trammel, Sproule, Candelario, Clark, to name the more prominent) all lead to biographical dead ends. Of Thomas Hammersly's list of army officers serving the United States immediately preceding 1849, there are twenty-nine officers surnamed "White" (855–856). Winnowing from Hammersly's list those who resigned their commissions entirely too early to fit the background of McCarthy's character Captain White, as well as those who died after 1849 or 1850, leaves only one officer, a Joseph A. White, whose command disbanded on July 15, 1848.[12] But the chance discovery of White's name brings the search little closer to locating a fully developed source for McCarthy's episode.

McCarthy probably invented the filibustering troop, a bit of fiction well within the tradition of the historical romance. The editor's postscript to Chamberlain's narrative indicates that Chamberlain may have accompanied Walker on his southern California expedition of 1853 (299). Since McCarthy was familiar with *My Confession*, he was familiar with Chamberlain's being associated both with Glanton's scalping raids and with filibustering.

---

11. Interviews in person and by telephone with the historians Gilbert Joseph, Ralph Smith, Caesar Caballero, Roger Lotchin, Mark Wasserman, Oscar Martinez, Evelyn Hu–DeHart, Thomas Burdett, Michael Hunt, and Linda Hall have produced no "historical" information on McCarthy's Captain White expedition, by time, place, or name.

12. In *Agents of Manifest Destiny*, Charles Brown mentions a First Lieutenant Joseph A. White, who "sought from among the discharged soldiers of the American army" for volunteers to fight against the Indians in the Yucatán in 1848 (33). "Details of Colonel White's expedition (he had promoted himself two grades in rank from the one he held in the American army) are scarce," Brown writes, adding that a newspaper article by G. H. Tobin (published in 1849) contains the "fullest account" (34). George Henry Tobin is listed in Spurlin (198). Spurlin also lists private John A. White as serving two hitches as a Texas volunteer in the Mexican War in Ben McCulloch's companies (198, 199).

Details of Captain White's death, the preservation of his head (69), and his body being fed to hogs (70) are similar to the circumstances surrounding the death and treatment of Henry Alexander Crabb, the leader of an unsuccessful "support" expedition into Sonora in 1858 (Forbes 7). But for a single survivor, Crabb's entire troop was killed by Mexicans. His own head was severed and "preserved for a time in vinegar [?] it was finally thrown away [presumably offensive] as it was being taken to Ures," and the fragmentary remains of Crabb and his men were "mangled by hogs and coyotes" (Forbes 23). Crabb's expedition (like McCarthy's) has a sixteen-year-old male survivor. In both accounts the leader of the party is decapitated, his head preserved, and his body fed to hogs. That McCarthy pulled historical details from outside the strict chronology of *Blood Meridian* is not hard to accept.[13]

Two last items suggest that McCarthy's filibuster is a construction. One concerns a phrase that occurs in an account of Walker's expeditions and in a remarkably similar context in McCarthy. The historian Frederic Rosengarten, Jr., writes:

In February 1855 Walker gave up his newspaper work and devoted himself completely to organizing his second filibustering expedition. This time, unlike what occurred during the Sonora debacle, the United States authorities in California gave Walker their *tacit approval*. Major General John E. Wool, commanding the Pacific Division, went even further—he shook Walker heartily by the hand and stated that he not only would not interfere with the Nicaraguan colonization enterprise, but wished it complete success (75; my emphasis.)

McCarthy's White says, "We have the tacit support of Governor Burnett of California" (34). "Tacit support" is not "tacit approval." But the fact that "tacit approval" relates to filibustering expeditions and the government of California reduces the likelihood of an incidental use of the phrase. The occurrence of this phrase, the details of Crabb's death, Chamberlain's presence as a filibusterer only after the Yuma-ferry massacre all suggest that McCarthy synthesized the Captain White expedition from various sources.

A final commentary on the novel's filibustering scene is invited by the mention of both Governor Burnett of California and General William Jenkins Worth during this episode. White's trip toward Sonora takes place after the spring of 1849 (5) and before July 21 of that year (165). General Worth "assumed command of the Military Departments of Texas and New Mexico" on December 26, 1848, "and established his headquarters at San Antonio" (Wallace, *General* 186). He was the first commander of this new department, but died during the cholera epidemic of that winter and spring on May 7, 1849 (Wallace,

---

13. After the Yuma-ferry massacre, California sent Colonel Morehead and his troops to Yuma to punish the Indians. The expedition was a $120,000 waste of time that nearly bankrupted the "infant state" (Guinn 258–259). Stout concludes his recounting of Morehead's expedition with the thought: "Thus, an outlaw wanted for numerous crimes in Texas, [Glanton] . . . very likely set in motion the series of events that led to the first filibuster into Mexico following the war of 1846–1848" (39).

General 187). The Mennonite's warning, then, that Worth would jail the filibusterers "to a man" must have occurred before the middle of May (40).[14] Worth's dates can be seen to match McCarthy's use of Worth's name. But Peter H. Burnett took the oath of office as first governor of the state of California in December 1849 (Melendy and Gilbert 25). Worth's death came months before Burnett became governor. Some aspect of McCarthy's scene needs amplification.[15] The suggestion that White's filibustering is McCarthy's invention is made more compelling, given these irreconcilable dates.[16]

John Joel Glanton

[D]isplaced emigrants [were] . . . turning into horse thieves, gamblers, and even murderers. One set up a business killing Apache Indians and selling scalps to the Mexican government for two hundred dollars each, and collecting two hundred and fifty for each prisoner. If Indians were scarce, he even killed Mexicans to profit from their scalps. (Horgan, *Great River* 787)

This nameless profiteer can only be John Glanton: these comments include all the elements of the Glanton legend. Associated with Major Michael H. Chevallié, Glanton was, historically, an emigrant seeking the gold of California who took a scalp-hunting job with Chihuahua in order to finance the rest of his trip (Smith, "John Joel Glanton" 9; Wharton 34–37). Given the facts that the Indians soon moved, very sensibly, away from the scalpers' range, and that so much money was paid for scalps, the killing of dark-

14. This date allows time for the news of Worth's death to travel to outlying areas: Lieutenant Whiting had been in the desert and did not learn of the general's death until almost three weeks after the event (Whiting 349). Yet suggesting that news of Worth's death had been delayed is also a problem, since this filibustering scene takes place in San Antonio de Bexar, the site of Worth's administrative headquarters.

15. The presence of Burnett's name in Goodman's letter (see the Massacre Accounts section, Chapter 10) authenticates, to some extent, McCarthy's decision to mention Governor Burnett in his novel.

16. The point is perhaps minor, and may be lost on anyone other than another Tennesseean, but it is the case that both filibustering Walker and freebooting Crabb were natives of Tennessee (Rosengarten 9; Forbes 7). Eight of the historically verifiable characters in *Blood Meridian* are also Tennesseeans: the Reverend Robert Green (J. M. Carroll 113); Governor Peter Burnett (Melendy 25, Burnett 1); Captain John Glanton (Woodward, "Side Lights" 7; D. Martin 142), though Glanton's birth is probably more properly placed in South Carolina (Chamberlain 268; Smith, "John Joel Glanton" 14); Doctor Able Lincoln (Woodward, *Feud* 26), though his birth is better placed in New York (D. Martin 138–139); Ben McCulloch (Samuel Reid 23); Lieutenant Cave Couts (D. Martin 128); General Patterson, also known as "Anderson" (Foreman 336; Woodward, *Feud* 24); and Sarah Bourdett (Woodward, "Great Western" 4). Information of this sort necessarily qualifies the assertions that *Blood Meridian* is McCarthy's first novel set outside the South (Arnold, "Cormac McCarthy" 1036; Winchell 307), since McCarthy appears to have brought a good many out of Tennessee with his kid. No other state is as well represented in McCarthy's novel of the opening years of the American Southwest.

haired Mexicans in outlying regions was a temptation to Glanton, and a less-than-problematic moral issue to a former Texas Ranger and a Mexican War veteran (Clemens, *Gray* 269).

Clearly, McCarthy did not limit himself to a single source. Two accounts of the Yuma ferry during the spring of 1850, Arthur Woodward's *Feud on the Colorado* and Douglas Martin's *Yuma Crossing*, are the most detailed and the "closest" to McCarthy's.

In *Feud* (20–30), Woodward quotes what appears to be the full text of the deposition that William Carr gave in San Diego. The attack took place on April 23 at noon. Glanton, it is said, was killed by the blows of a club, and his body was shot with arrows. Additional information in *Feud* from Carr's Los Angeles deposition (see the Massacre Accounts section, Chapter 10) includes his story of three men who were cutting poles and were approached by Indians wanting to "help" with the work. Carr took an arrow in his leg during the attack (a doctor in San Diego later removed it for five hundred dollars). Patterson, "Callahan" (not McCarthy's spelling), Caballo en Pelo, and Lincoln and his dogs are all mentioned in *Feud*. Also included in these pages is a partial quotation from a story concerning the massacre, published in the *Daily Alta California* on January 8, 1851.[17] The writer of the letter "mistakes" Anderson for Patterson, and dates the massacre April 21, 1850. The writer also specifies that a gang member named "Brown," held in jail in San Diego, had bribed a guard to make good his escape. Brown robbed this "deserter." The writer then relates that, "as he tells me," Brown went north until Governor Burnett talked him into acting as a guide on Morehead's ill-conceived, punitive expedition against the Yumas. A circumstance of this sort (three known survivors, none of them Brown) may suggest that Brown either turned away from Yuma after his escape from jail, or, what seems more likely (since Glanton had given Brown $500 with which to bribe the guard), was possibly headed back to Glanton at the ferry when the massacre occurred. And this is McCarthy's scenario. Woodward's *Feud* reproduces enough of the story for this conclusion to be drawn.

Douglas Martin's *Yuma Crossing* is the other major telling of the Yuma massacre that closely matches McCarthy's (138–150). Martin quotes several passages from Cave Couts's *Diary* (128–136) and reproduces a letter dated April 1850 from Able Lincoln to his mother, concerning the ferry business, including mention of the howitzer, the gang's presence, the great amounts of money he has made, and the danger that he senses around himself.[18]

---

17. Taken from the *Daily Alta California*, the full text of this letter is presented in the Massacre Accounts.

18. Lincoln's published family history places Doctor Able B. Lincoln's birth in New York (D. Martin 139). Lincoln writes that he has hired "12 Americans, deserters of the army, that I am paying $100 a month, also 10 Americans that I pay $40 a month each. These men I have all armed with Colt revolvers for which I paid $75 each" (141).

Providing background to introduce Glanton, Martin writes, "Chihuahua merchants who had suffered losses in numberless Indian raids financed an expedition of extermination" to be led by Glanton (143).[19] Martin notes the "nasty whispers" that arose after Glanton's second (and last) Chihuahuan expedition (144). His note of two dead and three wounded at Jesús María gives more numerical information than is provided by other accounts and agrees with McCarthy's version of that fight. He notes that "Callaghan" (McCarthy's spelling) was shot by the gang. He counts but one trip to San Diego, during which a man was thrown in jail. In Martin, Glanton is killed by a "hatchet," and Lincoln by a stone and a club (147). They were, he says, both burned with their dogs. William Carr, Joseph Anderson, and Marcus L. Webster escaped downstream. Martin's account (1954) does not include Holden (who was first identified in *My Confession* [1956]), nor mention the gang's tricking of the Yumas into coming within the howitzer's range.[20]

Of interest to an assessment of *Blood Meridian*, Martin twice makes the point that history repeats itself: "As sure as history had repeated itself here [at the crossing] in the past, it would repeat again, and the Yumas would exact a bloody toll once more at the edge of the Colorado" (137). In the middle of his Glanton story, Martin returns to this thought:

It is rather interesting to note that [the Yumas] chose the same strategy their ancestors had planned to use with Captain Diaz, 310 years before. It was the sound military theory of divide and conquer and this time it worked.

Diaz had frustrated the plot to wipe out his force by his alertness to signs of trouble. But when Glanton came back from San Diego he and four of his men sat down to a big dinner, at which they got into their supply of fresh liquor and then went to sleep. (146)

McCarthy's novel is replete with allusions to repetitions and reexaminations. One of *Blood Meridian*'s epigraphs, from the *Yuma Daily Sun*,[21] is as graphic a statement of the theme of repetition as can be imagined to preface a novel about nineteenth-century scalp

19. Douglas Martin's inclusion of Chihuahuan merchants brings Riddle and Speyer to mind, but can also suggest governor Angel Trías, who, Mark Wasserman notes, was "a successful businessman as well as politician. . . . he took over his grandfather's mercantile business in Chihuahua during the 1820s. . . . He lost much of it, however, in the disruptions of the Indian and civil wars" (23).

20. The particulars of the "howitzer" with which Holden bluffs his way to freedom during the massacre (275) are elusive bits of historical trivia. McCarthy calls it a twelve-pounder with "a bore the size of a saucer" (260). In Dr. Lincoln's letter to his mother, he writes of "a small piece of artillery which I purchased of the American consul at Guaymas" (D. Martin 141). Chamberlain notes "Washington's Battery of six pounders" during the Mexican War (106). Naming Lincoln's "artillery" as a "howitzer," the weapon that Glanton uses to surprise the Yumas during their prearranged attack, suggests the "blunderbuss," "six-pounder," or "howitzer" (Thrapp 11) with which James Johnson surprised the Mimbreños.

21. McCarthy quotes, in advance of the novel proper, from the *Yuma Daily Sun* of June 13, 1982: "Clark, who led last year's expedition to the Afar region of northern Ethiopia, and UC Berkeley colleague Tim

hunting. The Indian dressed in a Spanish breastplate in the novel's first view of the Comanches (52; cf. 140) may even be an allusion to the early Spanish explorer Melchior Diaz's contact with Native Americans in 1540.[22] Details tend to confirm McCarthy's recourse to Martin's version of the Yuma-ferry massacre story (the Chihuahuan merchants, the men killed and wounded at Jesús María, Lincoln, Callaghan, the hatchet), especially considering Martin's observation that "this" had all happened before.

William Carr's deposition in Los Angeles (1850, published 1903), attested to by Joseph A. Anderson and Marcus L. Webster, is a document of obvious importance to the composition of *Blood Meridian*, whether as original newspaper reportage in 1849 or as republished in 1903.[23] Of basic interest, though: the account gives April 23 as the massacre date, mentions the limited number of shots the escaping men could depend on, and notes Black John Jackson as the man drowned and lost in the river. All these items enter *Blood Meridian*. The arrow in Carr's leg is an arrow in the kid's leg. David Brown's name is, too, contained in Carr's deposition (as it is in Goodman's *Daily Alta* account from 1851), though not in the newspaper stories from the spring of 1850. Indeed, from Carr can

---

D. White, also said that a re-examination of a 300,000-year-old fossil skull found in the same region earlier shows evidence of having been scalped."

22. Harlan Hague writes: "With a force of twenty-five men, Melchior Diaz in 1540 marched from northern Sonora to the Gulf of California and on to the mouth of the Gila River." Hague's note digresses, and then continues: "From that moment, bad luck plagued the Spaniards. After some difficulty with the Yumas, the soldiers crossed the Colorado," found they could advance no farther, and went back into Sonora by the way they had come (26).

23. The question of Chamberlain, Tobin, Webster, and Hitchcock, as the only group of massacre survivors separated from the camp because they were cutting poles at the time of the attack, when compared to the account that Carr, Anderson, and Webster give of their remarkably similar activities, becomes an issue of the credibility of one account or the other (or both). Chamberlain's editors suggest that Chamberlain was either the Carr or Anderson of the deposition (299), having given a false name to screen his desertion from the army. This explanation accounts for some of the similarities between the deposition and Chamberlain's version, but Carr may be, I think, eliminated from consideration as Chamberlain. The deposition's speaker desired, he swears, to kill sleeping Indians whom the three moved past in the night following the massacre. Only that his companions "were unwilling to have it done," the deposition asserts, prevented this additional bloodshed. Since the Chamberlain of *My Confession* found Glanton's and Holden's treachery toward the Indians singularly disgusting, he is probably not Carr, given Carr's desire for blood here. Of Anderson, no assessment is possible, though the thought that Chamberlain is not any of Carr's three (and therefore not Anderson either) derives from the different reasons each group gives for having survived the attack. Chamberlain's group was on its way out of camp when the attack took place, having already determined to leave, while there was nothing voluntary about the Carr group's departure. Given the lies contained in the deposition (when compared to Chamberlain's account) regarding the gang's treatment of the Yumas, Chamberlain's "reasons" for departing might be expected to show the three survivors to the alcalde of Los Angeles in a better light than is apparent in Carr's tale. Ralph Smith writes, in a letter cited above, "It seems the more that is written on the Yuma crossing affair the more confusion and contradiction are added." His point is well taken, and the reader of these notes who inclines to puzzles may compare texts at leisure.

come a reading of Glanton's death from an edged steel weapon, not a club, since the pole-cutting party gave a hatchet to a Yuma Indian who, before he ran from them, "was cutting very near the head of one" of the party (52). Carvings on the handle of the death weapon aside (*Blood Meridian* 275), the deposition gives the novelist historical latitude for the thought that the survivors were directly intertwined in Glanton's death.

Chamberlain's contact with the gang was limited to the period of time after the gang's employment by Chihuahua (259–297). Chamberlain provides a portrait of Glanton as having been fervently religious (274, 276) and of Sarah Borginnis (*Blood Meridian* 256–258) as a laundress (see her section below), gives the scene of the lottery of arrows (280–281), notes the ferry of wagon bodies (287), and documents a Glanton gang disguised as Indians for some of its raids (272, 275; cf. *Blood Meridian* 153).[24] He also draws a portrait of Judge Holden as his immense, mercurial, knowledgeable, and practically indestructible adversary. Granted that McCarthy's debt to Chamberlain for character and incident is deep, nevertheless, in an abbreviated list, McCarthy brought to his Chamberlain: Reverend Green, Toadvine, Grannyrat the Mier (and Chihuahua) prisoner, the Van Diemen's Lander, Speyer, the kid as a filibusterer, the gang's scalping business in Chihuahua City, fortune tellers, a living wife for Glanton (Chamberlain only mentions a murdered fiancée), stories of Holden and gunpowder and of Holden on Cooke and Blackstone, stories of fights at Nacori and Jesús María, Dr. Lincoln at the ferry, the Yuma chief's green goggles, pet dogs for Lincoln and Glanton, two trips to San Diego, the farrier story, and a funeral pyre for those massacred at the ferry.

Newspaper versions of the massacre at the Yuma ferry often form the basis for later narratives. Quoted in Massacre Accounts (Chapter 10) are accounts from successive editions of the *New York Daily Tribune*. The item "The Indian Troubles on the Colorado," attributed to the *Alta California* (July 8, 1850), does not mention Glanton's scalp-hunting. He is identified as an outlaw in Texas and Mexico, but no charges are named. Glanton's gang is said to have broken up the Indians' ferry and to have demanded that the Indians not even swim their own goods across. In exasperation, then, the "aborigines" rose up to murder them. "Justice," the author writes in his story, was done by the Indians.

The second *New York Daily Tribune* story, "Massacre of Eleven Americans by the Yumas Indians—Further Particulars" (July 9, 1850), is noted to be the "extract" of a *Sacramento Transcript* story of the "30th ult," and appears to be an abridgement of Carr's Los Angeles deposition (yet the massacre is said to have occurred on April 21). The details of the splitting of the Anglo party into groups on both sides of the river before the Yuma attack began, which Carr and Douglas Martin mention, are given. A scene in which the

---

24. Contributing to this McCarthy scene of a burning wagon train (153) is Chamberlain's statement that any straggling army marcher risked being tortured and could expect to have his "privates cut off and crammed into his mouth," and then be "left to die" (69).

pole cutters distrust the motives of the Indians desiring to "help" them is also provided. The survivors are said to have seen Glanton's dead body just before their escape downriver. Mexican eyewitnesses claim that Lincoln was awakened by the blow of a rock to his skull, and that when he arose, he was clubbed to death; "Another woman related the death of Glanton in the same manner." The burning of the corpses is noted, as is that dogs were "burned alive with them." A list of the names and birthplaces of the dead men closes the account.

Ralph Smith's article "John Joel Glanton, Lord of the Scalp Range" (1962), dependent on Chamberlain, provides no Couts, no Lincoln or Callaghan at the ferry. This is the longest and most detailed article devoted entirely to Glanton (9–15). Only in this article does Glanton's gang make more than two scalp-hunting expeditions. Two of the expeditions are out of and back to Chihuahua, but Smith determined that Glanton also made trips to El Paso in order to sell scalps and stock (which amounted to profiteering, since Chihuahua had invested money for provisions and arms for Glanton's expeditions). Glanton makes three progressively less "successful" trips on Chihuahua's behalf. Smith writes that Glanton fought Gómez but did not kill him. Smith's article is followed by "A Select Bibliography on Scalp Hunting" (16). Chamberlain, David Lavender, Horace Bell, Mayne Reid, George Ruxton, M. L. Crimmins, Richard Irving Dodge, John T. Hughes, and twenty more names are found there, suggesting that Smith's article may well have contributed a ready-made pattern of research for McCarthy's work on the novel.[25]

Jay J. Wagoner mentions Couts, Lincoln, the killing of Callaghan, a massacre date of April 21, 1850, a trip by Glanton to San Diego, the three survivors, and the notice that the dogs of the men were tied to their bodies and burned on a pyre (305–306). This account, though brief, distinguishes the deaths of Lincoln, who was clubbed, and Glanton, whose head was "split . . . open with a hatchet" (306), the only account besides Douglas Martin's wherein Glanton dies in this way.

Thomas W. Sweeney's *Journal*, edited by Arthur Woodward, relates an Anglo traveller's conversation with the Yuma chief Santiago concerning the ferry massacre in which Santiago had played a part (132–137). Sweeney had also spoken, he writes, with one of the survivors of that massacre, and notes that chief Santiago's story "tallied" with the survivor's story "exactly" (133). It is said that the Indians tricked the gang with kindnesses and in this way lulled their defenses. These accounts, Indian and survivor, note only one trip for supplies to San Diego, and that three men escaped by boat, floating down the Colorado until they began a trek westward across the desert. Sweeney says that he "also heard that all three of the fugitives subsequently died violent deaths" (137). His remark is the only one discovered that in some way unites the fates of all three survivors. Sweeney

---

25. In this same vein, Kenneth Hufford's articles contain bibliographies of firsthand accounts of travel over the Gila Trail, and are of interest. He notes Emory, and has one of the only references to Whipple.

notes two Chihuahua expeditions, but does not mention travel in Sonora. He provides no death details.

John Russell Bartlett's account of Glanton's death (2:174–176) is one of the earliest published (1856, apparently second only to the newspaper accounts), and does not mention Lincoln, but rather substitutes "Dr. Langdon," of Louisiana, for the ferrymaster. Several later accounts preserve this name version. Bartlett describes "Gallantin" as a "fugitive from justice," though no mention of scalp hunting is made. He describes a trip made by Glanton to San Diego during which a soldier was killed, but no other men are mentioned. He remarks on the rise in ferry rates under Glanton to four dollars a head. He specifies that twelve to fifteen men were killed in the massacre and that three escaped, but, again, no names are included. Bartlett does add the assertion that the Yumas had, before Glanton's time, tricked travellers into relaxing their guard and had then killed them (see 2:144–145).

Owen White's romanticized account of Glanton's career is one of the fullest, though not the most objectively presented (143–159). White's story begins with an account of Glanton's young and beautiful wife and their baby girl. He follows Glanton into Chihuahua and to Jesús María, relates the Mexican-flag incident (*Blood Meridian* 193), and mentions T. B. Sanford, Frank Carroll, and Mangas Colorado, saying that Glanton and Mangas went "drinking" in Tucson. In the "late summer" of 1849, Glanton arrives at the Colorado, where he met Dr. Langdon (153–154). The Indian's white ferryman is killed. An argument with a Mr. Brodie over the possibility of his entering the ferry business as a third partner apparently convinces Brodie to retire from the scene, but only after he had invested in the construction of a new ferryboat. White mentions a westward supply trip and the jailing of a man. Others accompanying the prisoner go back to the ferry. Glanton heads for San Diego to get his man free and takes twenty-five thousand dollars for a bank deposit. Glanton "hangs" the alcalde in order to effect the release of his man. On the party's return to the ferry, a Yuma attack at midnight kills them all. White's story concludes with Brodie suing for his "invested" share of the company's bank deposit, with the balance going to Glanton's widow and child. This account joins Jesús María details to the ferry story and includes Mangas Colorado. It also provides two trips to San Diego. But in its details, White's story does not include the deaths of any men at Jesús María, does not use the name "Lincoln," and does not mention Brown's bribery of his guard in San Diego or any death details or a funeral pyre. In White, the bodies float down the Colorado to the sea (see Crimmins, below).

Jeremiah Clemens, in his novel *Bernard Lile* (1856), devotes three pages to John Glanton (226–229). He first describes Glanton as a "youth" who:

had not seen more than twenty-two summers. His cheek was smooth and almost beardless; his frame slender and light. There was a peculiar glossiness about the long, raven hair that hung around his neck, and but for the firm lip, and the flashing eye, he might have been mistaken for a woman in disguise. But that slight frame was knit of twisted steel, and the white hand that brushed back his flowing hair had shed more blood than would have furnished its owner a crimson bath. (226–227)

Chamberlain describes Glanton with similar hair and coloring, but with a torso that has become "thick-set" (39–41, 267). To a man in *Bernard Lile* named Tom Simpson, Glanton says:

"There is exactly where we differ. I'm thinking of the girls all the time, and curse me if I haven't killed half a dozen Greasers for no other reason in the world than because I thought it would delight the black-eyed, orange-cheeked damsels to get rid of the infernal brutes."
    "You killed [the Mexican husbands] more because you was a born devil, John, than anything else," replied the volunteer, lying down upon his blanket with the air of a man who intended to put an end to the conversation. (227–228)

Glanton's banter with the volunteer reaches an impasse. Tom will not discuss Bernard Lile with him. Tom says:

"I don't know anything to tell you, John, and wouldn't do it if I did, unless [Lile] said so."
    "Well," said Glanton, rising, walking behind Simpson, and putting his hands on his shoulders, "if you wont [sic] tell me anything, I'll tell you something."
    He stooped, as if to whisper in his ear, and catching the member in his teeth, bit it sharply. With a hasty exclamation, the hunter turned to grasp his tormentor, but the active youth had bounded beyond his reach, and with a loud laugh disappeared in the darkness.
    "Plague take the boy," muttered Simpson, rubbing the smarting member, "he's brought the blood." (228–229)

Glanton's name is associated with violence, but this is the only instance of ear-biting.[26] Tom doesn't seem to find the episode uncharacteristic of Glanton, and the impression is left with the reader that Tom probably will not carry a grudge. These are hardy folk, the volunteers. *Blood Meridian*'s most prominent instance of ear-biting is that of Glanton's horse biting the ear of an Indian subchief's horse when the gang meets Mangas Colorado (228–229).
    Robert Eccleston, in his diary of 1849, notes a "Glantom" who had fought three hundred Indians led by chief Gomez during a dawn raid near Presidio (137–138). He later mentions Glanton and the "Biddle" horse (usually glossed "Riddle," for the American trader and consul in Chihuahua, Bennet Riddells), which Glanton had sold for two hundred dollars (183). Eccleston's third mention of John Glanton regards an agreement made between Glanton and John Coffee Hays. Hays desires to make a treaty with Indians in

26. Elliot Gorn's article on the fighting styles of southern plain-folk men, with biting as an integral technique, may be of some interest to the reader of *Blood Meridian* regarding Glanton's biting, and regarding the scene of the death of white John Jackson (killed by a black man) as well.

the vicinity of the Santa Rita mines and asks Glanton to hunt scalps elsewhere—or to enter the area after his trip—so that his peace negotiations will not be disturbed (232).

Colonel Crimmins's article "John Glanton" (1940) names the "Brown Brothers." Crimmins mentions Glanton's wife and baby in San Antonio (see Crimmins, quoted in H. Bailey Carroll, below). He notes two Chihuahua expeditions, including the attack on an Ojinaga Indian camp along the Concho River. He mentions the cutting down of a Mexican flag, Tucson, and Mangas Colorado. He places Glanton at the ferry in late summer of 1849 with Dr. Langdon. The Indian's white ferryman is killed. Men ride to San Diego for supplies and one of them is arrested. Glanton then goes to San Diego to free his man and to make a bank deposit. Crimmins is one of the relatively few authors to enumerate scalping expeditions. The close of this article seems to inform McCarthy's image of Callaghan's headless body floating down the Colorado with a buzzard perched on its back (*Blood Meridian* 262; see the Callaghan section, below).

Charles D. Spurlin's book (1984) is a collection of lists of names, from enlistment records, of Texas volunteers in federal service during the Mexican War. Glanton, at age twenty-seven, is noted as a private in Company F from May 24, 1847, until March 1, 1848 (97, 95). Again shown as twenty-seven, and still a private, Glanton served in Captain Walter P. Lane's Company A from the time of his transfer from Company E on September 1, 1847, [*sic*] until mustering out on June 30, 1848 (151–152). Glanton is listed as a first lieutenant, age thirty, in Benjamin F. Hill's company from October 27, 1848, until December 17, 1848 (125). Spurlin's lists contain hundreds of names, including those of Ben McCulloch, Mabry Gray, Michael Chevallie, George Henry Tobin, John A. White, a Trammel, and a James Hobbs.

George W. B. Evans's journal entry for July 24, 1849, mentions "Glantin" capturing "a very aged squaw" and having "a Mexican to shoot and scalp" her (133; *Blood Meridian* 97–98). Of the several accounts of this incident, Evans's is the only one that attributes both the killing and the scalping to one gang member (see otherwise Smith, "John Joel Glanton" 10).

J. Frank Dobie's book *Apache Gold and Yaqui Silver* (1939) contains several items of interest. His chapter "Scalp Hunter's Ledge," concerning a lost outcrop of silver ore, mentions John Glanton, giving Lane's account (below) of Glanton's killing of a Mexican civilian. This paragraph also mentions "the Brown brothers" and Charlie Brown's Congress Hall saloon at Tucson. Glanton's end does not enter into this account, though "the Prussian Jew Speyer" and "the Englishman Johnson" (in the Mangas Colorado section) are mentioned (266). Dobie's book also includes a separate bibliography of "the scalp hunters of northern Mexico and their activities" (363–366), which contains some items (in its twenty-seven citations) not found in the usual scalp-hunter bibliographies, particularly the Ober and Bourke books examined below.

Horace Bell's account (1881, reprinted 1927) of Glanton (273–280) mentions Frank Carroll and W. T. B. Sanford at Jesús María, and the flag incident, though the insult causes no deaths. Bell refers to a mention of John Glanton as a protégé of Mabry Gray in Jeremiah Clemens's novel *Mustang Gray*.[27] Bell mentions Riddle and Abel as suppliers of the scalper's gang, mentions Mangas Colorado and a feast of seven bullocks that fed the gang and the Indian band at Tucson. Of the Brown brothers, Bell writes:

The two Browns were not of kin, Dave being a red-headed, good-natured American, while Charley was a quarter-blood Cherokee. Dave was hung at Los Angeles in 1854, by an irate mob of California Mexicans, most of whom were his personal friends, and hung him only in vindication of principle. That is to say, the Americans of the Angel City were in the habit of amusing themselves by hanging some luckless Mexican, and the Mexicans wished to show that they could play at the same game, and so seized on poor Dave as a fit subject for demonstration, apologized for the liberty they were taking with him, which Dave laughingly accepted, and was then swung up. Dave had always lived the life of an unprincipled fellow, he died in vindication of a principle, that is, to show that the native Californians knew how to hang a man in the most approved gringo fashion.

Poor Dave set a most beautiful example to the young people who witnessed his interesting taking off. He said he had committed a great many crimes, but not of sufficient magnitude to deserve hanging. The only great crime he had ever seriously contemplated was running for councilman of our pure and lovely municipality, and should he have done so, and been elected, and have served, then "I would have felt that I deserved death"; "but fortunately," said Dave, "in going into the presence of the great Judge, I can at least claim that I was never either mayor, or member of the Los Angeles city council." Alas! poor Dave, his crimes were many, but these last mentioned were not charged up against him in the kingdom come.

The other Brown also fell a victim to principle. He went to Nicaragua under the banner of manifest destiny, and died in vindication of the principles thereof. (279–280)

In C. L. Sonnichsen's *Tucson* (78), a photograph of the interior of a saloon built in 1868 includes figures identified as the saloon's owner, Charles O. Brown, and his son William, which tends to undermine Bell's point regarding "Charley" and "manifest destiny."[28] Bell's account does not include ferry information.

Ralph Smith's article "'Long' Webster and 'The Vile Industry of Selling Scalps'" (1961)

27. This citation is probably an error, and may be the continuation of some earlier error. There is no substantive mention of John Joel Glanton in *Mustang Gray*. Clemens's novel *Bernard Lile* (1856), published two years earlier than *Mustang Gray*, does have a scene in which Glanton says he will join Gray at Camargo during the Mexican War (227), but Gray at Camargo, in *Mustang Gray* (290–293), does not meet up with John.

28. Horace Bell's story of Charley [*sic*] Brown and Nicaragua must also be compared with John Cady's assertion that he had worked for Charles Brown in Tucson beginning in late 1870 and that he was also "chef in the Brown household" during that time (57–58).

mentions Glanton and includes a description of him based on Chamberlain (108–109). This article includes references to Jesús María, the cut flag, Sanford and Carroll. Mangas Colorado is mentioned. Allusion is made to a hunt of "Navajo" Indians. A substantial portion of the end of this article is based on Chamberlain: Holden is named, the four Yumas killed by Glanton's gang are mentioned. Lincoln and Glanton are, in this article, beheaded.

In "Poor Mexico, So Far from God and So Close to the Tejanos" (1968), Smith mentions Chevallié, John Joel Glanton, and their contracts with the state of Chihuahua. Holden is mentioned and referenced to the Chamberlain source.[29] Included in the Jesús María episode is Sanford's name as well as that of Roy Bean.[30] Killed there, Smith states, were David and Robert Sanderson, in a fight that "put an end to a guerrilla carousal of several days" (102). This article does not number the gang's expeditions in Mexico, does not mention the Yuma massacre, but does list the names of many gang members unavailable to this researcher in any other place. Interestingly, McCarthy does not incorporate into *Blood Meridian* any of the many Mexican gang members whom Smith names.

In "Apache Plunder Trails Southward, 1831–1840" (1962), Smith notes Glanton as a scalp hunter (23). Smith also mentions Glanton's "fleecing" of the Mimbreños tribe of Apaches in New Mexico, a tribe led by Mangas Colorado (25; see *Blood Meridian* 228–231, 242).

Smith's article "The Mamelukes of West Texas and Mexico" (1963) notes the presence in Glanton's gang of a "negro" (67). On the same page, Smith notes: "With painted faces and absorbed in magic, taboos, and obi superstition, [the scalp-hunting Mamelukes, many of them black men] exhibited an appearance of savagery that must have equalled that of the Indians they were hunting." The "ritual" awakened in Black John Jackson's "dark blood" (81), his association with the gypsy family (99), his killing of the white Jackson (107), and his robes that match the judge's (273) come to mind at this description.

Smith's article "The Scalp Hunter in the Borderlands, 1835–1850" (1964) mentions Glanton (18), and mentions Chamberlain's arrow-lottery story.

Julius Froebel (1859) mentions Glanton as a scalper killed at the Yuma ferry (350–351). He also provides one of the only accounts of Glanton's home life in San Antonio. Froebel presents a portrait of John's wife (a woman other than the earlier fiancée, whom the Indians had killed) as having been praised by the community for her devotion to him: she would not let a posse chasing John come into their house until he had made his escape. Of Glanton's life before scalping, Froebel writes that he "shot men for sport on the high road" (440). He adds that Glanton "usually . . . murdered weak and defenceless men,"

---

29. Smith ("'Long' Webster" 114, "John Joel Glanton" 12) consistently states Holden's height as six feet in his moccasins, not "six feet six" in his moccasins, as cited by Chamberlain (271).

30. Sonnichsen's *Roy Bean* includes a version of Bean's flight to, and then from, Jesús María (26).

making a distinction between Glanton and another outlaw, Bill Hardy, who would arm his opponents before he killed them (441). The cowardice that Froebel attributes to Glanton, though not confirmable by any other source, is reminiscent of Chamberlain's comments about Holden (272). The arming of opponents before they are killed suggests the shooting of Owens by Black John Jackson (*Blood Meridian* 234–236).

H. Bailey Carroll, in his column in the *Southwestern Historical Quarterly* (January 1944), reproduces F. B. E. Browne's hand-drawn map from 1851 (facing page 306) of an area in Texas between San Antonio and El Paso; a looping trail in the southwest corner is designated as the "Rout taken by Glanton in search of Indians." Carroll asks if any reader can identify unknown parts of the map or the reference to Glanton. In response to the query, in the April 1944 issue, Colonel M. L. Crimmins answers that Glanton was from San Antonio and that he had left a widow, Joaquina Menchaca (see also Crimmins, below). These were, Crimmins notes, the "parents of John William, born 1847, and Joaquina Margarita, born 1849" (430).

General Walter Lane, a Mexican War veteran, writes in 1887 of having let John "Glandon" escape a military inquiry into his shooting, under questionable circumstances, of a fleeing Mexican (56–57). Lane recounts that he told Glanton "to skip for San Antonio, as Gen. Taylor was bound to have his scalp [for the shooting], and I could not protect him" (59).

According to Colonel Richard Irving Dodge (1883), Glanton was "notoriously cold-blooded" (245). Dodge includes a brief notice of Glanton's daylight attack on a winter camp of Indians on the American side of the "Grand Cañyon" of the Rio Grande, in which two hundred and fifty scalps were taken. There is no mention of Chihuahua, of the number of scalping expeditions Glanton made, or of the name of the tribe Glanton and his men attacked.

Sonnichsen's *Pass of the North* (1968) mentions Glanton and Major Chevalier as scalp hunters (131). Sonnichsen notes that in the winter of 1849–1850, Glanton's gang took two hundred and fifty Mescalero scalps in Santa Elena Canyon. Sonnichsen's account is not detailed enough to mention the number of scalping expeditions that Glanton made.

Sonnichsen, in *Tucson* (1982), mentions Cave Couts and Glanton and refers to Chamberlain (34). This very brief account circumstantially places Couts in Tucson, but only as Major Graham's command was "passing through" in 1848 (34).

John C. Cremony, who travelled with Bartlett's Boundary Survey Commission, tells a story (1868, rpt. 1983) of "John Gallantin" herding twenty-five hundred sheep out of Mexico on his way to California by way of the Yuma ferry (112–113, 116–117). Glanton and his men were killed there by the Yumas, clubbed to death after the Yumas had feigned friendship. "Not a soul of his band escaped death," Cremony writes, though Caballo en Pelo is said to have been Cremony's informant, and the information is said to have been provided to him (within months of the massacre) in the fall of 1850. His mention of "double-barreled shotguns" as prime causes of death in Arizona and New Mexico during the 1850s may perhaps give some "authenticity" to the episode of David Brown's argument with the farrier (*Blood Meridian* 265–268).

In J. P. Dunn's *Massacres of the Mountains* (1886, rpt. 1958), "John Gallantin" scalped for the state of Chihuahua, and when he and the gang fled, they are said to have rounded up and taken with them twenty-five hundred head of sheep to the Yuma ferry crossing in 1851. Yuma chief Caballo en Pelo first professed friendship for Glanton, but "suddenly fell upon them" (316). In the page immediately preceding the Glanton story is an account of the Mimbreños closing the road to the Santa Rita del Cobre mines after James Johnson's attack on Chief Juan José Compá (see Mangas Colorado, below). Dunn remarks that of the several hundred miners and their families who fled from Santa Rita to Chihuahua City for safety from the Apaches, only four or five men survived ambushes along the way.

Hubert Howe Bancroft, in *History of Arizona and New Mexico* (1889), mentions Cave J. "Coutts" as the first ferryman at Yuma. He mentions a "wheeled boat" that had been built on Lake Michigan and brought overland to the crossing as a ferryboat by an entrepreneur. Bancroft names Lincoln and Glanton, cites the killing of the "opposition" ferryman, the massacre, and three escapees. His account does not provide death details. He footnotes the possibility that Glanton was "Galantin" the sheep drover, and names the escapees as "C. O. Brown," "Joe Anderson," and "another" (486–488). Joseph Anderson is the name of one of the survivors who gave a deposition in San Diego after the massacre, but C. O. Brown is not.

J. M. Guinn's *History of California* (1907) notes a dependence on Bancroft's *Arizona and New Mexico*, though Guinn's account, for the purposes of this project, is interestingly divergent from Bancroft's history. Guinn gives no scalp-hunter details. He writes of the survivors' depositions given before Alcalde Don Abel Stearns of Los Angeles, including Jeremiah Hill's deposition (printed along with Carr's deposition in the same periodical). Guinn gives a date of February 12, 1850, for the arrival of the gang at the ferry. He also notes that April 25 was "two days after the massacre." Guinn states that Lincoln was a native of Illinois and a relative of President Abraham Lincoln, "facts" that Douglas Martin's version of the ferry massacre lays to rest. Guinn writes that "Anderson," not Patterson, gave the Yumas their ferry; that Lincoln was clubbed to death; and that Glanton was killed "in the same manner" (258). Guinn's account contrasts with McCarthy's on the points at which the depositions vary from the novel.

In the installment of Arthur Woodward's article "Scalp Hunters of Chihuahua" that was published in 1938, he relates Glanton's story briefly. Glanton's "scrapes" in San Antonio are mentioned, as is his scalp hunting. Lincoln is named. The bashed heads and burned bodies at the massacre are noted. Woodward includes no count of the number of Chihuahua expeditions and no survivor information.

Woodward's "Side Lights on Fifty Years of Apache Warfare, 1836–1886" (1961) provides the reader little Glanton information not already provided in "Scalp Hunter."

John Bourke's *On the Border with Crook* (1896) briefly tells the story of the "Englishman Johnson" firing a cannon into a group of Mimbreños Apaches (117–118). He identifies Glanton as an "Irishman," apparently confusing Glanton with the Irish-born scalp-hunter James Kirker. Bourke also notes that Glanton's "first 'victory' was gained over a band of Apaches with whom he set about arranging a peace in northern Chihuahua," (117) in a story not elsewhere recorded, but not far removed from Glanton's "trick" on the Yumas in *Blood Meridian* (256, 260–262).[31] Ruxton's name is included as the source for some of Bourke's information. Bourke notes the Yuma massacre of the ferrymen, but gives no names or death details.

Joseph Allen Stout, Jr., mentions Glanton as someone who scalped both Indians and Mexicans, but who "cleverly blamed the Indians in the area for such massacres" (39). He does not mention the number of expeditions made. Stout's version gives no death details, but includes the note that "some" survived the massacre at the ferry.

Grant Foreman, whose book includes the overland journal of Captain R. B. Marcy, tells the Glanton massacre story (335–336). Lincoln and Patterson are named along with the men otherwise listed in the *New York Daily Tribune* article of July 9, 1850, on the massacre. The date of April 21 is given for the fight.

Donald E. Worchester notes both Glanton and James Kirker as having worked for Chihuahua as scalpers. He places Glanton in Sonora. The massacre is described as "poetic retribution" (47).

John H. Cady's reference to "the infamous 'Doc' Glanton and his gang" does not mention any scalp hunting, but does briefly mention the gang's murder of the Yumas' white ferry pilot; "the Glanton gang was subsequently wiped out by the Indians in retaliation" (27). Such is the extent of Cady's mention of Glanton—strictly hearsay—in his otherwise personal memoir.

Donald MacCarthy's "Chihuahua Scalp Hunters" (1929) ends with the coy remark that "the above article is largely derived from the late Major Horace Bell's *Reminiscences of a Ranger*," which had been reprinted in 1927.

McCarthy gives Glanton a roundness of character, a personalization, not generally found in the histories or personal narratives that mention him. The following paragraphs provide the reader of *Blood Meridian* with a streamlined key to McCarthy's details of Glanton's character.

Glanton allows the gypsy family to accompany the gang to Janos, though he warns them, "I promise you nothin" (90). Glanton "seemed to simply reckon [the black and

---

31. Bourke's thought may be a conflation of the Glanton and Hays agreement noted above.

white Jacksons] among his number and ride on," though the other men watched the antagonism between the two with apparent interest (81). Black Jackson "looked to where Glanton sat" during his confrontation with white Jackson at the fireside, yet "Glanton watched him" without any apparent choosing of sides or preferences (106). After the beheading, "Glanton rose" (107). In bloody circumstances McCarthy's Glanton does not absolutely need to participate.

At the Santa Rita mines, Glanton met squatter miners and "shook his head at the wonderful invention of folly in its guises and forms" (117). Fools though he thought them, Glanton nevertheless gave the miners "a half pound of rifle-powder and some primers and a small pig of lead" for their defense as the gang rode out (119).

As the gang moved through the mountains, Glanton picked up an aspen leaf, one of the "golden disclets," "and turned it like a tiny fan by its stem and held it and let it fall and its perfection was not lost on him" (136).[32] Though bloody himself and perhaps mad, this Glanton is a character who recognizes "perfection" in a "lonely aspen wood."

In McCarthy's further development of this character, Glanton asks Cloyce Bell, "You let women see that thing?" (234). Bell's brother, the idiot, is the "thing" to which Glanton refers, his remark indicating some regard for propriety.

McCarthy's Glanton, after the scalping expeditions, took stock of his men and his situation one night as he stared "long into the embers of the fire" (243). Glanton's past and future are assessed on this page, and he is seen to have "usurped to contain within him all that he would ever be in the world"; "he claimed agency," and this is a claim that Holden turns to later in the book (330). And in some final act of apparent mercy, Glanton has the alcalde loosed from his hanging before he is dead (271).

Albert Speyer

A note in Josiah Gregg's *Diary* identifies the trader Albert Speyer as "a Prussian Jew" and a "prominent Santa Fe trader from 1843 to 1848" (197). On the "particular trip" in the late spring of 1846, to which the note belongs, Speyer:

created considerable excitement because he happened to be carrying two wagonloads of arms and ammunition that the governor of Chihuahua had ordered in 1845. Speyer travelled rapidly in order to escape United States cavalry trying to intercept him, as well as to reach New Mexico early enough to obtain a certificate from the custom house before the United States took it over. (197)

---

32. Lester Ballard dreams: While he was riding a mule "on a low ridge," "each leaf that brushed his face deepened his sadness and dread. Each leaf he passed he'd never pass again. They rode over his face like veils, already some yellow, their veins like slender bones where the sun shone through them. He had resolved himself to ride on for he could not turn back and the world that day was as lovely as any day that ever was and he was riding to his death" (McCarthy, *Child of God* 170–171).

Speyer's commendable commitment to his arms-importing deal with Chihuahua was also, given that the Mexican War started in 1846, treasonous trade with the enemy. But to be fair, Speyer was not the only trader to find it more profitable to sell arms to threatened Chihuahua. Of the 315 wagons that originally accompanied the army's southward march on Chihuahua, Ralph Smith writes, "One trader after another slipped from Doniphan's [American military] tow until more than fifty wagons reached Chihuahua City before the Battle of Sacramento." The net result was that Chihuahua was no longer a "poorly armed" city, as the scouts had advised Doniphan ("King" 40–41).

Speyer's name comes up several times in the narrative of James Hobbs, who rode with James Kirker's scalp-hunting gang in the early 1840s. Along with American trader Riddle, Speyer supplied many of the gang's needs.[33] Hobbs notes that Speyer seems to have acted as a go-between, on occasion, for the sale of scalps to Chihuahua (71). He also says that the traders Riddle and Speyer occasionally "cached" incoming goods until they could negotiate to reduce import duties to a bare minimum. A customs official would meet the traders at midnight a mile outside the city and escort their wagons into town. The official would be paid a hundred dollars, "more than he could make in a month out of government," Hobbs writes, and each of his "file of ten soldiers" would be paid "a dollar, a pair of shoes, and a bottle of whisky" (77–78).

After a successful scalping expedition, then-governor Trias brought musicians to the gates of the city to greet his returning warriors (Moorhead 150). Kirker and Hobbs were "presented" with new suits of clothes from Speyer's store and treated to a "complimentary dinner at Riddle & Stephens's hotel" (Hobbs 95; see also the Riddells section, below).

McCarthy's scene involving Speyer has several parallels to the historical accounts. Speyer meets the gang on the "outskirts" of the city (81). He is described as a "Prussian jew" (82). Speyer says that the Colt six-shooters "were contracted for the war," in an apparent reference to the guns having been overbought for sale to Chihuahua during the Mexican War (83). Mexican soldiers (ten and an officer) are involved in both Hobbs's and McCarthy's scenes ("Ten or a dozen," 83). The soldiers in McCarthy, even though "convinced" that the trading is sanctioned by the governor, are paid off through the coins "doled" to Sergeant Aguilar (85).

Other outside influences on the Speyer scene can be noted. Frederick Adolphus Wislizenus writes that when Speyer's servant discharged pistols in a "court-yard" in a "remote corner" of this city, as a preliminary to cleaning them, the concussions brought him "in contact with the Mexican authorities" (48–49), just as Glanton's pistol-firing attracted Sergeant Aguilar. Furthermore, Glanton's choice of animal targets in the courtyard seems related to what James Greer reports about John Coffee Hays's target practice:

33. Hobbs spells the name "Speyers."

At Washington-on-the-Brazos, Hays inspected the pistols of his latest recruits. He reloaded the new weapons and was standing with one of them in his hand as he talked of guns. Just then "He observed," related Webber, "a chickencock some thirty paces off in the square, which was just straightening its neck to crow. 'Boys, I'll cut that saucy fellow short,' he remarked, as he leveled and fired quickly at it. Sure enough, the half-announced clarion note of chanticleer was lost in the explosion as the bird fluttered over dead with a ball in its head." (35)

The texts are clearly linked by the similarity of Hays's and Glanton's choice of live targets and by the fact that both men demonstrate handguns before their groups.

Consul Bennet Riddells

The spellings "Riddle" and "Stephens," apparently unique to James Hobbs's narrative, are the spellings McCarthy uses in *Blood Meridian*.[34] Bennett Riddells is often mentioned by travellers to Chihuahua City before, during, and after the Mexican War. Riddells was born in South Carolina, and by 1850 had been a trader in Mexico, in and around Saltillo and Chihuahua, for twenty-one years (Riddells, letter to Clayton). The American consul in Chihuahua immediately preceding Riddells's first tenure resigned on May 4, 1849, as noted in a letter posted from Mexico City. The first correspondence from Riddells listed in the Consular Register of the State Department of the United States is a letter dated August 27, 1850. The register notes Riddells's resignation as consul on receipt of a letter written on February 21, 1851. Two other men then held the post of consul in Chihuahua. Riddells appears in the register as consul in Chihuahua for a second period of time, beginning with a letter written on June 8, 1852. This second term lasted until December 1, 1852, when Riddells again resigned, noting that it had "become necessary to remove to the Port of Mazatlan on the Pacific (Mex)" (letter to Crittenden).

Historians who mention Riddells as American consul in Chihuahua make no distinctions regarding his terms of service. He may have been consul in Chihuahua when Glanton's gang first rode in to town. He is described as "acting American consul in the city" by McCarthy just after the gang's return, on July 27, from its first Chihuahuan expedition that included the kid (171). This date falls in the period between the resignation

---

34. Spellings of Riddells's name vary: "Bennet Riddells" (Bartlett 2:430) or "Bennett Riddells" (Lister 113). In Wislizenus, the hotel is the "Rittels & Stevenson" (48). Max Moorhead notes that "Benjamin Riddells and a man named Stevenson" (later noted as "Stevenson or Stephenson") operated a hotel for transient merchants (117–118). "Benjamin Riddle" and John Abel are named the suppliers of Glanton's first expedition (MacCarthy 523; Smith, "John Joel Glanton" 9). Neither of these accounts mentions Stephens. Riddells's signature is plainly "Riddells" in his letters cited below. Mr. Riddells' first name, in his correspondence, is abbreviated. A letter from Mr. Green, consul in Chihuahua after Riddells's first term, concerning the return of Riddells's consular bond, spells Riddells's given name as "Bennet" (letter, August 28, 1851), as does Bartlett.

of the earlier consul and the first correspondence between Riddells, as consul, and the State Department. Since McCarthy presents Riddells as "acting consul," his sources of information on Riddells appear to be early documents or copies of them. If these assumptions regarding McCarthy's research are correct, then it is interesting to note that McCarthy chooses James Hobbs's spelling for Riddells's name. W. I. Riddle, of San Antonio, was a "merchant" (Greer 54), and Hobbs's spelling aligns these two men. Given this spelling, Riddells also becomes a "Riddle," bribing customs agents, smuggling, and fronting money for scalpers.

Governor Angel Trias

Of the governor of Chihuahua who hired Glanton for scalp hunting, McCarthy writes that Trias "had been sent abroad as a young man for his education and was widely read in the classics and was a student of languages" (168). John Russell Bartlett, in charge of a United States Boundary Commission in 1851–1853, surveying the border between the United States and Mexico in anticipation of the Gadsden Purchase, published a thousand pages on his experiences. The second volume of his account contains a description of Trias remarkably similar to McCarthy's:

General Trias, who was for several years Governor of the State of Chihuahua, is a gentleman of large wealth and fine accomplishments. After receiving his education he went to Europe, where he spent eight years travelling in various parts, although he remained most of the time in England and France. He is well versed in several of the European languages, and speaks English with great correctness. Of English literature he told me he was very fond; and he considered that no native appreciated the beauties of Shakspeare and Milton better than he. With Addison and the belles-lettres writers of England he was also familiar. (2:426)[35]

At Trias's banquet for the Anglos, Holden sat at the governor's right hand, "and they at once fell into conversation in a tongue none other in that room spoke at all saving for random vile epithets drifted down from the north" (169), recalling Chamberlain's remark that Holden "conversed with all in their own language" (271). The novel's Tobin says that Holden and the governor "sat up till breakfast and it was Paris this and London that in five languages" (123).

When McCarthy writes of the banquet held in honor of the scalp hunters' trophy-laden return to Chihuahua City, he notes:

Patriotic toasts were drunk, the governor's aides raising their glasses to Washington and Franklin and the Americans responding with yet more of their own country's heroes, igno-

---

35. Bartlett's *Narrative* was published as two volumes in one binding.

rant alike of diplomacy and any name at all from the pantheon of their sister republic. (169)

This detail, and particularly McCarthy's depiction of the gang's ignorance of Mexican heroes, probably springs from Bartlett's mention that at a dinner hosted by General Trias in honor of the Boundary Commission:

Patriotic toasts were drunk, and among those given by the Mexicans were Washington and Franklin. In return we gave the heroes of the Mexican revolution, Iturbide, Hidalgo, Allende, and Jimenez (2:427; cf. 2:435.)

McCarthy's alteration of Bartlett's detail stresses that the gang was ignorant, and certainly in comparison with Bartlett's surveyors, they might well have been. McCarthy also, thereby, further alienates the gang from civilized company.

Grannyrat

McCarthy's character Grannyrat appears to be a conflated rather than a particular historical character.[36] Still, the novel's introduction of Grannyrat is rich in historical references. Grannyrat's participation in the Mier campaign and the taking of Chihuahua links him to the Mexican War. General Lane, in his memoirs, describes a Captain Lewis as having been a Mier prisoner held at Chihuahua City, where he paved streets during his detention (73). Details of this sort may inform McCarthy's Chihuahua prisoners' cleaning of the streets (74). The "Old Bill," to whom Grannyrat refers (77), is Colonel William Alexander Doniphan, who was a reputedly brilliant commander.[37] Captain White tells the kid that "when Colonel Doniphan took Chihuahua City he inflicted over a thousand casualties on the enemy and lost only one man and him all but a suicide" (33), and that his troops were "unpaid irregulars that called him Bill, were half naked, and had walked to the battlefield from Missouri" (34).[38] Grannyrat's (and the captain's) familiarity of address is

36. McCarthy's character named "Chambers" (104) is introduced as a man who had fought in the war in Doniphan's command, and who had been one of the "Mier" prisoners, yet a cross-check of lists of men of both campaigns does not confirm a "Chambers." William Connelley notes the discharge of a Private "John Chambers" from the Doniphan command after the Mexican War (569). But Joseph McCutchan, in his "List of men comprising the command of Col. Wm. S. Fisher, In 1842, '43 & '44, In the Campaign Known as 'The Mier Expedition,'" does not show a "Chambers" among them (192–201).

37. It is unlikely, given the details associated with the mention of this person, that the reference is to the well-known mountain man "Old Bill" Williams of whom Alephus Favour wrote.

38. Connelley, in a note in his book on Doniphan's expedition, writes at some length on the "true origin" of the Doniphan family and of William Doniphan himself:

The founder of the family was Carmac, King of Munster, A.D. 483. The ancient name was Donnaghadh, which signifies "Destroying."

consistent with James Hobbs's remark that some of Doniphan's volunteers would call him "'colonel,' some 'Doniphan,' simply, while others, to abbreviate it, called him 'Bill'" (158).

Grannyrat's use of the word "dance" (77) to characterize the Comanche attack on White's filibustering expedition is the first of many allusions to the dance, which become so prominent by the book's final chapter. Grannyrat also introduces the novel's first indication of Anglos scalping Indians, in his story of the one-hundred-year-old Lipan Indian mummies whose hair was taken for sale to Durango (77–78). This scalping story is McCarthy's interpolation (see the Wislizenus section in Chapter 3). The novel's introduction of Glanton's scalping band occurs three paragraphs later, foreshadowed by this deliberate alteration of the source account. Grannyrat's appearance in the novel, then, links the recent wars in the Southwest, in which he participated, to the story *Blood Meridian* is about to unfold.

Bathcat

McCarthy's character Bathcat does not appear to be a verifiable historical figure. He is *Blood Meridian*'s "fugitive from Vandiemen's Land" (86). As with "Bexar" for "San Antonio," McCarthy correctly uses Tasmania's name in 1849, Van Diemen's Land (changed in 1854), as if to emphasize, after all, that the transience of "nomenclature" is one of McCarthy's preeminent themes (172).

Bathcat's participation in scalp hunting is an appropriate occupation for a dispossessed nineteenth-century Van Diemen's Lander, for it was at that time that the aboriginal population of Van Diemen's Land faced extinction. In 1842, William Lanne, the "last man" of the aboriginal population of the island, was a child of six or seven (Bonwick 393). There were to be no more children of that race. Bathcat's presence reminds us that Spaniards killed natives, the Dutch killed natives, and the English colonists in both America and Australia killed natives: "as Cotton Mather reports of the English American Colonies: 'Among the early settlers, it was considered a religious act to kill Indians'" (Bonwick 68–69; see also Drinnon 457). Bathcat has found his niche killing more "aborigines" in the novel (87; see also 173): as a transported prisoner, Bathcat could never return to England or his home in Wales (R. Montgomery Martin 346). In addition, emigrants from Australia to California at that time were held responsible for the beginning of thievery in that state.[39] Since McCarthy's inclusion of Bathcat in Glanton's gang

---

But [Colonel Doniphan] was himself a typical Celt—of immense stature, noble appearance, brilliant parts, fearless, of great moral courage, sanguine, faithful, just, poetic in temperament, the champion of the down-trodden, eloquent beyond description, and without doubt entitled to be classed among the greatest orators that ever lived. (18)

39. Governor Burnett writes:

During the year 1848 there were very few, if any, thefts committed in California. The honest miners

of scalpers is apparently his own invention, Bathcat's presence expands the novel's world of reference beyond Texas, Mexico, and the Southwest to encompass the rest of the colonized world as well. Through this character, McCarthy enhances the validity of Holden's contention that violence drives men's destinies.[40]

Mangas Colorado

On April 22, 1837, in the Sierra de las Animas of present Hidalgo County in southern New Mexico, trader James Johnson brought together the Mimbreño Apaches of his friend chief Juan José Compá in order to feast and trade with them (Worchester 37–38). As the Indians stood together, examining the goods, Johnson gave a sign and a concealed cannon loaded with grapeshot and chain was fired, cutting into the unsuspecting Indians, killing, it is said, dozens.[41] Small-arms fire from the whites who had stood to the side killed many more. Johnson himself killed chief Juan José. Johnson, it turned out, had been hired by the Mexican state of Sonora to hunt scalps (Worchester 38; Smith, "Scalp Hunter" 5). The story of the concealed cannon entered scalp-hunting legend.[42]

It was Mangas Colorado (Red Sleeve) who united the surviving Mimbreños. Mangas Colorado was "a huge man, some said six feet, six inches tall, with," Thrapp says, "a proportionate brain and intelligence" (12). Cremony writes of Mangas's size and "far more than an ordinary amount of brain strength" (47) as well as the "atrocious cruelties" of which he was capable (177–178). When McCarthy mentions Mangas Colorado, he introduces the reader to yet another of the several larger-than-life historical characters of his

---

kept their sacks of gold-dust in their tents, without fear of loss. Men were then too well off to steal. Toward the close of that year some few murders and robberies were committed. But in 1849 crimes multiplied rapidly. The immigrants from Australia consisted in part of very bad characters, called "Sydney Ducks." These men soon began to steal gold-dust from the miners, and the latter showed them no mercy. In most mining camps they had an alcalde, whose decisions were prompt and final, and whose punishments were severe and most rigidly inflicted. (204; see also Wilson, 161)

40. The writer of a California newspaper story in 1851 used a reference to Van Diemen's Land that involved the westward transportation of the Indians of the eastern United States: "It was fortunate that the eastern states had a kind of Van Dieman's land on the western side of the great river where they could transport those poor red children of the forrest. It is not so, however, with California. If we drive the poor Indian from his old hunting grounds . . . it is to the mountains and starvation that we give him" (*Daily Alta California*, January 12, 1851). Bonwick's apology for English colonists' treatment of aborigines in Van Diemen's Land, that such treatment is universal, seems confirmed in this account.

41. Woodward names the white leader "John" Johnson ("Scalp Hunters" [March] 5).

42. Mayne Reid's Seguin answers the charge of a similar incident of trickery in his novel (67). McCarthy's Glanton's "howitzer trick" on the Yumas is not verifiable in its details, though it is said that Glanton and his men shot and killed four Yumas with handguns (Chamberlain 288–289). It may be that the "howitzer" in McCarthy's scene echoes Johnson's betrayal of Juan José.

novel. William Doniphan, Judge Holden, Sarah Borginnis, and Mangas Colorado are all of imposing physical stature. The Anasazi, to whom Holden refers in *Blood Meridian* (146), are also thought to have been "a tall people, some standing over 6 feet tall, with a relatively heavy bone structure," and may be classed in this group (Trimble 32). The Yuma chief Pascual is, John Ross Browne writes, "the longest of his tribe" (59). Samuel Chamberlain, one historical analogue to the kid, was himself six-two (Chamberlain 4).

McCarthy's novel seems to collect such characters, but for what purpose? The judge's narrative import takes advantage of his massive stature. Sarah Borginnis, the wife, laundress, and cook to a great many of the Army of the West, is sized appropriately. But Mangas and Doniphan lose some of their eminence when introduced into the novel. Grannyrat's reference to Doniphan is in diminutive form. What appears to be at work, though, is more an enhancement of Holden and Borginnis than a diminution of Mangas and Doniphan: both Captain White and Grannyrat praise Doniphan, and McCarthy's description of the depopulated Santa Rita del Cobre mines (113–119) is no small compliment to Mangas Colorado's strength.

To meet him on horseback in 1850 was not a laughing matter.[43] He had been chief of the Mimbreños since 1837 and would be chief until his death, in 1863. Dunn writes that after Johnson's massacre of Juan José's band, Mangas led other Mimbreños to kill fifteen trappers, but:

> Their vengeance did not stop at this. The copper mines of Santa Rita were furnished with supplies from the city of Chihuahua by guarded wagon-trains (conductas) that brought in provisions and hauled back ore. The time for the arrival of the train came and passed, but no train appeared. Days slipped away; provisions were almost exhausted; the supply of ammunition was nearly gone. Some of the miners climbed to the top of Ben Moore, which rises back of the mines, but from its lofty summit no sign of an approaching conducta was visible. Starvation was imminent. The only hope of escape for the miners and their families was in making their way across the desert expanse that lies between the mines and the settlements. They started, but the Apaches, who had destroyed the train, hung about them, and attacked them so persistently that only four or five [of three or four hundred] succeeded in reaching their destination. (315–316)

This is the Santa Rita del Cobre mining town that McCarthy describes as "abandoned these dozen years past when the Apaches cut off the wagontrains from Chihuahua and

---

43. Hughes, though, presents a portrait of the Mimbreños under Mangas that might have tempted the unwitting to laughter (Glanton, in McCarthy, is hard pressed to keep a straight face when he first meets the Yuma chiefs). Hughes writes: "To turn the scorching rays of an almost vertical sun from their faces, and preserve their eyes, some of them used a fantastic kind of shield, made of raw-hide and dressed buckskin; while others of them employed a fan of twigs, or a buzzard's wing, for the same purpose. They were armed in part with Mexican fusils, partly with lances, and bows and arrows." (80). Hughes's eye "shield" made of "a buzzard's wing" is presumably the source for McCarthy's "eyeshield made from a raven's wing" (110).

laid the works under siege" (113; also see Emory 58). It was Mangas Colorado who isolated the town (Baen 56). It is of note that Dunn's account describes "four or five" survivors *from* the town in 1837, and McCarthy's scene brings four men and a boy back *into* the town.

History places Glanton at the Santa Rita mines in mid-October 1849, where he and Colonel "Jack" Hays "met General José María Elías, commanding more than 400 Sonoran cavalrymen from Ures. His force had just defeated a small Apache band nearby and had taken five scalps and nine pairs of ears, which were nailed to their field pieces. This fight shattered all hope of effecting a conference with the Apaches; the Glantonians left Hays about twenty-five miles west of Santa Rita for a better scalp range" (Smith, "John Joel Glanton" 11). This account also describes a meeting between General Elías and Glanton. McCarthy, though, describes Elías as commanding five hundred troops, and his "meeting" with Glanton in the novel is a bloody affair (205).[44]

In the novel, when Glanton and Mangas meet outside Tucson, as the historians say they did (Crimmins, "John Glanton" 280), McCarthy has already tangentially introduced Mangas by writing of the Santa Rita mines. Baen remarks of Mangas: "Victorio, his second in command, and he would take turns at drunkenness and debauchery so that the Apaches would never be without an effective leader" (56). Mangas's occasionally debilitating drinking bouts are consistent with McCarthy's Mangas, who wants a barrel of whiskey as apology for his man's injured horse (230–231).

Mangas's historical enmity was toward the Mexicans who had hired James Johnson. W. H. Emory, meeting Mangas at this same midcentury time, writes in his journal:

[October 20] The general sent word to the Apaches he would not start till 9 or 10. This gave them time to come in, headed by way of their chief, Red Sleeve. They swore eternal friendship to the whites, and everlasting hatred to the Mexicans. The Indians said that one, two, or three white men might now pass in safety through their country; that if they were hungry, they would feed them; or, if on foot, mount them. The road was open to the American now and forever. [Kit] Carson, with a twinkle of his keen hazel eye, observed to me, "I would not trust one of them." (60)

Richard Irving Dodge's words on Indian card-cheating, which define the winner as the most successful at "manipulation" (328), are ironically appropriate to Glanton's deception of Mangas with the short keg of whiskey, an incident that appears to be McCarthy's own invention (241–242).[45]

---

44. Bancroft notes that Sonora had "only" 527 men defending its territory in 1850 (*History of Texas* 671). His account is in line with McCarthy's figure for Elías's troops (205).

45. Also see Cremony on his perception of Indian ethics (285–286).

Sarah Borginnis

Sarah Borginnis, the "Great Western," is not difficult to locate in the literature of the old Southwest. The surnames ascribed to the "Great Western" are remarkably various. She is, depending on the narrator, Sarah Borginnis, or Sarah Borinis, or Sarah Bourdett, or Burdette, or Sarah A. Bowman, or Madame Sarah Borginnis-Davis, or Mrs. Davis nee Borginnis, or Mrs. Bowman-Phillips.[46] Sarah's nickname derived from her size, comparing her to the largest steamboat built to that day, the *Great Western*. Woodward writes she stood six feet tall ("Great Western" 4). She was thirty-three years old in 1846. Lt. Whiting describes her delighted greeting when they met in El Paso a few years after the Mexican War. "Her masculine arms," Whiting writes, "lifted us one after another off our feet" (Woodward, "Great Western" 4). Sarah, no doubt, could easily have "handed [James Robert Bell] down" out of the cart in which he rode so he could be bathed in the river (*Blood Meridian* 257). She is also described in several accounts as a laundress and a bit inclined to army men. Woodward places her at Yuma in the "early 1850s, possibly 1852" ("Great Western" 4). Chamberlain's stories of Sarah Borginnis contribute to an assessment of the Sarah Borginnis character of *Blood Meridian*, since Chamberlain's "Sarah Borginnis" is, apparently, the only instance of her name with exactly this spelling. Chamberlain writes:

a train of three large Chihuahua waggons came in sight around the bend of the road by the Obispado, preceded by a horsewoman who was recognized by all as Sarah Borginnis, the celebrated "Great Western." She rode up to Colonel Washington and asked permission to accompany the expedition; the Colonel referred her to Major Rucker, who informed her that if she would marry one of the Dragoons, and be mustered in as a laundress, she could go. Her ladyship gave the military salute and replied, "All right, Major, I'll marry the whole Squadron and you thrown in but what I go along." Riding along the front of the line she cried out, "Who wants a wife with fifteen thousand dollars, and the biggest leg in Mexico! Come, my beauties, don't all speak at once—who is the lucky man?"

Whether the thought that the Great Western had one husband in the 7th Infantry and another in Harney's Dragoons made the men hesitate, I know not, but at first no one seemed disposed to accept the offer. Finally Davis of Company E (the same that flogged Dougherty) said, "I have no objections to making you my wife, if there is a clergyman here to tie the knot." With a laugh the heroine replied, "Bring your blanket to my tent tonight and I will learn you to tie a knot that will satisfy you, I reckon!"

46. Sarah Borginnis: Chamberlain 241; Sarah Borinis: Chamberlain 202; Sarah Bourdett: Woodward, "Great Western" 4; Bourdett: Samuel Reid 135, Woodward, "Sweeney" 256; Burdette: Woodward, "Sweeney" 256; Sarah A. Bowman: Woodward, "Great Western" 5; Madame Sarah Borginnis-Davis: Chamberlain 256; Mrs. Davis nee Borginnis: Chamberlain 242; Mrs. Bowman-Phillips: Woodward, "Great Western" 7. This listing does not include other references to the same person under her pseudonym. Whiting (in Woodward, "Great Western" 4), Wislizenus (75), and Hobbs (216) are examples of Sarah described familiarly as the "Great Western."

Such was the morals of the army in Mexico. Mrs. Davis nee Borginnis went down on E Company books as "Laundress" and drew rations as such. (241–242)

It is no surprise that McCarthy presents her as washing James Robert. Laundress is her trade, though Wislizenus writes that he had stayed at a hotel she had run in Saltillo (75). Chamberlain painted her portrait as a "Landlady" standing in front of a well-stocked bar with a great ornamented mirror hung on the wall above it (242).

Chamberlain also develops the much-married side of Sarah's character, like some Wild West Wife of Bath:

With the party from New Mexico ["collecting and drying fruit for the Santa Fe market"] was a man of remarkable size and strength. Madame Sarah Borginnis-Davis, the "Great Western," saw this Hercules while he was bathing and conceived a violent passion for his gigantic proportions. She sought an interview and with blushes "told her love." The Samson, nothing loth, became the willing captive to this modern Delilah, who straightway kicked Davis out of her affections and tent, and established her elephantine lover in full possession without further ceremony. (256)

Chamberlain's characterization suggests that he in some way found her behavior a bit forward. She was certainly memorable to the men who met her. Yet McCarthy does not present this wanton side of Sarah in her scenes. There is nothing lascivious about her bathing of the naked James Robert.

Other characters in the novel, among its few women, may be suggested by the Sarah Borginnis of Chamberlain's acquaintance. McCarthy writes: "An enormous whore stood clapping her hands at the bandstand and calling drunkenly for the music. She wore nothing but a pair of men's drawers and some of her sisters were likewise clad in what appeared to be trophies—hats or pantaloons or blue twill cavalry jackets" (334). The free spirit of Sarah Borginnis, her immense frame, and her love of the army, here represented in the uniforms and the scene's setting in a saloon, all have the flavor of Chamberlain's account of Sarah. The presence of the "enormous whore" also seems to counterpoint Holden's presence in this scene.

The Yuma Chiefs

The "riders were hard put to keep their composure," McCarthy writes, when first they laid eyes on Yuma Indian chiefs Caballo en Pelo, Pascual, and Pablo (254–255). Vereen Bell writes:

It is a nice, unliberal irony of McCarthy's story that the Indians in it are if anything more deranged and barbarous than the white men and more surreally discontinuous from any known patterns of human behavior. . . . They are wonders of the imagination, and yet we have the queasy feeling that we are being told, for the first time, the raw, unromantic truth about both sides of the war for the Southwest territories. (*Achievement* 123–124)

And the reader of the diaries and personal narratives of the period will not be "seeing" these three Indians (at this place, at this time) for the "first time." Lieutenants Whipple and Couts travelled together to the Yuma crossing in the fall of 1849 with a military detachment.[47] Each kept a diary. Bartlett later had access to Whipple's diary, and published extracts from it in his second volume. Browne visited the Yuma crossing many years after Couts and Whipple.

Caballo en Pelo is mentioned first in the novel. Little description is given of him, though Whipple characterizes him as the "famous war chief" of the Yumas who on that day (October 12, 1849) led an attack against a Maricopa Indian settlement (60–61). Mc-Carthy's note that Caballo en Pelo had lost an eye to the Maricopas (254), though not confirmed in Whipple, nevertheless may be based on Whipple's remarks.

Pascual is next mentioned by McCarthy, and a good deal of the description of the man centers on the bone and pendants that hung from his nose. In 1871, Browne writes:

Pascual, the doughty head-chief of all the Yumas, long known to fame as the longest of his tribe, predominated over the ceremonies. A grave, cadaverous, leathery old gentleman, with hollow, wrinkled cheeks, and a prodigious nose, through the cartilage of which, between the nostrils, he wears a white bone ornamented with swinging pendants, is Pascual the doughty. On account of the length of his arms and legs—which, when stretched out altogether, bear a strong similitude to the wind-mill against which Don Quixote ran a tilt—the mighty Pascual is regarded with much respect and veneration by his tribe. His costume, on the present occasion, consisted of a shabby military coat, doubtless the same worn in ancient times by his friend, Major Heintzelman, the embroidery of which has long since been fretted out by wear and tear, and the elbows rubbed off by long collision with the multitudes of office-seekers among his tribe. Of pantaloons he had but a remnant; and of boots or shoes he had none at all, save those originally furnished him by nature. (59–60)

Though both the coat and Pascual are worn threadbare in this account, the nose-bone ornament remains. Whipple describes Pascual as a minor chief (58).

---

47. Whipple conducted a scientific survey of the area. He describes the junction of the Colorado and the Gila: "The Colorado at the ferry, a short distance below the junction, is about twelve feet deep. The waters of the Colorado are almost opaque with clay, tinctured with the red oxide of iron. But the water is sweet, and, when allowed to rest, becomes limpid. The waters of the Gila are colored with a sediment nearly black, and have a brackish taste, making appropriate the Yuma name for it, 'Ha-qua-siéel'—meaning 'salt water'" (62–63). This is the junction of rivers of black and red, of South and Southwest, and, acknowledging Bartlett's similar assessment, is the "rio obscuro," or "dark river," of the novel's tarot prophecy (96).

In his green goggles, Chief Pablo is one of a kind. Whipple enters a note for Wednesday, October 3, 1849: "To-day came Pablo, grand chief of the Yumas, with his scarlet coat trimmed with gold lace, his epaulettes of silver wire, and, to crown all, green goggles. His legs and feet were bare, but he did not allow that to detract from the dignity of his manner" (56). Bartlett's version of Whipple's diary entry is faithful to Whipple's original, beginning with Pablo's "scarlet coat" to the end of the passage cited above (2:181). On October 5, Whipple again mentions Pablo:

To-day the Indians of the Yuma tribe held a grand council, in honor of our arrival; and, as Pablo Coclum, the great chief in epaulettes and green goggles, had been chosen under the Mexican reign, they determined to show their adherence to the United States by deposing their old chief, and, in a republican manner, electing a new one. The successful candidate was our old friend Santjago, captain of the band of the Cuchans at the lower crossing. He seems a good old man, and worthy of his honors. Upon his election, he was escorted to my tent for the customary presents, and promised good faith towards all Americans. (57)

The final diary entry is Cave Couts's.[48] Where Whipple's diary is in many ways an objective document, Couts gives the feel of the author toward his subject. Couts writes of Pablo:

Capt. Pablo, who met us last fall at Camp Salud y Salvacioun, stood near me, in his habitual costume, an old hat fantastically rigged, a red and fanciful military coat, buttoned up to the chin, with infantry epaulettes, three pairs of pants, different lengths, with shortest on the outside, reaching just below the knees, an old pair of shoes, several red strips around his waist, an old kind of sword, two feet long, leather scabbard brass mounted, which he held in his hands, protected from the sun by a pair of coarse black leather gloves, so stiff that all his fingers stood out like a fifer's eye on muster morning, and his eyes hid by a pair of green goggles, which he had robbed some unfortunate individual of. To his saddle he had a Mexican sabre attached, which he wore after their mode. (*San Diego* 35–36)

Almost unbelievably, these three Indians and their clothes are historical figures, not creations of McCarthy's imagination.

Callaghan

In *Blood Meridian*, a man named Callaghan operated the Yumas' ferry, "but within days [of Glanton's arrival] it was burned and Callaghan's headless body floated anonymously downriver, a vulture standing between the shoulderblades in clerical black, a silent rider

48. Couts has two diaries that include descriptions of trips to the Yuma crossing: *From San Diego to the Colorado in 1849*, quoted from in this section, and *Hepah, California! Hepah, California!*, which seems to contain little of interest to the reader of *Blood Meridian*.

to the sea" (262). Colonel Crimmins's otherwise suspect article "John Glanton of San Antonio" includes this report:

> under cover of the silent night, the former owners claimed their revenge. When the morning sun rose over the horizon one might see dark objects floating down the muddy Colorado. Buzzards were, even then, silently sailing overhead with motionless wings like miniature airplanes. Whenever one of these objects struck an obstruction and lodged, the buzzards nearby stopped too, and lit on it. (281)

Discounting Crimmins's "miniature airplanes," the reader is left with the bodies of the gang, with a similarity of location (the Colorado River, which empties into the sea), a similarity of anonymity (Callaghan headless, the bodies as "dark objects"), and the buzzards standing on dead bodies in the river. Crimmins's buzzards do not "ride" on down the river, as McCarthy's do, yet some of the novel's imagery may indeed have been derived from Crimmins's passage.

CHAPTER 3

Settings and Sources

The Leonids

The kid's birth during the Leonid meteor shower of 1833 may derive from George Frederick Ruxton's *Life in the Far West* (1849), in which the story of a character resembling the kid opens with a reference to 1833 as "the year it rained fire" (8).[1] The kid's birth is then associated with "fire," an important element in *Blood Meridian*, which is assessed in the essays "Tarot and Divination" (Chapter 5) and "Why Believe the Judge?" (Chapter 8). McCarthy writes: "Night of your birth. Thirty-three. The Leonids they were called. God how the stars did fall. I looked for blackness, holes in the heavens. The Dipper stove" (3).

A birth during the Leonids of 1833 would have been on about November 12.[2] Therefore, the astrological sign under which the kid was born is Scorpio (October 23–November 21). Scorpio is ruled by the planet Mars, a "violent planet," and by Pluto, "the planet of secrecy" (McIntosh, "Scorpio" 177).[3] Leo, the constellation from which the night's meteors appeared to descend, is ruled by the sun and has among its characteristics generosity and kindness (McIntosh, "Leo" 176).[4] Born under the influence of Scorpio, McCarthy's kid has a "taste for mindless violence" (3) and tends to secrecy and kindness.[5] Holden's charge that the kid had shown "clemency for the heathen" (299)—even given

---

1. The kid's birth in 1833 lets the novelist McCarthy, born in 1933, examine what life might have been like had he been born a hundred years earlier.

2. Some confusion exists regarding the day or date of the Leonids of 1833. A *Raleigh Register* story in an edition headed Tuesday, November 19, 1833, dates the event as having occurred on "Wednesday morning last." From this information, the Leonid shower took place on the morning of November 13, and not, as Peter Brown (and others) write, "on the morning of 12th November" (205).

3. The planet Pluto, first sighted in 1930, brings a question of anachronism to this presentation, but C. W. Roback (1854) links to Scorpio a quality of "secrets," a relationship into which this planet, once discovered, was fit.

4. Fred Gettings notes in his discussion of meteors that the "origin-point" of periodic meteor showers "has been used by some astrologers as the basis for interpretation" in genethlialogical (i.e., destiny-forecasting) astrology (200). Warren Kenton illustrates a "cosmic clock," with the zodiacal houses in a circular arrangement, that marks Scorpio as "death" and associates this sign with Pisces' "privacy" and Cancer's "security" (8). Roback's volume on astrology contains a chart, reproduced here, that displays a connection between the constellation Leo and a person's heart (82).

5. Kenton parallels Scorpio in his remark that there is an "unconscious intelligence of the arms and legs

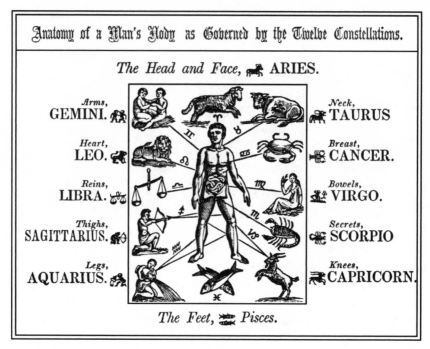

Astrological Signs and the Body, from Roback (82)

the novelist's refusal to provide scenes to confirm it—is prefigured astrologically in the novel's first page. Such prefiguring extends even to the last of the book: just as a mythological griffin has a lion's body, Fort Griffin seems the kid's astrologically appropriate place of destruction, out of his natal association with the Leonid meteor shower, which incarnates influences the judge will kill to suppress.

But the Leonids, in literature, folk tradition, and science, can be found to bring to *Blood Meridian* a great deal more than even these influences. The Indians marked the year 1833 by picturing this one event.[6] Faulkner defines a year by referring to the shower.[7]

---

in contrast to the conscious awareness of the mind and heart of a person" (30; Roback 82). Distinctions of conscious intelligence and unconscious awareness call to mind the context of the epigraph from Paul Valéry with which McCarthy opens the novel (see also the essays "Tarot and Divination" and "Why Believe the Judge?"), and suggests the marked difference between the judge's remarkable intelligence and the kid's unreflective personality.

6. Dodge devotes several pages and illustrations to a seven-decade calendar of the Sioux. In a widening spiral on buffalo skin, each year is represented by a drawing of a key event of the year. For the white man's 1833, a pictograph of a meteor shower is the year's memorable event (399–405; see also Capps 20–21, for an illustration of this "calendar" in color).

7. In "The Bear," Faulkner designates 1833 as the "yr stars fell," and adds that a son was born in June of that year to a mother who died (269).

Only after the Leonids of 1833 was a scientific hypothesis was put forward regarding its cause: "In 1834, two Americans, Olmsted and Twining, suggested that the annual Leonid showers were caused when the Earth passed through a cloud of meteor particles each November. . . . In 1864, H. A. Newton of Yale College, New Haven, reached the conclusion that perhaps the most dense part of the Leonid meteor cloud was only met with at intervals of approximately 33 years. . . . As a result Newton boldly predicted that the Leonids would recur as a *spectacular* display in 1866" (Brown, *Comets* 206). Science had caught up to the Leonids by the shower of 1866, and it, too, *was* spectacular.

But for that "night the stars fell" in 1833, in "the year it rained fire," there had been no analysis, no prediction, no warning. It is the greatest shower ever recorded. Peter Brown cites "a cotton planter in South Carolina [who] recalled his own experience" of the event:

I was suddenly awakened by the most distressing cries that ever fell on my ears. Shrieks of horror and cries of mercy I could hear from most of the negroes on three plantations, amounting in all about six or eight hundred. While earnestly listening for the cause, I heard a faint voice near the door calling my name. I arose, and taking my sword, stood at the door. At this moment I heard the same voice beseeching me to rise, and saying, "Oh, my God! the world is on fire!" I then opened the door and it was difficult to say which excited me most—the awfulness of the scene, or the distressed cries of the negroes. Upwards of one hundred lay prostrate on the ground; some speechless, and some uttering the bitterest cries, but most with their hands raised imploring God to save the world and them. The scene was truly awful; for never did rain fall much thicker than the meteors fell towards the earth,— east, west, north, and south, it was the same! (205–206)

A newspaper account in the *Raleigh Register* nearly a week after the shower described the "many who rarely bestow a serious thought in retrospect on a life of sin, [who] seemed now to hear a voice in nature, as 'twere of God . . ." (November 19, 1833). This account concludes, as do others, with a sense of embarrassment that the fear and repentance were all for nothing.

But McCarthy's reference to the Leonids does not limit his frame of historical reference simply to a night of reckoning for the guilt-ridden. J. W. Wilbarger's *Indian Depredations in Texas* (1889) opens with his brother scalped and left for dead, though he lived (12). This event in 1833 was "the first blood shed in Travis County at the hands of the implacable savages" and "was but the beginning, however, of a bloody era which was soon to dawn upon the people of the [Little] Colorado" (13). If 1833 and Texas need correlation, perhaps Wilbarger's bloody scalping, indicating the beginning of open hostility between the Anglos and Indians, may serve. Certainly the novel's end in Fort Griffin lends a sense of closure to this pattern, since, with the end of the buffalo in Texas, all possibilities of Indian independence from the whites vanished (see the section on Fort Griffin, below).

Too, there seem to be as many "traders" in *Blood Meridian* as there are fights with In-dians.[8] It was in the fall of 1833, David Lavender notes, that Charles Bent applied for the United States government license of his brother William's newly built trading house.[9] Bent's Fort (in present-day Colorado) was to become the trading center of the West for the next forty years: "The move could not have come at a more propitious time. The year before, John Jacob Astor had noted silk hats on British men and had foreseen the end of the demand for beaver felt" (139). Lavender's note of the loss of a market for beaver fur in 1833, a significant change in the western economy, suggests McCarthy's theme of cyclic extinctions. McCarthy may have been thinking of this "change" in the West when he picked 1833 as the year of his protagonist's birth: Lavender's title for the chapter about the opening of Bent's Fort is, interestingly enough, "The Night the Stars Fell." The Leonids of 1833 are woven into the opening and ending of his chapter. As it closes, Lavender writes:

And now, on November 12, 1833, the very firmament was cracking open, tumbling down the stars. While the skies dripped fire, while William Bent and other traders watched from the fort's unfinished walls, the visiting warriors decked themselves in full battle regalia of feather and paint, lance and shield. They could not fight this fearful thing. But at least they could die like men. They mounted their horses. Women cried and children shrieked; in the fort the dogs howled back at the chorusing wolves. Chanting their death dirges above the din, the warriors rode in single file around the tepees, under the shadow of the great mud bastions.

The next morning the sun shone again. The young men laughed at their alarm, and sto-ries of the night the stars fell passed into folk tale. Nonetheless, the symbol of death stood above them, unrecognizable because from its vast walls seemed to come the luxuries of a fuller life. Better if the dirges had been for this, the white man's earthen fist henceforth clenched unshakably about the people of the plains. Little though Bent, St. Vrain & Com-pany may have intended the doom, or even thought about it, the arrows of an aboriginal faith were forever blunted, the star of the Cheyennes could do nothing but dim. (143–144)

Insofar as McCarthy's novel has as a theme the transience of the dancer on the world's center stage (331), the Leonids are themselves a predictable, transient, and, as well, an appropriately terrifying metaphor. Opposed to this predictability, though, is the sense of

8. Riddle and Speyer are traders in *Blood Meridian*, but there are other characters in the novel whose biographies include evidence of backgrounds as traders. Governor Burnett of California had been a trader in his youth (Burnett 29). General Worth is praised by General Logan as a man who, beginning life "in the humble capacity of trader's clerk," and "from a position of a purely commercial character, became one of the most distinguished military officers in the regular army of the United States" (547). Wasserman writes of Governor Angel Trias of Chihuahua as "a successful businessman" (23). Bartlett writes of Angel Trias's two estates (2: 418–419). And Sanford and Carroll, who flee Jesús María with the gang, are noted by Horace Bell as the "only American traders" in town (276).

9. Lavender appears to be a source for McCarthy's description of Mexican buffalo-hunting "ciboleros," examined below.

the kid's nativity embodied in the novel's opening, whereby the shower is depicted as both miraculous and ominous at once, signalling an epic—probably not a mock-epic—tradition.

The Comanche Attack

Pages 52 through 54 in *Blood Meridian* introduce the reader to Comanche power in the Southwest in the 1840s. Though intending to filibuster in Sonora, the book's Anglo party of forty-six had apparently taken a westbound shortcut across southern stretches of Chihuahua and cut across a Comanche war trail as well. These three pages of conflict are as full of energy and strangeness as any in McCarthy's novels.

The chaos of this battle scene distances us from our cinema- and television-inspired notions of cowboy-and-Indian fights. But before television were the diarists, the personal narrators, and the historians. It is out of their stories that McCarthy has woven this battle. The historian J. W. Wilbarger and the army journalist W. H. Emory give accounts of two encounters with Indians, one a battle, one a show of power:

Early in the morning of August 8, some few of the inhabitants of Linnville observed in the distance a perfect cloud of dust, caused, as they supposed, by a vast *caballada* of horses, being brought in from Mexico for trading purposes. By throwing themselves on the sides of their horses, and riding in this way, the Indians had completely concealed themselves from the vision of the unsuspecting denizens of the village. Imagine their consternation and utter dismay, when one thousand red savages, suddenly rising in their saddles, dashed upon the defenseless town, when many of the inhabitants were fast asleep. The alarm was given as soon as the discovery was made. Resistance was not thought of, and panic stricken, men, women and children, young and old, rushed for the boats which were anchored near by in the shallow water. The scene amid the confusion which prevailed was one never to be forgotten by the survivors of that terror stricken people. The war whoop of the wild Comanche commingled with the screaming of women, the crying of the children, and the groans of the dying and wounded almost beggars description. (Wilbarger 26–27)

The Indians concealed behind their horses are found in McCarthy's tale, to the utter dismay of the filibusters when the true number of Indians dawns on them. Wilbarger's story concludes, as does McCarthy's, on the groans and screams of victims.

Emory's story may have provided McCarthy with a further description of Indians appearing from within a cloud of dust:

When within a few miles of the town, we saw a cloud of dust rapidly advancing, and soon the air was rent with a terrible yell, resembling the Florida war-whoop. The first object that caught my eye through the column of dust, was a fierce pair of buffalo horns, overlapped with long shaggy hair. As they approached, the sturdy form of a naked Indian revealed itself beneath the horns, with shield and lance, dashing at full speed, on a white horse, which,

like his own body, was painted all the colors of the rainbow; and then, one by one, his followers came on, painted to the eyes, their own heads and their horses covered with all the
strange equipments that the brute creation could afford in the way of horns, skulls, tails,
feathers, and claws.

As they passed us, one rank on each side, they fired a volley under our horses' bellies
from the right and from the left. Our well-trained dragoons sat motionless on their horses,
which went along without pricking an ear or showing any sign of excitement.

Arrived in the rear, the Indians circled round, dropped into a walk on our flanks until
their horses recovered breath, when off they went at full speed, passing to our front, and
when there, the opposite files met, and each man selected his adversary and kept up a running fight, with muskets, lances, and bows and arrows. Sometimes a fellow would stoop almost to the earth to shoot under his horses' belly, at full speed, or to shield himself from an
impending blow. So they continued to pass and repass us all the way to the steep cliff which
overhangs the town. (37)

Emory here creates a stronger sense of the Indians as shocking to the narrator than does
Wilbarger. Claws and skulls decorate Emory's Indians. The first object to appear, in both
Emory and McCarthy, is a buffalo-horn helmet. McCarthy's Indians are depicted as totally alien to the filibusterers, as if from "regions beyond right knowing where the eye
wanders and the lip jerks and drools" (53). They are no less bizarre to the reader.

McCarthy's characterization of some of the Indians as dressed in "biblical" fashion
might well come out of Bartlett's mention of deerskin helmets worn by them (1: 328,
illus. 329), or from Ruxton's note in *Adventures in Mexico and the Rocky Mountains* (1847)
of a "turban" worn by Indians (313). Bartlett's illustration, which shows a full-sized skull-
cap edged with a border, with feathers gathered on its crown in a plume that falls to the
back of the cap, is not dissimilar, but for the feathers, to caps worn in Old Testament illustrations from a child's Bible.

McCarthy's description of the Comanche dress as "attic" might also suggest that Mc-
Carthy was aware of Emory's observation of his meeting with Mangas Colorado, of which
he wrote:

By this time a large number of Indians had collected about us, all differently dressed, and
some in the most fantastical style. The Mexican dress and saddles predominated, showing
where they had chiefly made up their wardrobe. One had a jacket made of a Henry Clay
flag, which aroused unpleasant sensations, for the acquisition, no doubt, cost one of our
countrymen his life. Several wore beautiful helmets, decked with black feathers, which,
with the short shirt, waist belt, bare legs and buskins gave them the look of pictures of antique Grecian warriors. (61)

Emory's observation of helmets and Greek warriors may, indeed, inform McCarthy's
pages (see also Chamberlain 278).

Or the modern historians Joseph Cash and Gerald Wolff might be as close in detail
as Emory to McCarthy:

Apache Headdress, from Bartlett (1: 329)

The warrior was very careful of his appearance when preparing for battle, much as the ancient Spartan fighters had been. They painted the face and the body red, but also used black, yellow, green, and blue paint. There were myriad designs, each suited to the particular warrior and chosen in conjunction with his own personal medicine and wishes. They took great pains with their hair, wearing it long, parting it in the center with the part painted, and wearing it in braids on each side. The scalplock would fall from the top of the head. Frequently the side braids were wrapped with fur, cloth, or other materials, and a single feather was frequently worn in the scalplock. Many warriors plucked all the hair from their body, including the eyebrows, and occasionally tattooed their bodies as did the women. The men would also pierce their ears for earrings. (Cash and Wolff 20–21)

Though interesting to consider as a possible influence on McCarthy's scene, Grecian and colorful, Cash and Wolff's description is hardly as wild or aggressive as Emory's. Still, Cash and Wolff may have provided McCarthy with descriptions of the Indian's manner of grooming his hair before a battle. They mention that the side braids were "wrapped with fur, cloth, or other materials." As Colonel Richard Irving Dodge remarks in *Our Wild Indians*: "Comanches and Kiowas comb the hair back from the face and plait it, with additions, in a single long tail, ornamented with silver or plated buckles, and often reaching nearly to the ground" (52). Sources such as these may inform McCarthy's note of the Indians' braids having been long enough to trail on the ground.

Dodge's book is a rich vein of authentication for the details of this scene:

I was present at probably the most important council of late years, between whites and Indians. Turkey Leg, a Cheyenne chief of considerable prominence, came into the council lodge, a buffalo robe tightly folded around him, though it was warm weather. Over his head and face he wore an ordinary green veil. Over that, perched on the very top of his head, and at least two sizes too small for him, was a tall straight-bodied stove-pipe hat. When he rose to speak, he retained the hat and veil, but dropped his buffalo robe, disclosing his other apparel, which consisted of a calico shirt and a pair of moccasins. (299–300)

Last year I met Little Chief, and the other Northern Cheyennes, on their return from Washington. They were riding through southern Kansas, en route to their agency, and everywhere they created a sensation. A brawny buck with white shirt, elaborate necktie and felt hat, had buckskin leggings, and moccasins, and held over his head a lady's parasol. Another, buttoned to the chin in a thick coat, had his nether extremities covered in the same way, was without a hat, but fanned himself incessantly with a huge gaudily painted Chinese fan. (300)

No more motley, ridiculous, overdressed, and undressed crowd can be found in the world, than a party of Indians "fixed up" to receive white company. (300–301)

The "green veil" becomes a "bloodstained weddingveil" in McCarthy (52). That Glanton's seventeen-year-old fiancée had been carried off, raped, and murdered by Indians just before their wedding (Chamberlain 268–269) might well justify a change in a "historical" detail (as the "green veil" into "weddingveil" appears to be), a change that foreshadows Glanton's appearance later in the novel.

Marcy's *Journal* mentions Indians carrying umbrellas (Foreman 263). But the Comanche characterized by McCarthy is perhaps best suggested by James Thomas DeShields:

Several of the Indian chiefs charged up in front of the Texans and hurled defiant arrows and spears at them. One of these daring chiefs rode a fine horse with a fine American bridle, with a red ribbon eight or ten feet long tied to the tail of his horse. He was dressed in elegant style from the goods plundered at Victoria and Linville, with a high-top silk hat, fine pair of boots, leather gloves and an elegant broad-cloth coat hind-part before with brass buttons shining brightly up and down his back. When he first made his appearance he carried a large umbrella stretched. He and others would charge upon the Texans, shoot their arrows, and retreat. (324)

Greer's biography of John C. Hays, which apparently relies on this DeShields story, more clearly characterizes the trouserless condition of the chief, an element prominent in McCarthy:

One of the most venturesome chiefs rode a fine stolen horse wearing a heavily decorated bridle. A ten-foot-long red ribbon streamed from the tail of this dancing charger. The rider wore a pair of gleaming calf boots, a high-topped silk hat, and an elegant broadcloth, swallow-tailed coat, worn backwards so that the bright brass buttons gleamed along his spine. He was trouserless and carried a large opened umbrella. (39–40)

McCarthy's depiction of the Indians' treatment of their enemies is graphic. It is probably appropriate, if only as supporting evidence and not as analogue or source, to cite DeShields on the treatment of enemies: "Though having lost one of their comrades in the fight, the Tonkawas were elated over the victory, and after scalping the dead and dying Wacos and Comanches, cutting off their hands, feet, arms and legs, and fleecing strips of flesh from their thighs and breast, they were ready and anxious to return to their village and engage in their usual cannibal-like and mystic war dance" (287).

Ciboleros

During the first scalp-hunting expedition, Glanton's gang crosses paths with a party of Mexican buffalo hunters, *ciboleros*. McCarthy describes them as:

dressed in skins sewn with the ligaments of beasts and they sat their animals in the way of men seldom off them. They carried lances with which they hunted the wild buffalo on the plains and these weapons were dressed with tassels of feathers and colored cloth and some carried bows and some carried old fusils with tasseled stoppers in their bores. The dried meat was packed in hides and other than the few arms among them they were innocent of civilized device as the rawest savage of that land." (120)

Within contemporary historian David Lavender's *Bent's Fort* is a description of:

Mexican ciboleros, buffalo hunters, more than a hundred of them, who had been out on the plains killing and drying meat. Their arms and equipment were primitive bows and arrows slung over their backs, crude lances bedecked with ribbons and carried perpendicularly in holders on the front of the saddles, a few ancient fusees whose barrels were stoppered against the weather by plugs of wood likewise fluttering with parti-colored streamers. (98–99)

The similarities between these accounts, the types and descriptions of the weapons, and a comparison of McCarthy's phrase "old fusils with tasseled stoppers in their bores" to Lavender's "a few ancient fusees whose barrels were stoppered against the weather by plugs of wood," all tend to suggest that McCarthy was probably aware of Lavender's description. But this description does not account for all of McCarthy's details. Wislizenus also discusses ciboleros. He writes:

While we were travelling to-day over the lonesome plain, men and animals quite tired and exhausted, on the rising of a hill before us quite suddenly appeared a number of savage looking riders on horseback, which at first sight we took for Indians; but their covered heads convinced us soon of our mistake, because Indians never wear hats of any kind: it was a band of Ciboleros, or Mexican buffalo hunters, dressed in leather or blankets, armed with bows and arrows and a lance—sometimes, too, with a gun—and leading along a large train of jaded pack animals. These Ciboleros are generally poor Mexicans from the frontier settlements of New Mexico, and by their yearly expeditions into the buffalo regions they provide themselves with dried buffalo meat for their own support and for sale. Their principal weapon is the lance, which in riding they plunge so adroitly into the buffalo's flanks, that they seldom miss their aim. They are never hostile towards white men, and seem to be afraid of the Indians. In their manners, dress, weapons, and faces, they resemble the Indians so much, that they may easily be mistaken for them. The company which we met with consisted of about 100 men and some women, and they felt rather disappointed when we told them how far they had to travel to find the buffalo. (12–13)

McCarthy's ciboleros, in their primitive clothing "sewn with the ligaments of beasts" and bearing themselves "in the way of men seldom off" their horses, are similar to Wislizenus's "savage looking" ciboleros dressed in "leather or blankets," who "resemble Indians so much, that they may easily be mistaken for them."

The Hueco Tanks

McCarthy describes the Hueco Tanks as "almost within sight of the town of El Paso" and as a "group of natural stone cisterns in the desert" (172–173). Bartlett writes that the tanks are located in "mountains" and are a very good source of water (1: 133–134). Sonnichsen quotes Captain John Pope's words on them from 1854: "About fourteen years ago . . . these Arabs of New Mexico, the Apaches, having made a desperate foray upon the Mexicans, retreated with their plunder to these mountains, the Huecos, thirty miles east of El Paso. The Mexicans surprised and surrounded them, hemming them up in the rocky ravine forming the eastern tank. Here an engagement took place, in which the Indians were totally defeated and nearly exterminated, only two or three escaping. It is said that upwards of one hundred of them were killed" (*Pass* 95).

Searching for scalps, Glanton may have believed these Hueco Tanks a likely spot to find both water and Indians.

Jesús María

Jesús María was one of Mexico's great silver-mining areas, as was Santa Rita del Cobre for copper. John Woodhouse Audubon's travel took him into the town:

Four hours and a half of most precipitous descent brought us to a luxuriant growth of pine and spruce, and passing through one of the wildest and most picturesque gorges I have ever seen, we came to the extraordinary little town of Jesus Maria, situated at the junction of two little torrents of clear, beautiful water, tumbling in noisy, joyous splashing from rock to basin, and carrying away the rubbish from this half-civilized settlement of miners as it passes through the town. (120–121)

It is, presumably, into one of Audubon's "torrents" that the judge casts his new-bought puppies (192).[10] The junction of these two streams is analogous to the junction of the Gila and Colorado rivers, where the gang is massacred and black John Jackson is lost in the water.

A number of descriptions of roads similar to the one in *Blood Meridian* occur in the literature of that time. Emory writes of one such hazardous road within a mile of the Gila River, where a "pack slipped from a mule, and, though not shaped favorably for the purpose, rolled entirely to the base of the hill, over which the mules had climbed" (61). A few pages later in his account, Emory describes another road, no less hazardous, which took eight and a half hours to travel:

The metallic clink of spurs, and the rattling of the mule shoes, the high black peaks, the deep dark ravines, and the unearthly looking cactus, which stuck out from the rocks like the ears of Mephistopheles, all favored the idea that we were now treading on the verge of the regions below. Occasionally a mule gave up the ghost, and was left as a propitiatory tribute to the place. This day's journey cost us some twelve or fifteen mules. (66)

Emory's second description carries a more developed sense of the effect such a trail has on the traveller, though it is not a description of the road west out of Jesús María. Only in Josiah Gregg's *Commerce of the Prairies* is a characterization of this road found. He begins with a description of the road east of town, and then states that the road west is "also extremely perilous." The eastern road, he says, "winds so close along the borders of precipices, that by a single misstep an animal might be precipitated several hundred feet." "I was shown the projecting edge of a rock over which the road had formerly passed. This shelf was perhaps thirty feet in length by only two or three in width" (294). Mc-

---

10. Central to McCarthy's "A Drowning Incident" are puppies drowned in a stream. In a related scene in McCarthy's *The Orchard Keeper*, John Wesley Rattner wants back a hawk he had given up for a bounty (77–79, 232–233); see also Harrogate's dead bats (*Suttree* 206–219), though here emotions of sorrow and longing (present in "Drowning" and *Orchard Keeper*) turn into hilarity.

Carthy's description of the road west out of Jesús María seems historically accurate, whether or not Gregg is his resource.

As Glanton's gang rides west out of Jesús María, it encounters a "conducta of one hundred and twenty-two mules bearing flasks of quicksilver for the mines." "Bad luck. Twenty-six days from the sea and less than two hours out from the mines" (194). In a bad mood, the gang pushes ahead, shooting the muleteers and shouldering fifty of the mules off the trail. The animals and their flasks tumbling over the hill explode in a slow-motion verbal simulation.

Audubon's journal note for July 28, 1849, graced with a sense of forbearance alien to Glanton's gang, may have provided McCarthy with a source for his scene: "We did not leave camp until nearly noon, waiting for a train of one hundred and eighty-two mules packed with nothing but flasks of quicksilver; the usual length of trains is about forty to fifty, with six or eight men" (129).

One other note on this scene involves McCarthy's phrase "twenty-six days from the sea." Quicksilver is necessary to refine silver from ore (Gregg, *Commerce* 295–297). Bartlett writes of the New Almaden cinnabar mine located thirteen miles from the bay of San Francisco. It may be that McCarthy refers to quicksilver from the New Almaden mines in his scene on the cliff-side trail. According to Bartlett, "there was but one other mine in the world, that of Almaden in Spain, where the operation [of quicksilver refin-ing] was carried on on a large scale" (2: 57). Just as Cortés's manufacture of gunpowder from New World sources freed him from absolute dependence on the whims of the king's bishops (Cortés 325), so, too, did the New Almaden mine free the New World's silver mining and refining economy from dependence on Spanish quicksilver. The New World supported the technology of guns with volcanic sulfur deposits, and it also literally made its own money.

The Wild Bull

The particular account informing McCarthy's scene in which gang member James Miller is attacked by a wild bull has not been found, though Bartlett does write of wild herds (1: 256, 258, 397). Nevertheless, Phillip St. George Cooke records, in his journal of 1846–1847, that as his party travelled westward from Santa Fe and approached "San Pedro" (footnoted in the text as being in the southern part of modern Cochise County, Arizona), several wild bulls showed themselves and some of these attacked. Horses and mules were gored, some wagons were charged and knocked into the air, and some men injured (142–144). Private Keysor's "journal," in a note attached to this entry of Cooke's, adds, "These bulls were very hard to kill; they would run off with half a dozen balls in them unless they were shot in the heart. The Indians apparently had killed off the cows" (144).

McCarthy's scene involves the goring of one man's horse (223–224). He refers to old Spanish brands on the bulls' hips. The gang is then in an area between Santa Cruz and Tumacacori, heading north to Tucson. Cooke's journal entry shows many bulls attacking, does not mention the brands, and takes place to the east of McCarthy's area. Nevertheless, in both accounts only bulls are seen. The western edge of Cochise County is less than thirty miles east of McCarthy's San Bernardino setting. Perhaps some specific local account informs McCarthy's scene of the goring of Miller's horse, but Cooke's account may have provided some historical inspiration for McCarthy's scene.

The Meteorite

Depending on the reader's assessment of Judge Holden's strength, either of two outside accounts of the Tucson meteorite-anvil mentioned in McCarthy may suffice. Holden wins a series of three increasingly difficult bets by finally walking ten feet with it lifted above his head (240). The commonly available story of a meteorite used as an anvil is from gold-rush traveller Asa Bement Clarke. He saw such a meteorite at a blacksmith's shop, describing it as "a natural curiosity. It was a piece of native iron from a neighboring mountain, used for an anvil, and the only one in the shop. It was between three and four feet long, with two large legs, which were firmly set in the ground, all in one piece,

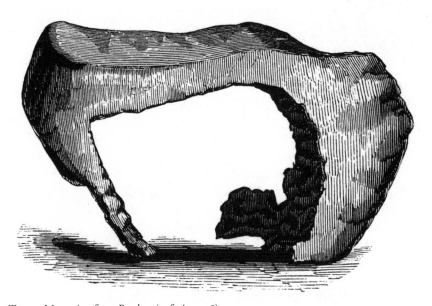

Tucson Meteorite, from Bartlett (2: facing 298)

and judged by our men to weigh two thousand pounds. I hammered it and found it malleable" (68). Sonnichsen adds "Pacheco," as the blacksmith's name, to his story of this anvil (*Tucson* 36). James Officer, basing his version on Clarke, notes a meteorite in a Tucson blacksmith's shop, "presumably that of Ramon Pacheco" (229).

Another account of what must be the same anvil-meteorite, though some details differ, is provided in John Russell Bartlett. In Tucson he examined:

> a remarkable meteorite, which is used for an anvil in the blacksmith's shop. This mass resembles native iron, and weighs about six hundred pounds. Its greatest length is five feet. Its exterior is quite smooth, while the lower part which projects from the larger leg is very jagged and rough. It was found about twenty miles distant towards Tubac, and about eight miles from the road, where we were told are many larger masses. The annexed drawing [facing 298 in Bartlett] gives the appearance of this singular mass. (2: 297–298)

These accounts seem to have been blended in *Blood Meridian*. Pacheco's name does not appear in Bartlett's account, but is associated with Clarke's (though is not in Clarke's), and McCarthy does include the name.[11] At the same time, Bartlett's estimate that the anvil weighed six hundred pounds, given McCarthy's scene in which Holden walks with it above his head, does not make such an imposition on the reader's credulity as would Clarke's estimate of 2,000 pounds.

June 11, 1850

It wasn't early morning, and it wasn't remotely June 11, 1850. Toadvine and Brown were not hung together (311). But, as McCarthy's Holden did tease him (161), the historical David Brown died hung by the neck.

Harris Newmark writes that on October 13, 1854, "a good-for-nothing gambler, Dave Brown" killed "Pinckney Clifford, in a livery stable" (139). Newmark continues: "the lawless act created such general indignation that vengeance on Brown would undoubtedly then and there have been wreaked" had Mayor Stephen C. Foster not intervened: "In order to mollify the would-be Vigilantes, Foster promised that, if the case miscarried in the courts and Brown was not given his due, he would resign his office and would himself lead those who favored taking the law into their own hands" (139). Tried and convicted of Pinckney's murder on November 30, Brown was sentenced to hang on January 12, 1855, "the same date on which Felipe Alvitre, a half-breed Indian was to pay [a like] penalty" for murder (139).

---

11. In point of fact, McCarthy's characterization of the anvil as shaped like a "great molar" (240), a comparison not present in either Bartlett or Clarke, may well be derived from his contact with Bartlett's illustration of the meteorite, reproduced here.

Newmark notes that Brown's "attorneys worked so hard and so effectively for their client that on January 10th, or two days before the date set . . . the Supreme Court granted Brown a stay" of execution (139). Alvitre "was hanged in the calaboose or jail yard, in the presence of a vast number of people, at the time appointed" (139). The Supreme Court's stay of Alvitre's execution would arrive days too late. That Brown was not hung early on the twelfth "proved too much for the patience of the populace," and "to focus the indignation of the masses," Foster, "true to his word, resigned from the office of mayor and put himself at the head of the mob" (140). By afternoon, "Poles and crowbars were brought, and a blacksmith called for," and "In a few minutes, Brown was reached, dragged out and across Spring Street, and there hanged to the cross-beam of a corral gateway opposite the old jail, the noose being drawn tight while he was still attempting to address the crowd" (140). A special election reinstated Stephen Foster as mayor. The trusted Foster would also serve as superintendent of schools.

"Louis" Toadvine, as Holden names him in *Blood Meridian* (282), here seems an historical dead end.

What remains for consideration is the novel's June 11, 1850, when McCarthy's "two bound figures rose vertically from among their fellows" (311). In the United States House of Representatives on that day, "the noise in the Hall was so great that the Chair could not hear what was said by gentlemen. It was impossible to get along with anything like regularity unless order was preserved" (*Congressional* 1171). Representative Volney Erskine Howard, of Texas, had delivered a speech "Against the admission of California, and the dismemberment of Texas" (772–778). A bill by Representative Doty, of Wisconsin, to admit, with boundary provisions, the state of California to the Union would be read (*Congressional* 1171). Questions of the final marking of boundaries between states and of boundaries with Mexico, because they were intertwined with questions of slavery in the West, were the bedlam order of the day.

Two months before, Henry Foote, of Mississippi, had confronted Thomas Hart Benton, of Missouri, with a pistol on the Senate floor. Indeed, on this same day in June, delegates from nine southern states were meeting at McKendree Methodist Church in Nashville, Tennessee, to discuss their resentments of the federal government.[12] Arguments for secession were publicly raised there, and would be raised again when this confederacy met again as planned in the fall. The West was now politics. McCarthy's Toadvine had "run plumb out of country" (285), and on this day his Toadvine and Brown ran out of time.

---

12. The convention met June 3 through 11 (or 12). One hundred of these southern states' 175 representatives were Tennesseeans.

Fort Griffin

On barbed-wire fences, like symbols of the new order of affairs over the controlled range lands, dead, skinned coyotes were impaled in a frieze—twenty or thirty of them at a time. They were stretched in midair with a lean, racing look of unearthly nimbleness, running nowhere; and their skulled teeth had the smile of their own ghosts, wits of the plains. In the dried varnish of their own amber serum they glistened under the sun. The day of unrestrained predators was over. (Horgan, *Heroic Triad* 233)[13]

Doniphan, Kearney, and Sloat had taken United States territorial claims to their westernmost reach—the shore of the Pacific—during the Mexican War. The open ranges of "unrestrained predators" thirty years later were much smaller parcels. Barbed wire was "first used in 1875 to fence pastures in which with fewer and less skillful cow boys the herds could be restricted and more easily managed" (Horgan, *Heroic Triad* 232). In fact, the novel's epilogue is literally a description of digging postholes using a throw-down tool (337), a step toward the fencing of open range. The advance of such work is incremental. McCarthy characterizes the pause of a worker at a hole and his walk to the next spot in a metaphor of clockwork mechanisms, as "monitored with escapement and pallet." In the world of the analogue clock face, the turn of the sweep hand shows these advances and pauses, and the hand's motion is circular and endless, much like McCarthy's eternal cycles of dancers.

In its allusive language, this epilogue also contains reference to the novel's destructive dances of conflict and overthrow, as in McCarthy's choice of a rocky stratum to underlie the dirt in which the hole is cut. His phrase "fire in the hole," a result of steel tool jaws striking rock (further explored in the essay "Why Believe the Judge?" Chapter 8), is today's call warning of blasting (akin to the cry of "timber" in logging), both for mining and as a preliminary step in construction. In addition, "fire in the hole" is also a military call warning of loose live hand grenades. Thus, McCarthy's phrasing links his literal description of posthole digging with the destruction of warfare. And the railroad linking San Diego and El Paso in 1877 sewed the eastern United States to the southwestern land.

Fort Griffin, Texas, the town in which the man (the adult kid) dies, barely outlasted him.[14] The post, established in 1867, was a central supply point for buffalo-hide hunters

---

13. Very early in *Blood Meridian*, McCarthy writes of "darker woods . . . that harbor yet a few last wolves" (3). In the fourth paragraph of *The Confidence-Man*, Melville writes of a peddler at the St. Louis steamboat landing who "hawked, in the thick of the throng, the lives of Measan, the bandit of Ohio, Murrel, the pirate of the Mississippi, and the brothers Harpe, the Thugs of the Green River country, in Kentucky—*creatures*, with others of the sort, one and all exterminated at the time, and for the most part, *like the hunted generations of wolves in the same regions*, leaving comparatively few successors" (my emphasis).

14. McCarthy writes that the man "crossed the Double Mountain Fork of the Brazos River" on his way to Fort Griffin (316). As was earlier noted regarding McCarthy's use of the names "Bexar" and "Van

in the 1870s, yet "by the summer of 1879, scarcely a hunter remained in Fort Griffin" (McHugh 276). McCarthy's choice of Griffin in the "late winter" of 1878 for the setting of his novel's close prefigures the historical "closings" of the West ("Knitting the Winds," Chapter 7, expands the thought). The decline of southern buffalo herds hurt Griffin's trading economy, but not nearly as badly as it hurt those Indians whose only traditional source of food, shelter, and clothing had been extinguished (McHugh 286–287; Dodge 296).[15] For all the years of Indians fighting with the Spanish and Anglos, of scalp bounties, of trickery, raids, and massacres, the extinction of the buffalo finally "controlled" the Indian menace (McHugh 285).

The "bonepickers" (317–323) who wander through the novel's last chapter are a no less vanished but verifiable part of Texas history than are Fort Griffin and the buffalo. When the use of bone phosphorus for agricultural fertilizer was discovered in the nineteenth century, buffalo skeletons became significant commodities in the economy of the West. Larry Barsness provides photographs of bone piles in front yards (135), bones on the prairie (136), and bones in rows along the railroad right-of-way (139). The dryness of the western climate had preserved buffalo bones for generations. It is estimated that the skeletons of 178,500,000 buffalo were shipped east, "three to five times the total buffalo thought to inhabit the continent when the Spaniards arrived" (Barsness 137). John Cook writes:

I saw in 1874, the year before the great buffalo slaughter began in earnest, a rick of buffalo bones, on the Santa Fé Railroad right-of-way, and twenty miles ahead of the track from Granada, Colorado, piled twelve feet high, nearly that wide at the base, and one-half mile long. Seven, eight, nine, and ten dollars per ton was realized from that alone. (196)

The railroads even built spurs into areas for no reason other than access to buffalo bones (Barsness 134).

All evidence, apparently, of the buffalo, and therefore of the Indian, was swept from the West when the formerly nuisance bones went east for the farmers. McCarthy's description of the harvest of buffalo bones into "windrows," surreal though it may seem, is faithful to history.

Diemen's Land," the intervening century saw this fork change names to the "Salt Fork of the Brazos in the southern part of Stonewall County, Texas" (Foreman 373). Griffin was on the Clear Fork of the Brazos (Barsness 124).

15. Of a treaty as sadly ironic in its conditions as can be found, Ralph Smith writes: "During one of these Comanche outbreaks in 1878, Charles Goodnight, owner of the JA Ranch in Palo Duro Canyon, made probably the last private treaty that the Comanches ever entered. For the goodwill of Chiefs Quanah Parker and White Wolf, Goodnight promised to give the Comanches two beeves every other day until they could find buffalo" ("Fantasy" 49).

Samuel Chamberlain, My Confession

Union Army general Samuel Chamberlain's handwritten personal narrative, *My Confession,* chronicling his adventures in the Southwest of the late 1840s, rediscovered by a private collector at a bookseller's in 1956, was probably written as much as a hundred years earlier (Chamberlain 2–3). It was serialized in *Life* in three abridged parts during the summer of 1956, with, as well, its "obvious mistakes and exaggerations . . . winnowed out" (July 23, 1956; 68). In the fall of that year, Harper brought out a hardbound edition of the full narrative. With identical pagination, this edition continued in print in Bison paperback.

Chamberlain's travels with the Glanton gang were published in *Life* only in an abstracted version. Several pages of Chamberlain's flight west after the Yuma-ferry massacre are printed as ordinary text, but the problem with this presentation, for the reader of *Blood Meridian,* is that the many mentions of Holden that appear at this point in the complete Chamberlain text have been omitted. The reader of the full version wonders whether the *Life* editors believed Chamberlain here exaggerated, or whether they simply refused to accept that such an improbable character could have existed at all.

Early in Chamberlain (19–20), he watches a fight on a muddy steamboat landing at Alton, "Illinoise," that breaks out between porters of several hotels over Chamberlain's custom: "the porters of the Franklin House crowed considerable over the less fortunate ones of the Eagle and Alton Hotels" (19). "[C]overed with mud, cold, wet, and hungry," Chamberlain seated himself on a wheelbarrow and watched the fight play out (20). The fact that a fight takes place in a muddy setting in Chamberlain gives his pages only the barest of analogues to McCarthy's fight across the mud between Toadvine and the kid (9–11); nevertheless, Chamberlain's fight involves a trip to a hotel, and the novel's scene that follows the kid's muddy fight involves a violent excursion to a hotel.

Chamberlain fought a man and "was afraid I had received my death wound, and this idea made me determined that my destroyer should keep me company" (36), a sentiment that may guide the novel's Tobin to say to the kid, as the kid removes an arrow from David Brown's leg by pushing it through, that Brown would have "took you with him" had the kid failed (161–163). On the same page, Chamberlain writes of having pinned an adversary to the ground with a bayonet through his neck, though "the weapon had passed through the thick muscles of the neck without touching a vital part, making a painful but not a serious wound" (36). The injured man survives, as does Tobin, who is shot in the neck by Holden in the novel (290).[16]

---

16. Still, when Lieutenant Britton Davis writes of a "little dried-up Irishman with a terrible brogue," Sergeant Conn, who was shot "full in the throat" and recovered, McCarthy's more likely source is present. Davis writes that the bullet "made a ghastly hole, pushed aside the jugular vein (so the surgeon claimed), grazed the vertebra, and passed out, leaving a hole the size of a silver dollar" (35).

As he begins his travels into the Southwest, the youthful Chamberlain is held at, and then released from, the "Old Spanish Jail at San Antonio," and flies, half crazed, into the countryside (41–42). He awakens one morning three weeks later to find himself thirty miles from San Antonio at Castroville, and is told that he had been found "lying near the road entirely nude and insensible" (42). It is possible that the discovery of the "nude" Chamberlain may have inspired McCarthy's early scene of the kid "lying naked under the trees with his rags spread across the limbs above him when another rider going down the river reined up and stopped" (28).

Chamberlain recounts an episode from the Mexican War in which American volunteer soldiers butchered "over twenty Mexicans" in retaliation for the murder of an American (87–88). What is notable, other than that no soldier was punished for the murders, is that the Mexicans were scalped by the Anglos, and that "A rough crucifix was fastened to a rock [at the scene] and some irreverent wretch had crowned the image with a bloody scalp" (88). McCarthy's penitents (313–315) are massacred in the shelter of a cross they carry with them. The two stories have some resemblances, but do not appear to expand or define each other (see also Bourke 239).

Chamberlain writes of a hard army ride at night: "A faint new moon gave a weird light to the scene as we rushed on in flight. Horses fell in the prairie dog holes, men were thrown . . . prairie dogs barked, snakes rattled, owls hooted and flew up from beneath and men cursed at our headlong flight" (109). On foot, the kid follows tracks made by the gang at night, and "could tell by the small rocks overturned and holes stepped into that they had passed at night" (216). All such night-ride risks are tallied by David Brown, who responds to the question of Apaches' hunting the gang at night, with "They wont ride at night"; when asked why not, "Brown spat. Because it's dark" (242).

In *Blood Meridian*, "small worms worked in the open wound" on Sproule's arm (67). When Chamberlain sees war wounded in a hospital, he writes, "maggots and vermin crawled in and out of their undressed wounds" (137).

Chamberlain writes, "Common prudence should have caused us to retire" from a Chihuahua saloon "full of ugly looking cutthroats." But Chamberlain and his army fellows go on, wanting to dance, since "a fandango was in full blast." Still, after one of the "Anglos" cried out, "I am cut"—a Mexican had knifed him in the side—Chamberlain "fired over the heads of the crowd and shot the bravo in the back" as the "ugly yellow belly [was] sneaking for the door" (248). This Chamberlain scene contains several of McCarthy's elements present in his scene of the knifing of Grimley at Nacori (178). Chamberlain's "Common prudence" can become McCarthy's "These details should have stood the workers entering the cantina in better stead," and Chamberlain's "fired over the heads of the crowd" is apparent when Holden "leveled [his pistol] above the heads of the men" in the cantina and "shot the drunk" who had knifed Grimley.

Chamberlain writes of the Southwest: "The air was so warm and dry that it took all the life out of the command, men and animals seemed to lose all of their vitality and dry up, waggons fell to pieces, tires came off, spokes came out, constant halting to repair broken-down waggons soured the disposition of all" (257). McCarthy draws this moment into a five-sentence paragraph beginning: "The wagons drew so dry they slouched from side to side like dogs" (45).

Chamberlain (280–281) is McCarthy's source for *Blood Meridian*'s lottery-of-arrows scene (205–209). Chamberlain is distraught at the gang's "merciful" murder of four of its wounded after a fight with the Apaches: "Glanton made a short but forceable speech, the drift of it was 'that *mercy*, and our safety demanded the death of these four, and that the laws of the desert sanction it.' I was horrified and expressed myself freely, but the execution was ordered" (280). Chamberlain tells another story from the Mexican War (280–281) that may shed some light on *Blood Meridian*'s scene. The tale concerns a group of Rangers travelling with the United States Army in Mexico (173–174). One of their number had strayed from the group, then gotten drunk and into trouble: he tied a church's cross behind his horse and dragged it through the streets of a Mexican town, where it struck and bloodied the parish priest. Townspeople lassoed the Ranger, tied him to a cross, and "flayed" him until his skin hung in strips. When the Rangers found their lost one, he was "yet alive and in his awful agony cursed all and everything and begged his comrades to shoot him and end his sufferings. He was cut down and finding him beyond hope the Rangers' Captain put a bullet through the brains of the wretch."

Clemens, commenting on Ranger units of the American army during the Mexican War, writes in *Mustang Gray*:

Fighting was their vocation; and the idea of refraining from so favorite an amusement at the bidding of any civil officer, however high his station, was so great an absurdity, that they were more disposed to regard it as an indifferent hoax, than a matter of serious import. Law was with them an obsolete word; and they submitted to no control save that which was necessary to their military efficiency. The Highlanders of Scotland had their hereditary chieftains, whose lightest word was implicitly obeyed. The Ranger of the Prairie had no superior except the officer who was for the time being in command. When the objects of an expedition were accomplished, he was on a footing of perfect equality with his commander. He was free to stay or go—to select another leader, or to set up for a leader himself. Thus it often happened that the captain of to-day was a private in the ranks to-morrow. All this was so perfectly understood, that no jealousy or heart-burning ever followed. Whoever planned a foray was its commander, unless he voluntarily gave way to some one who knew the country better, or had greater experience than himself. The subordinate officers were elected by the men. (235)

Historically, Glanton is a commander among former Rangers (Chamberlain 267). After the encounter with Elías in *Blood Meridian*, his decision to sort among the wounded for the ones to be killed "mercifully" recalls both Chamberlain's Glanton's execution of his wounded and Chamberlain's story of the Ranger shot by his commander. McCarthy's kid, not having begun his training as a Ranger, leaves the wounded Shelby to his own determination of what is most "merciful" (207–209). "Ranger" ethics are neither Chamberlain's nor, apparently, the kid's.

George Frederick Ruxton, Adventures in Mexico and the Rocky Mountains

Early in his mid-nineteenth-century eyewitness account, the Englishman Ruxton provides a description of the town of Vera Cruz which probably informs McCarthy's "sopilotes" scene (59). When McCarthy misspells the Mexican word for buzzard as "sopilotes," his choice of spelling would seem to identify his source as in Ruxton.[17] Ruxton writes:

One hundred years ago [Vera Cruz was] a flourishing commercial city, [and] like everything in Spanish America, it has suffered from the baneful effects of a corrupt, impotent government. Now, with a scanty population, and under the control of a military despotism, its wealth and influence have passed away. The aspect of the interior of the town is dreary and desolate beyond description. Grass grows in the streets and squares; the churches and public buildings are falling to ruins: scarcely a human being is to be met, and the few seen are sallow and lank, and skulk through the streets as if fearing to encounter, at every corner, the personification of the dread vomito [cholera], which at this season (August) is carrying off a tithe of the population. Everywhere stalks the "sopilote" (turkey-buzzard), sole tenant of the streets, feeding on the garbage and carrion which abound in every corner.

The few foreign merchants who reside here, remove their families to Jalapa in the season of the vomito, and all who have a few dollars in their pockets betake themselves to the temperate regions. The very natives and negroes are a cadaverous stunted race; and the dogs, which contend in the streets with the sopilotes for carrion, are the most miserable of the genus cur. Just before my window one of these curs lay expiring in the middle of the street. As the wretched animal quivered in the last gasp, a sopilote flew down from the church-spire, and, perching on the body, commenced its feast. It was soon joined by several others, and in five minutes the carcase was devoured. These disgusting birds are, however, useful scavengers, and, performing the duty of the lazy Mexicans, are therefore protected by law. (12–13)

Ruxton stresses an "insatiable passion for gambling" on the part of the Mexicans, "which is at the bottom of this national evil," that is, the powerlessness of "justice" (31). Gambling is also present in Ruxton's scene of the knifing of a man at cards (as mentioned in the essay on tarot, Chapter 5), a killing to which "no one present paid the slightest attention" (44), and a story that may inform McCarthy's description of a knifing in the bar at Janos (102–103).

Ruxton writes: "The stranger in Mexico is perpetually annoyed by the religious processions which perambulate the streets at all hours":

17. Ober correctly spells this word for vultures "*zopilotes,*" and notes its derivation "from the Aztec word '*zopilotl*'" (177–178).

A coach, with an eye painted on the panels, and drawn by six mules, conveys the host to the houses of dying Catholics who are rich enough to pay for the privilege: before this equipage a bell tinkles, which warns the orthodox to fall on their knees; and woe to the unfortunate who neglects this ceremony, either from ignorance or design. On one occasion, being suddenly surprised by the approach of one of these processions, I had but just time to doff my hat and run behind a corner of a building, when I was spied by a fat priest, who, shouldering an image, brought up the rear of the procession. (35)

This paragraph presumably informs McCarthy's paragraph of the kid and other prisoners in the streets in Chihuahua City, who observed, as they moved about their work, that:

A small bell was ringing and a coach was coming up the street. They stood along the curb and took off their hats. The guidon passed ringing the bell and then the coach. It had an eye painted on the side and four mules to draw it, taking the host to some soul. A fat priest tottered after carrying an image. The guards were going among the prisoners snatching the hats from the heads of the newcomers and pressing them into their infidel hands. (75)

Ruxton's "annoyance" might also have contributed a setting to *Blood Meridian*'s bar fight at Nacori (177–178; see also Ruxton, *Life* 188–189).

    Ruxton presents a scene in which, mistaken for his dog, a thief or beggar is sleepily invited to share Ruxton's blanket (73). McCarthy's anchorite scene early in the book, in which the kid "woke sometime in the night [after having 'muttered like a dreaming dog' in his sleep] with . . . the hermit bent over him and all but in his bed" (20), shares characteristic elements with Ruxton.

    Ruxton travels through the Mal Pais "volcanic region" (79), which the novel's gang traverses in Tobin's tale of the judge and gunpowder (129). Ruxton writes of the Mal Pais as an "evil land":

The Mexicans, as they passed this spot, crossed themselves reverently, and muttered an Ave Maria; for in the lonely regions of the Mal Pais, the superstitious Indian believes that demons and gnomes, and spirits of evil purposes have their dwelling-places, whence they not unfrequently pounce upon the solitary traveller, and bear him into the cavernous bowels of the earth; the arched roof of the prison-house resounding to the tread of their horses as they pass the dreaded spot, muttering rapidly their prayers, and handling their amulets and charms to keep off the treacherous bogles who invisibly beset the path. (81)

In the novel, Tobin declares, "little devils with their pitchforks had traversed that fiery vomit," leaving "little hooflet markings" (130).

    Ruxton includes a scene in which Indians advance on a group of Mexicans who think the Indians are their returning bullfighters (97). Their misperception may have shaded McCarthy's construction of *Blood Meridian*'s Comanche attack scene (52), since Ruxton also discusses the depredations of the Comanches in the Chihuahua area (101–102; see also 125). He mentions "a German named Spiers" (110; see also the Speyer section, above).

He describes a house, the roof of which had been "torn off, and from the upper walls [the Indians] had shot down with arrows all the inmates" (129). This detail of Mexicans shot from the upper walls of a building (with holes hacked as ports in the roof) appears also in McCarthy (60).

Of the feast of Las Animas, which occurs in *Blood Meridian* while the gang is at Jesús María (190–191), Ruxton writes:

It happened to be the feast of Las Animas, when money is collected by the priests for the purpose of praying souls out of purgatory, which on this day is done by wholesale. If money is not to be had, the collectors, usually children, with little boxes which have holes in which the coin is dropped, receive corn or beans; the contribution of my landlord being a couple of tallow candles, which no doubt were efficacious in getting some unhappy soul out of several years' pawn, and perhaps were useful in greasing the way, as the donor remarked, to the exit of some orthodox pelàdo [*sic*]. (142)[18]

"The faces of the women [at Socorro] were all stained with the fiery red juice of a plant called *alegria*, from the forehead to the chin. This is for the purpose of protecting their skin from the effects of the sun, and preserving them in untanned beauty to be exposed in the fandangos," Ruxton observes (183). This type of detail (McCarthy's source apparently provides him with information on red hematite, a red ochre, "almagre") obviously invests the narrator's remark, as the gang enters Ures, that "Females of domestic reputation lounged upon the balconies they passed with faces gotten up in indigo and almagre gaudy as the rumps of apes and they peered from behind their fans with a kind of lurid coyness like transvestites in a madhouse" (200; see also 69).

Ruxton seems a source for the term "possibles," which McCarthy uses when Sproule asks the kid, "Did you not save any of your possibles?" (56; see also 17, 140). Ruxton writes: "Ammunition, a few pounds of tobacco, dressed deer-skins for moccasins, &c., are carried [by trappers] in a wallet of dressed buffalo-skin, called a possible-sack. His 'possibles' . . ." (243).[19] This word, again in quotation, is capitalized in Ruxton's itemized subheading for Chapter 31, as "'Possibles' overhauled" (283; see also Favour 112, 113; and Ruxton, *Life* 17, 232).

Adventures also contains the information that two men in "rapid consumption" whom Ruxton met found that they "now were . . . perfectly restored, and in robust health and spirits" after having lived in the Mexican mountains (288). Sproule says in *Blood Meridian* that he had "come out here for my health" as a result of a consumptive condition (58).

18. "Pelàdo, literally skinless, meaning, in Mexico, the ragged, coatless vagabonds who loaf about the towns and villages" (Ruxton, *Adventures* 125; see also Ruxton, *Life* 187).

19. To a mountain man, this bag was every bit as vital to survival as his rifle. He called it his "Possibles" bag because without its contents, it "ain't possible" (Lermayer 87).

George Frederick Ruxton, Life in the Far West

Ruxton's "novel" of adventures begins with a reference to "the year it rained fire," adding that "every body knows when that was" (8).[20]

In *Life*, Indian scalp hair is decorative fringe on leggings (12), a detail also used by McCarthy in describing his gang's trappings (78). Ruxton also includes the killing of a wounded Indian "for mercy's sake" (31), which may compare to the killing of the gang's own wounded (205–206).

One of Ruxton's characters, La Bonté, is "not yet entirely steeled by mountain life to a perfect indifference to human feeling" at the death of a friend (73). Ruxton later writes:

If truth be told, La Bonté had his failings as a mountaineer, and—sin unpardonable in hunter law—still possessed, in holes and *corners* of his breast seldom explored by his inward eye, much of the leaven of kindly human nature, which now and again involuntarily peeped out, as greatly to the contempt of his comrade trappers as it was blushingly repressed by the mountaineer himself (111; my emphasis).

This "sin unpardonable in hunter law" passage may well have influenced McCarthy's drawing of the kid, since the judge accuses him of having a "flawed place in the fabric" of his heart, of having "reserved . . . some *corner* of clemency for the heathen" (299; my emphasis).

Ruxton's *Life* also features a deception having to do with Indians drinking whites' whiskey (see the Mangas Colorado section, Chapter 2), and that "with the mountain men bets decide every question that is raised, even the most trivial" (78). Indians, Ruxton writes, will wager "stakes, comprising all the valuables the player possesses" (101). He writes of the mountain men's dancing in which a man seizes "his partner round the waist with the gripe of a grisly bear," in the steps of the Indian "'scalp' or buffalo 'dances,'" and that the "Mexicans have no chance in such physical force dancing" (187). His words presage *Blood Meridian*'s final scenes in Fort Griffin, in which a bear dances, the judge embraces the kid, and "the board floor" slams "under the jackboots" (324–335).

James Hobbs, Wild Life in the Far West: Personal Adventures of a Border Mountain Man

Items in James Hobbs's recollection parallel a remarkable number of details in *Blood Meridian*, and at least two define Hobbs's as a book McCarthy had used as a source text.

---

20. This sentence is glossed by the editor as "The 'Year the Stars Fell'—the meteoric shower of November 12, 1833" (8).

As noted in "Introductions" (Chapter 1), when Hobbs writes "some of the party said it looked barbarous; but I kept on scalping, saying that business men always took receipts" (409), he is uniquely a source for Glanton's "Get that receipt for us" (98), as he is uniquely a source (77) for McCarthy's spelling of Bennet Riddells's name as "Riddle" (83–84).[21]

But Hobbs's items can begin as early as his book's frontispiece engraving, "The Author [dressed] as a Comanche," which echoes Chamberlain's Indian-dress-deception items (272, 273–274), and can be found in *Blood Meridian* in Holden's story of the harness-maker dressed as an Indian (142), and also in the novel's scene of a small wagon train massacred by whites who disguised the crime as if it had been committed by Indians (153). Indeed, regarding a sense of McCarthy's *Blood Meridian*, Hobbs left home at sixteen (2); mentions Speyers (59), Speyers's offer for scalps (71), that Riddle can bring goods into Chihuahua without trouble (77), and that Speyers bribes soldiers (78); and relates that Speyers had bought clothes for Hobbs and scalp-hunting James Kirker (95).

Hobbs's "Riddle & Stephens's hotel" (95) is the only full historical match to McCarthy's "Riddle and Stephens Hotel" (167). Hobbs gives "Bill" for William A. Doniphan (158), a detail also in a Captain White story (34). Hobbs writes of "slaughtered" scalpers at the Yuma ferry crossing—here, read Glanton's gang—who had been "taking . . . women prisoners and keeping them in camp as long as they pleased" (213), which is found in *Blood Meridian's* Yuma-camp setting (272, 275). He writes that "Captain Hooper" of Fort Yuma "clapped ["two escaped desperadoes" from the massacre] into irons and sent them to California for trial" (214), which could have suggested *Blood Meridian's* hanging of Toadvine and David Brown (311). Hobbs also writes of "'The Great Western'" (216), who is the novel's Sarah Borginnis (256).

John Woodhouse Audubon, Audubon's Western Journal: 1849–1850

John Woodhouse Audubon, son of artist John James Audubon, travelled the Southwest, keeping a journal, at midcentury. He defines the word "Jacal" parenthetically as "a sort of openwork shed covered with skins and rushes and plastered with mud, here so full of lime and marl that it makes a hard and lasting mortar" (54), a word that McCarthy uses

---

21. Sergeant Holbrook uses the term "voucher" (in Carson 137). In a letter to his editor Quaife in 1926, former Ranger James B. Gillett writes "To scalp an Indian is a barbarous and inhuman act and I am ashamed now to admit that I helped to scalp an Indian we rangers had killed. I sewed a part of his scalp onto my revolver holster and with the long hair hanging down almost to my knee, wore it around over the frontier. Now isn't that almost like a savage? Yet we thought nothing of it at the time, but as we grow old we grow in grace, and I have many times knelt down and prayed to God for his forgiveness" (65).

in *Blood Meridian* to name a "crude hut of mud and wattles" that the filibustering troop comes across in its travel into the Southwest (48).[22]

Frank "Carrol" is mentioned in Audubon and even travels with his party, but this account does not indicate that he stays on at Jesús María (92, 106, 110). Cave Johnson Couts, as "Lieut. Coats," is mentioned (161, 164).

A probable source for McCarthy's tarot-reading tent show, which travels with the gang to Janos, is in Audubon's entry for June 13, 1849, at Cerro Gordo:

> Here we were visited by a member of a Mexican travelling circus, who asked our protection as far as El Valle, which we promised them. The party consisted of five, one woman and four men. The lady rode as we used to say in Louisiana "leg of a side," on a small pacing pony; the two horses of the ring carried only their saddles, two pack mules, four small trunks, and four jaded horses the rest of the plunder. The four men went on foot, driving the packs and continually refitting and repacking, the other three riding. One man had two Chihuahua dogs about six inches long, stuffed in his shirt bosom, another a size larger on the pommel of his saddle. A second man was in grand Spanish costume, on a small but blooded grey horse, with a large dragoon sword on his left, and a Mexican musket made about 1700, which would have added to an antiquary's armory. They told us they had everything they owned with them, so that if alone, and attacked by the Apaches, whom we hear of continually but never see, their loss would be a very serious one to them. (100–101)

Audubon visited the silver mining town of Jesús María, and notes that two rushing streams join there (120–121; see the section on Jesús María, above). The germ of the idea for *Blood Meridian*'s slaughter of the quicksilver train heading east into Jesús María (194–195) may, too, be found in Audubon when he writes for July 14, 1849: "Everything used [in Jesús María] is brought from the Pacific side, quicksilver, irons, wines and liquors; even flour is sometimes brought, but most of that comes from Sonora which is ten days' travel to the east" (121). In contrast to *Blood Meridian*'s nightmarish encounter, Audubon notes his party's forbearance, west of Jesús María, on July 28: "We did not leave camp until nearly noon, waiting for a train of one hundred and eighty-two mules packed with nothing but flasks of quicksilver; the usual length of trains is about forty to fifty, with six or eight men" (129).[23]

Angry at his losses in Jesús María and on treacherous mountain trails, Glanton simply shoves past such a supply train as this, McCarthy inverting Audubon's patience to satisfy his own narrative requirements.

Audubon's party included a man named Sloat travelling west with it to San Diego (138,

---

22. See also Bartlett, who uses the word "jackal" and writes of such buildings as "rude, being . . . built of upright sticks filled in with mud" (2: 392).

23. Ober mentions "a caravan of mules . . . nine fourteen-mule teams . . . used in transporting machinery and mining supplies to those far away camps in the mountains" (620).

174). An editor's footnote to the Audubon text quotes Amiel Whipple (see the Yuma Chiefs section, in Chapter 2) describing this man as "a son of Commodore Sloat" (165). McCarthy's novel includes Glanton's question to "a boy named Sloat," asking if "he were kin to the commodore of that name the boy spat quietly and said No, nor him to me" (204).

Audubon's party burned wood for charcoal in order to shape horseshoes (145), as McCarthy's judge burned wood to charcoal for the making of his gunpowder (128).[24]

Concurring with the novel's description of the Yuma ferry at the crossing of the Colorado, the *Western Journal* details it as "a boat" which "was really a large wagon body, made into a scow," and that "Lieut. Com. Coats" assisted their party with the loan of "his sergeant's boat, a wagon body caulked" (163).

As he reaches California, Audubon begins a series of entries depicting gambling. In one of the first of these scenes, at Stockton, sometime after November 9, 1849, he writes:

We went into the "Exchange Hotel," which might better be called the "Exchange of Blacklegs." Such a crowd as the bar-room of this hotel presents nightly, cannot be found except where all nations meet. Cards were being played for stakes everywhere, and the crowd around added to the picture, which once seen is difficult to forget. The tall, raw-boned Westerner, bearded and moustached like his Mexican neighbor beside him, the broadheaded German and sallow Spaniard, French, Irish, Scotch, I know not how many nationalities are here represented. I saw even two Chilians with their cold, indifferent air, all mixing together, each man on his guard against his fellow-man. The tight fitting jacket and flowing serape touch each other, all blending into weirdness in the dim light of a few candles, would that I had time and opportunity to sketch some of the many scenes I beheld. (187)

One wonders at the way in which men stay here day after day, gambling going on incessantly. Of course, the sharpers and experts get all the money, the poor dupes continue to put down gold-dust, even though every boat that leaves takes away professional card players and they have to return to the mines to dig. (188)

On Christmas Day 1849, "in this pandemonium of a city," San Francisco, Audubon enters in his journal:

Not a *lady* to be seen, and the women, poor things, sad and silent, except when drunk or excited. The place full of gamblers, hundreds of them, and men of the lowest types, more blasphemous, and with less regard for God and his commands than all I have ever seen on the Mississippi, [in] New Orleans or Texas, which give us the same class to some extent, it is true; but instead of a few dozen, or a hundred, gaming at a time, here, there are thousands, and one house alone pays one hundred and fifty thousand dollars per annum for the rent of the "Monte" tables. (193)

---

24. Bartlett also burns wood to charcoal for smithing (2: 315). This edition of Audubon notes Bartlett's *Personal Narrative* (168), Wislizenus, and Emory, among others (142).

I could almost fancy as we made our way to the open bay through the crowd of vessels, that I could hear the chink, chink of dollars as the gamblers put them down on the Monte tables, and a picture of the whole place, a regular Inferno, came before me as plainly as if I actually saw it. Every house, with rare exceptions, letting out their bar-rooms as well as all other available space, for gambling purposes, immense rents being paid for a mere shell of a house. (196)[25]

The reader will notice, above all, that both Audubon's *Journal* and *Blood Meridian* (324–335) concur in their depiction of the western saloon environment.

John Russell Bartlett, Personal Narrative of Explorations and Incidents

Bartlett was commissioner of a boundary survey marking the border of the United States and Mexico in the early 1850s, a border that determined the area of the Gadsden Purchase and so determined the final extent of the area of the contiguous United States. He published over a thousand pages on his experiences in the Southwest, a source for several particulars in *Blood Meridian*, notably his portrait of Governor Angel Trias and his description and illustration of the Tucson meteorite-anvil.

McCarthy describes a "Moorish churchdome" (21) at San Antonio de Bexar, a type of detail often highlighted in Bartlett. In his narrative, Bartlett writes of the "Moorish style" of the doorway of the Alamo at San Antonio (1: 41). The Texas missions of San José (1: 42) and Concepción (1: 44) are illustrated. Bartlett expands his remarks when he writes that, from the East, "the style was introduced into Spain by the Moors, and by the Spaniards was taken to Mexico. Moorish capitals and ornaments are still visible both in the fine dwelling and the humble cottage in northern Mexico" (1: 190, see also 2: 463).[26]

Bartlett describes two horses bitten by rattlesnakes (1: 84, 2: 342), though neither is said to have been bitten on the nose, as was McCarthy's "mad horse" at the Santa Rita mines (115).

In describing "rude paintings and sculptures, representing men, animals, birds, snakes, and fantastic figures," painted by Indians on rock outcrops, he notes that "some of them, evidently of great age, had been partly defaced to make room for more recent devices" (1: 170–171). This comment may have suggested the scene of the judge defacing such paintings (173). Given McCarthy's persistent theme of the newer dominating the older, here the newer rewrites or supplants the older's records.

Bartlett writes of "The most beautiful mirage I ever witnessed," which "seemed like the surface of a broad lake, the mountain peaks standing detached, like so many islands rising from the bed of its placid waters" (1: 218), and later of "*playas*, or dry lakes," of

---

25. See also Audubon 198, 212–214.
26. At Jesús María, McCarthy notes a fiddler playing a "Moorish folktune" (189).

which it was "utterly impossible" for the observer "to say, whether they contained water or not" (2: 371).[27] These remarks inform some of McCarthy's description of a mirage in which "The floor of the playa lay smooth and unbroken by any track and the mountains in their blue islands stood footless in the void like floating temples" (108; see also 46).

Bartlett recounts a story that resembles Dunn on the Santa Rita del Cobre mines (1: 228–229), also recounting Johnson's trick on the Indians on a later page (1: 323). He includes information on wild bulls in the Southwest (1: 256, 258, 397) and mentions the Indians' desire to get whiskey from the Anglos (1: 302, 2: 220). On two occasions Bartlett's text uses the uncommon word "sutler" (1: 303, 309), which also occurs in *Blood Meridian* (44, 201). He describes deerskin helmets worn by Apaches (1: 328, illus. 329), which, taken with Ruxton's note in *Adventures* of a "turban" worn by Indians (313), may inform McCarthy's detail, included in the novel's Comanche attack (52), of Indians dressed "in costumes attic or biblical." Here, too, is the term "*arriero* or muleteer," in a description of Mexicans at the copper mines (1: 358–359), a Mexican word McCarthy includes in his quicksilver-train incident (195). And Bartlett mentions that an Indian became alarmed when his portrait had been drawn (1: 444), much as had an old Hueco described by Holden in *Blood Meridian* (141).

Bartlett devotes attention to the Catholic Church in Mexico. He writes of thousands of dollars collected for the church, none of which seemed to benefit the parishes (1: 426). McCarthy's feast of Las Animas (a major feast in the Mexican religious calendar even today), which occurs while the gang is in Jesús María, is also described: "On the 'feast of the dead' the bells toll day and night; and in the evening, the graves and monuments are surrounded with lighted candles, and visited by the friends of the departed. These kneel by the graves, while the priest, with a choir of singers, goes from one to the other, singing as many prayers for the souls of the departed as the survivors choose to pay for" (1: 478–479).

Carl Sartorius describes this feast's link in the Mexican mind to ancient Aztec festivals honoring the dead (162). He also stresses the extreme poverty of the Mexicans, whose contributions to the church on this day constitute "a harvest-day for the priests" (165; see also, generally, 161–165). But an appreciation of the frontier's starkness, of its utterly desolate nature as McCarthy presents it, may benefit from the addition of a brief historical overview.

Anglos in Mexico, in mid-nineteenth-century literature, are often referred to as "hereticos," which arises out of the Mexican response to a culture more in line with the traditions of the Protestant Reformation than to Mexican Roman Catholicism. Though

27. Bartlett also footnotes mirages, quoting Alexander Humboldt: "This phenomenon has been observed in all quarters of the world" (1: 247).

the secularization of Mexico's Catholic properties formally dates to the mid-1850s, by the mid-1830s the "liberal reformers who chipped away at the Church's underpinnings managed only to weaken it in central Mexico, but they helped bring about its collapse on the frontier" (Weber 82). When McCarthy writes of "the great sleeping God of the Mexicans routed from his golden cup" (60), he may well be basing these sentiments on the historical record—that the Catholic God's "silence" in Mexico is in the 1840s deeper than ever before in post-Columbian times (cf. 34, 40, 111, 145, 146, 280, 293, 330). The landscape he depicts, dotted with abandoned churches, signifies not only a general fear of Indian incursions, but also an abandonment of the churches by the Mexicans. Only in places like Chihuahua City, in Nacori, and particularly in the isolated mountain town of Jesús María is the Catholic Church in *Blood Meridian* present in its traditional strength. Bartlett's description of a ruined mission in Sonora echoes McCarthy's vision of any number of abandoned structures: "Bats were already in full possession of the edifice, and hung from the projecting walls and corners, like so many black ornaments" (1: 414). The frontier is literally an abandoned and godforsaken place.

Bartlett writes several times of wolves in the Southwest. Pack mules that wandered from the train, Bartlett writes:

should they elude the Indians, their fate most inevitably was, in their enfeebled state, to become an easy prey to the hungry wolves, which in great numbers were constantly prowling about, making night hideous with their howlings; and not unfrequently so impatient were they to seize upon the poor animals, that they could be seen skulking close to our camp in broad daylight. (2: 2–3)

Some parts of the country, though, were barren to the degree that even wolves were not present, as evident in the untouched carcasses of dead animals (1: 101, 2: 128, 555).

In his second volume, Bartlett finds "crystallized sulfur" (2: 39–40), as does the judge in Tobin's telling of the gunpowder story (131). Bartlett describes the Colorado River as "dark reddish" (2: 150), a detail that may contribute to McCarthy's tarot prediction of a "dark river" (81, 96).

Bartlett writes of his "great relief," at one point in his travels, to have "perceived" that a group of men approaching him were "clad in dark coats, and that all wore hats, some of them black. This showed that they were neither Apaches nor Mexicans; for the former do not wear hats at all, and the latter at this season ["August 1st"] wear white calico shirts, with straw hats" (2: 327). Bartlett's relief is akin to the kid's relief, lost at one point between Indians and Mexican soldiers, to discover that an approaching group of "riders [Glanton and his men] wore hats" (218).

Near the hacienda of San Bernardino, Bartlett writes of meeting a Colonel Garcia:

with a detachment of two hundred Mexican troops from Tucson, on a campaign against the

Apaches. A more miserable set of men I never met, certainly none calling themselves soldiers. Some of them were destitute of shirts, others of pantaloons, and some had neither
coats nor hats. Some wore overcoats, without a rag of clothing beneath. They had seen no
Indians, as might be expected, although forty were observed here the day before. In all
probability the wily enemy had perceived them, and would follow them, in the hope of
stealing some of their animals, and piercing some of them with a lance or an arrow. (2:
328–329)

This account of Garcia appears to inform McCarthy's description of "Garcia's command,"
in which he writes: "Two days later they encountered a ragged legion under the command
of Colonel Garcia. They were troops from Sonora seeking a band of Apaches under Pablo
and they numbered close to a hundred riders. Of these some were without hats and some
without pantaloons and some were naked under their coats and they were armed with
derelict weapons, old fusils and Tower muskets, some with bows and arrows or nothing
more than ropes with which to garrote the enemy" (243).[28]

Bartlett notes that "Carrizal is an old dilapidated presidio, and now nearly depopulated; more than half the houses being tenantless" (2: 409). His description is not at vari-
ance with the novel's description of Carrizal (174–175).

Travelling east from San Diego, he passes Carrizo Creek, littered with bones (2:
126–128), and the well at Alamo Mucho (2: 132, 140–141), both places the kid reaches
heading west after the massacre.

As noted above, Bartlett seems McCarthy's source of information on Pacheco's Tucson meteorite-anvil. Bartlett also writes a long footnote on meteorites, accounting for
their falls by quoting Alexander Humboldt's prosaic explanation of them as "small masses
moving with planetary velocity, and revolving in obedience to the laws of general gravity in conic sections around the sun" (2: 459).

Adolphus Wislizenus, Memoir of a Tour to Northern Mexico

The German doctor Adolphus Wislizenus travelled the Southwest during the Mexican
War. Comments on geological and botanical items are the backbone of his book, but
McCarthy's use of Wislizenus's other details—regarding people and events—may be dis-
cerned.

Wislizenus left Independence, Missouri, in the company of his "enterprising country-
man, Mr. A. Speyer, whose name is very well known in the Santa Fe trade for his energy,
perseverance, and fearlessness" (5). Speyer is mentioned many times in Wislizenus's *Memoir* (13, 29, 42, etc.).

---

28. See also Wislizenus's description of Garcia's command, below.

Presented above, Wislizenus's description of ciboleros (25–26) probably helped shape McCarthy's account of them (120).

Wislizenus's note of a band of Mexican soldiers that he encounters in his travel may shade McCarthy's description of Garcia's soldiers (243). Wislizenus writes:

On riding to camp I was taken by surprise at hearing suddenly the warlike sound of a trumpet, and seeing a captain, with 30 Mexican soldiers and a flock of sheep, encamped near our caravan. The soldiers looked as poor and miserable as they could be. Some wore pieces of uniform; some were dressed in mere rags; some seated on mules, and some walked barefooted. All of them were armed with short lances, like the Ciboleros, but few had rusty guns. After all, they made no formidable appearance; and had no use for it, neither, because they appeared with the most friendly intentions. (16)

McCarthy's kid rides with Sproule in a "carreta" (67–68). The two heard its approach "like thunder" and felt its approach "in the ground." McCarthy describes the cart as "lumbering clumsily." Wislizenus writes of his encounter with a rustic cart of this sort:

Travelling this morning quietly over the plain, we heard in the distance of several miles a singular, awful noise, like a combination of falling rocks, breaking of bones, screams of an-guish and cries of children, but the deep impression which the mysterious concert had made upon my ears was but surpassed by the surprising effect, when with my own eyes I descried the wonderful machine whose action produced that unearthly music—a Mexican carréta. Imagine to yourself a cart, made without any nails or iron of any kind, with two solid wheels formed out of the trunk of a big tree, and in the circumference rounded, or rather squared, and with a frame of ox-skin or sticks fastened together by rawhide, and this machine then put in motion by three yoke of oxen, and carrying a load, which on a better vehicle one animal could transport much faster and easier, and you will have an idea of the primitive and only known vehicle used in Northern Mexico. (16–17)

Wislizenus characterizes rock formations along the Santa Fe road as "firm granite ground, thrown up from the bowels of the earth in one of the grand revolutions which, in time immemorial, have changed the nature of our globe" (19). Wislizenus's sense of the geology of the world is, then, akin to that sense of "revolution" that recurs in McCarthy's novel. Wislizenus writes, regarding the Mexican general Santa Anna's sense of the world, that "the wheel of fortune is always turning" for him (27).

He relates that "an old tradition reports that the Aztecs, in their migration from the north to the south of Mexico, made three principal stations—the first on the lake de Teguyo, (great Salt lake?) and the second on the Gila, and the third at Casas Grandes" (60), in a note that echoes in McCarthy's inclusion of the town of Casas Grandes as an emblem of the ever-changing nature of the world (139, 146).

Of the Spanish conquerors of the Indians, Wislizenus writes: "They found a great many Indian tribes and settlements, which they succeeded in christianizing in the usual Spanish way, with sword in hand, and made them their slaves. The villages of the christianized Indians were called *pueblos*, in opposition to the wild and roving tribes that refused such favors" (26). When Glanton's gang attacks pueblos (181, 204), one may wonder if these brutalities allude to the Christian "moral" when confronted with the amoral.

Wislizenus writes that during the Mexican War, "the treatment of the Texan prisoners is but one of the many instances where the cruelties of the Mexican men were mitigated by the disinterested kindness of their women" (27). This remark may well inform McCarthy's scene of the kid's transfer to the prison at Chihuahua, where a woman "smuggled them sweets under her shawl and there were pieces of meat in the bottom of the bowls that had come from her own table" (71).

Rather than pay for and display whole scalps, as in Chihuahua, the "refined New Mexicans show but the ears," and strings of these ears were used as "festoons" across the windows of the governor's palace at Santa Fe (28; see also Kendall 580). The gang members' "scapulars" of ears (78, [Bathcat] 87, [David Brown] 269–270) may come out of this Wislizenus detail.

As explicated in some detail in the tarot essay (Chapter 5), Wislizenus appears to be McCarthy's historical source for the St. Elmo's fire in *Blood Meridian*. Reproduced here in their entirety, these passages recount Wislizenus's mid-nineteenth-century "scientific" assessment of St. Elmo's fire and static discharges.

About noon [of August 16], while we were encamped, a thunder-storm came on, as usual in the rainy season. It rained awhile, and towards the end of the shower, the thunder disappearing in the distance, I perceived a most remarkable phenomenon in the mountains to our right, about 10 miles distant. Three pointed flames, apparently from one to two feet high, and of whitish lustre, were seen at once on a high barren place in the mountains; they lasted for about 10 minutes, and disappeared then as suddenly. The Mexicans told me that this phenomenon is not uncommon in these mountains, and that such a place had once been examined, and a crevice found, around which the grass was burnt. The popular opinion amongst the Mexicans seems to be, that such flames indicate silver mines. There can be hardly any doubt that the phenomenon is connected with electricity; but whether an inflammable gas, that emanates from a crevice, is ignited by lightning, or an unusual quantity of free electricity is developed by local causes, or superficial metallic layers should have some influence in producing it, are questions that can only be solved by a repeated and careful examination of the localities and circumstances. (43)

The great dryness of the atmosphere produces, of course, a very free development of electricity. By rubbing the hair of cats and dogs in the dark, I could elicit here a greater mass of electricity than I had ever seen produced in this way. Some persons, entitled to confidence, informed me that by changing their woolen under-dress in the night, they had at first been repeatedly frightened by seeing themselves suddenly enveloped in a mass of electrical fire. The remarkable flames that appeared after a thunder-storm in the mountains south of el Paso, already mentioned by me, were no doubt connected with electricity. I recollect also, from an account published in relation to the battle of Buena Vista, that during a sultry evening electrical flames were seen on the points of bayonets among the sentinels stationed in the mountains. Experiments made on the high table-land of Mexico with a fine electrometer, would no doubt give interesting results. (55).

Wislizenus must be the source for Grannyrat's story of the Lipan mummy burials. McCarthy writes:

There was a cave down there [that] had been a Lipan burial. Must of been a thousand indians in there all settin around. Had on their best robes and blankets and all. Had their bows and their knives, whatever. Beads. The Mexicans carried everything off. Stripped em naked. Took it all. They carried off whole indians to their homes and set em in the corner all dressed up but they begun to come apart when they got out of that cave air and they had to be thowed out. Towards the last of it they was some Americans went in there and scalped what was left of em and tried to sell the scalps in Durango. I dont know if they had any luck about it or not. I expect some of them injins had been dead a hundred year. (77–78)

Wislizenus's words, as he rode in the area between Chihuahua and Saltillo, are strikingly similar:

On the right hand, or south of us, a chain of limestone mountains was running parallel with the road. At the foot of a hill belonging to that chain, Señor de Gaba pointed out a place to me where some years ago a remarkable discovery had been made. In the year 1838, a Mexican, Don Juan Flores, perceived there the hidden entrance to a cave. He entered; but seeing inside a council of Indian warriors sitting together in the deepest silence, he retreated and told it to his companions, who, well prepared, entered the cave together, and discovered about 1,000 (?) well preserved Indian corpses, squatted together on the ground, with their hands folded below the knees. They were dressed in fine blankets, made of the fibres of lechuguilla [a type of agave], with sandals, made of a species of liana, on their feet, and ornamented with colored scarfs, with beads of seeds of fruits, polished bones, &c. This is the very insufficient account of the mysterious burying-place. The Mexicans suppose that it belonged to the Lipans, an old Indian tribe, which from time immemorial has roved and is yet roving over the Bolson de Mapimi. I had already heard in Chihuahua of this discovery, and was fortunate enough there to secure a skull that a gentleman had taken from the cave. At present, I was told, the place is pilfered of everything; nevertheless, had I been at leisure, I would have made an excursion to it. (69–70)

McCarthy's note that some of the mummies had been scalped may not be otherwise verifiable. The inclusion of this detail foreshadows the introduction of Glanton's scalp hunters, which occurs only a few pages later in the novel.

Sarah Borginnis appears in Wislizenus: "I stopped for some hours in the hotel of the 'Great Western,' kept by the celebrated *vivandière*, honored with that *nom de guerre*, and whose fearless behaviour during the battle of Buena Vista was highly praised; she dressed many wounded soldiers on that day, and even carried them out of the thickest fight" (75).

Though of only circumstantial interest, Wislizenus describes a "ferry boat, managed by a rope drawn across the river," which carried him to the Mexican town of Camargo (79). Jeremiah Clemens writes in *Bernard Lile* of Glanton's plan to go to Camargo at about this point in the Mexican War (227). A scene at Camargo in *Mustang Gray* does not mention Glanton (290–293). But the impression from these details is that Glanton was possibly familiar with this ferry at Camargo. Glanton's past crossed his present, then, at the Yuma ferry.

The twenty-nine-page "Botanical Appendix" to this *Memoir* appears to be McCarthy's source for some of the novel's vegetation detail. McCarthy's vivid simile in which the "bones of cholla" are "like burning holothurians in the phosphorus dark of the sea's deeps" (243) may have drawn inspiration from Wislizenus's words on the *Opuntia*, or cholla, cactus:

On Waggon-mound the first (flowerless) specimens of a strange *opuntia* were found, with an erect, ligneous stem, and cylindrical, horridly spinous, horizontal branches. . . . as it appears to be undescribed, I can give it no more appropriate name than *O. arborescens*, the *tree* cactus, or Foconoztle, as called by the Mexicans, according to Dr. Gregg. The stems of the dead plant present a most singular appearance; the soft parts having rotted away, a net work of woody fibres remains, forming a hollow tube, with very regular rhombic meshes, which corresponds with the tubercles of the living plant. (89–90)

McCarthy's "holothurians," or sea cucumbers, are also radially symmetric around a central tube.

Wislizenus had, early in his volume, written of the yucca, or palmilla, as having a wood "too porous and spongy to become very useful; nevertheless, in the south the poorer classes build their huts entirely of this tree" (36). He remarks of the *Opuntia vulgaris* (prickly pear): "Charming as are all the brilliant flowers of the cactus family, more charming yet, to use no harsher expression, are their thorns, hooks, and prickles. A man collecting them ought either to provide himself with nerves of iron, to become insensible against pain; or, better still, with iron gloves, to handle them unpunished" (8). Such details may well have led McCarthy to find in the symmetric and woody cholla a fuel appropriate to the gang's campfires, itself as dangerous as the men riding with Glanton.

John Hughes, Doniphan's Expedition

Hughes was a soldier under Doniphan's command during the Mexican War. He records a night's march on the desert (128) similar to McCarthy's night-march scene of the filibusters (46–47). The elements common to both include a "military" expedition travelling at night, a lightning storm on the horizon with flashes illuminating distant mountains, the desert winds and the sand prominently mentioned, and animals failing for lack of water.

Hughes may provide background for McCarthy's scene of the gang's public bathing on its first return to Chihuahua with the kid:

Bathing is regarded, in Mexico, as one of the choicest luxuries of fashionable life; to which practice both sexes are much addicted. In Chihuahua there are many bath-houses, and pools of beautiful water, conveniently arranged for public accommodation. These are constantly filled by the young and gay of both sexes, promiscuously splashing and swimming about, with their long black hair spread out on the water, without one thought of modesty. (120)

McCarthy's note that "Citizens of both sexes withdrew along the walls and watched the water turn into a thin gruel of blood and filth [as the gang bathed] and none could take their eyes from the judge who had disrobed last of all" (167) can take an imprimatur from Hughes's observation of Chihuahuan customs at the baths. Too, with its inventory of scarred wounds, McCarthy's scene raises questions of will and chance, desire and fate.

Hughes's diary provides at least two more notable influences on McCarthy's novel. The first appears as an analogue to the kid's experience in the mountains as he and Tate attempt to escape from Elias's scouts. McCarthy's Anglos had "rolled in their blankets" to sleep in the foot-deep and still-falling snow that night. The Mexican scouts were "five men and they came up through the evergreens in the dark and all but stumbled upon the sleepers, two mounds in the snow one of which broke open and up out of which a figure sat suddenly like some terrible hatching" (211). In Hughes:

Having no tents, the soldiers quartered on the naked earth, in the open air; but so much snow fell that night, that at dawn it was not possible to distinguish where they lay, until they broke the snow which covered them, and came out as though they were rising from their graves; for in less than twelve hours the snow had fallen thirteen inches deep in the valleys, and thirty-six in the mountains. (70)

The several elements common to both passages suggest that McCarthy was aware of Hughes when writing his snow scene in *Blood Meridian*.

Hughes's influence is also apparent in another comparison of scenes. Following the snow scene, and while the kid continues to avoid Elías's troops, he watches a "senseless" battle from a perch on the mountainside, a "collision of armies": "The distant horsemen rode and parried and a faint drift of smoke passed over them and they moved on up the deepening shade of the valley floor leaving behind them the shapes of mortal men who had lost their lives in that place" (213).[29] Hughes's scene is viewed from the vantage of a mountainside, and describes a battle remarkably "senseless" in its own way. McCarthy's

---

29. "Senseless" appears here as a pun on "meaningless," and is used more literally on the succeeding page as an adjective describing "half frozen, his feet" (214).

"collision" leaves men dead on the valley floor. Only the intervening distance provides the kid with an illusion that nothing of the battle is tactile. For him, all is distant and visual.

Hughes's comparable scene is a genuinely illusory battle. The body of troops in which Hughes marched had split into two trains at a fork in the road. General Kearney and his men had headed toward the Indian pueblo village of Santo Domingo on flat ground. The remainder of the troops, including Hughes, followed a fork that ran up onto a spur of the mountains. Before Kearney's dragoons vanished from his sight, Hughes saw that:

The chief, or alcalde of Santo Domingo, at the head of about seventy dashing cavaliers, with a white flag, came out to escort the general into town, by way of winning favor, and also thereby intending him a compliment.—They made a sham charge upon the general, and performed several evolutions about him, displaying consummate horsemanship, and brandishing their pointed lances, as if to show what they were capable of doing, had their intentions not been peaceable and friendly. The whole of their movements were plainly beheld by the volunteers, from an eminence two or three miles distant. At first, we were impressed with the belief that a skirmish was taking place between the forces of the alcalde and the general; but as we did not see the flash of their guns, or hear the roar of the canon, and, after some time, saw the Indians and the general's troops all move off together towards the village, we were satisfied of the sham, and concluded the general might drink his wine and puff his cigaritos without our aid; so we moved onward. (43)

Both McCarthy's "collision" scene and Hughes's "display" fight are observations from a distance and from the advantage of a height. Also, though for different reasons, the sound of the attack is absent in both accounts, giving each a "senseless" aspect. The similarity of McCarthy to Hughes in this comparison is not as close as that found in their "snow" scenes, but they appear nevertheless analogous.

Mayne Reid, The Scalp-Hunters

Just as "sopilotes" and "ciboleros" are rare or peculiarly spelled words that provide relatively unique clues to McCarthy's probable sources for them, his use of the Scottish term "thrapple" (throat, windpipe) in the scene of Glanton's death (275) links him to a specific source, Mayne Reid's novel *The Scalp-Hunters* (185[2]). Late in the book, a Coco Indian, El Sol, a member of scalp-hunter Seguin's band, has killed an attacking Indian. A witness, one of the white scalpers, answers the main character's question about the outcome of the fight:

"How was it?"
"'Ee' know, the Injun—that are, the Coco—fit wi' a hatchet."
"Yes."
"Wal, then; that ur's a desprit weepun, for them as knows how to use it; an' he diz; that Injun diz. T'other had a hatchet, too, but he didn't keep it long. 'Twur clinked out of his hands in a minnit, an' then the Coco got a down blow at him. Wagh! it wur a down blow, an' it wan't nuthin' else. It split the niggur's head clur down to the thrapple. 'Twus sep'rated

into two halves as ef't had been clove wi' a broad-axe! Ef'ee had 'a seed the varmint when he kim to the ground, 'ee'd 'a thort he wur double-headed." (213)

"Hack away you mean red nigger," Glanton calls out in *Blood Meridian*, "and the old man raised the axe and split the head of John Joel Glanton to the thrapple" (275).[30] Such co-incidences, and in books on scalp hunting, support the thought that McCarthy had read Reid's novel.

J. Frank Dobie, Apache Gold and Yaqui Silver

Dobie's book contributes setting and flavor to *Blood Meridian*. Twentieth-century historian Dobie appears to be a source of information for a conversation of one of McCarthy's characters. Dobie quotes a treasure seeker:

I had my hat over my face so as to shut out the fierce light and was dozing off when all at once something aroused me. I think it was the sudden ceasing of the horses to graze. A grazing horse makes a kind of musical noise cropping grass and grinding it, and men out, with their lives depending on horses, often notice that music or the absence of it. Anyhow, when I raised up, I saw every animal with head up and ears pointed to the range of mountains we had last crossed. I looked too and saw a thin, stringy cloud of dust. (282–283)

At one point in the novel, Tobin draws an analogy between the sound of God's voice and the kid's experience with the sounds of horses:

At night, said Tobin, when the horses are grazing and the company is asleep, who hears them grazing?
Dont nobody hear them if they're asleep.
Aye. And if they cease their grazing who is it that wakes?
Every man.
Aye, said the expriest. Every man. (124)

From Dobie's comments on men and horses, McCarthy has made an analogy of God's felt presence. Dobie refers to "men out, with their lives depending on horses" and the music of horses cropping grass, and both points are important to McCarthy's novel of hunters in the desert Southwest, whose fights with Indians are characterized as "dances" (77).

When Dobie writes that "Thomás was pinching the end off a shuck cigarette . . . [and] took a coal of fire in his fingers to light it" (329), he may have suggested McCarthy's detail of his gang members reaching into fires for live coals (86, 126; see also the essays "Tarot and Divination" [Chapter 5] and "Why Believe the Judge?" [Chapter 8]).

---

30. McCarthy's "mean red nigger" appears in Chamberlain (264).

In an appendix, Dobie presents "A Note on Scalphunters in Mexico," a twenty-seven-item bibliography that includes the Ober and Bourke books assessed immediately below.

Frederick A. Ober, Travels in Mexico

The Dobie bibliography on scalp hunting overlaps many other bibliographies, particularly those of Smith and Brandes, but is unique in bringing Ober to light. Ober's narrative concerns a period some twenty or thirty years after *Blood Meridian*'s moment in Mexico. It contains several items not otherwise mentioned in the literature, but appearing in *Blood Meridian* as both substance and allusion.

Ober illustrates two "serenos," or night watchmen (286), and writes that their call "always [ends] up with 'Tiempo seréno,' or, 'All serene' (287). This mention of their call presumably informs McCarthy's "sereño" detail (100, 103), though the spelling in the novel (as examined in the "Languages" section, in Chapter 4) is not Ober's.

Perhaps significantly for *Blood Meridian*'s depiction of Judge Holden, Ober writes that the Aztec's god of war was depicted in statues as a "very fat" man (306, illus. 314). Ober himself ascended the smoking volcano Popocatepetl (375, 391–395), from which, according to William Henry Prescott's *History of the Conquest of Mexico*, Cortés obtained his sublimated sulfur. Ober's sustained mentions of Prescott (315, 398, 476, etc.) may have provided a link to Cortés's and Bernal Díaz's accounts of the first manufacture of gunpowder in the New World.

Ober also describes *carretas*, or carts "without a particle of iron in their composition" (583), though McCarthy may have taken his "carreta" (67) from any number of sources (as discussed in the Wislizenus section, above). Ober mentions mule teams used to transport mining supplies (620), the Mexican Proyecta de Guerra (1837), by which Chihuahua first offered scalpers bounty money (627), and his view of Indians "engaged in their favorite pastime of *monte*, or Mexican cards" (633).

John G. Bourke, On the Border with Crook

Dobie's bibliography on scalp hunting lists Bourke's book, which recollects his years in the army under General George Crook. But more interesting than Boutke's brief mention of Glanton (117–118) is that his first several hundred pages present a portrait of the Southwest in the 1870s that is uncannily close to McCarthy's novel in several respects: first, in Bourke's sense of the hellish conditions of that country; then, among other items, in the discovery of conquistador's armor in the Southwest at midcentury; in the power of the night sky; in the resemblance of Apache and Hebrew customs; in the mention of Charles O. Brown and his Congress Hall saloon; and in the strength of the Apaches' desire for card playing. Still, Bourke's book is not a confirmable source, yet his words are interesting both as background to a reading of the novel and as resonating with the concerns on which McCarthy builds his narrative.

In the opening pages of *Blood Meridian*, McCarthy's Reverend Green calls the saloons of Nacogdoches "hell, hell, hellholes" (6). McCarthy's characterization is little removed from Bourke's opening paragraph, which speaks of the "Gadsden Purchase," the land of Tucson, and the Yuma crossing:

Dante Alighieri, it has always seemed to me, made the mistake of his life in dying when he did in the picturesque capital of the Exarchate five hundred and fifty years ago. Had he held on to this mortal coil until after Uncle Sam had perfected the "Gadsden Purchase," he would have found full scope for his genius in the description of a region in which not only purgatory and hell, but heaven likewise, had combined to produce a bewildering kaleidoscope of all that was wonderful, weird, terrible, and awe-inspiring, with not a little that was beautiful and romantic. (1)

McCarthy mentions an Indian clad in conquistador's armor (52). Bourke himself possessed "a suit of armor which had belonged to some Spanish foot-soldier of the sixteenth century" (7) and which had been found intact around the bones of that soldier "in the extreme southwestern corner of the State of Texas, more than twenty years ago" (8). The geographic locations of McCarthy's and Bourke's armor appear identical.

Bourke touches on Indian "war customs" in a manner in some ways reminiscent of McCarthy's Holden's cycle of dancers and the universal harshness of battle:

[W]e have become grounded in the error of imagining that the American savage is more cruel in his war customs than other nations of the earth have been; this, as I have already intimated, is a misconception, and statistics, for such as care to dig them out, will prove that I am right. The Assyrians cut their conquered foes limb from limb; the Israelites spared neither parent nor child; the Romans crucified head downward the gladiators who revolted under Spartacus; even in the civilized England of the past century, the wretch convicted of treason was executed under circumstances of cruelty which would have been too much for the nerves of the fiercest of the Apaches or Sioux. Instances in support of what I here assert crop up all over the page of history; the trouble is not to discover them, but to keep them from blinding the memory to matters more pleasant to remember. Certainly, the American aborigine is not indebted to his pale-faced brother, no matter of what nation or race he may be, for lessons in tenderness and humanity. (115)

The Arizona night sky, powerful in *Blood Meridian*, is also present in Bourke's most sweeping of claims: "The stars shone out in their grandest effulgence, and the feeble rays of the moon were no added help to vision. There is only one region in the whole world, Arizona, where the full majesty can be comprehended of that text of Holy Writ which teaches: 'The Heavens declare the glory of God, and the firmament showeth His handiwork'" (27).

McCarthy's note of the Comanches in "biblical" dress (52) can find some parallel in Bourke's mention of a widowed "Apache squaw" who was displeased with her husband's family: "I do not remember in what this ill-treatment consisted, but most likely none of the brothers of the deceased had offered to marry the widow and care for her and her little one, as is the general custom, in which the Apaches resemble the Hebrews of ancient times" (47).

Bourke first mentions playing cards in a paragraph more modern in its insights into urban archaeology than might be expected of a soldier in Arizona in the 1870s:

The age of the garbage piles was distinctly defined by geological strata. In the lowest portion of all one could often find arrowheads and stone axes, indicative of a pre-Columbian origin; superimposed conformably over these, as the geologists used to say, were skins of chile colorado, great pieces of rusty spurs, and other reliquiae of the 'Conquistadores,' while high above all, stray cards, tomato cans, beer bottles, and similar evidences of a higher and nobler civilization told just how long the Anglo-Saxon had called the territory his own." (63)

Bourke illustrates the problem the "tenderfoot" had with geography (see "Introductions," Chapter 1). Here, he takes chronology into account as well:

It took some time for the ears of the "tenderfoot" just out from the States to become habituated to the chronology of that portion of our vast domain. One rarely heard months, days, or weeks mentioned. The narrator of a story had a far more convenient method of referring back to dates in which his auditory might be interested. "Jes' about th' time Pete Kitchen's ranch was jumped"—which wasn't very satisfactory, as Pete Kitchen's ranch was always getting "jumped." "Th' night afore th' Maricopa stage war tuk in." "A week or two arter Winters made his last 'killin' in th' Dragoons." "Th' last fight down to th' Picah." "Th' year th' Injuns run off Tully, Ochoa 'n' DeLong bull teams."

Or, under other aspects of the daily life of the place, there would be such references as, "Th' night after Duffield drawed his gun on Jedge Titus"—a rather uncertain reference, since Duffield was always "drawin' his gun" on somebody. "Th' time of the feast (i.e., of Saint Augustine, the patron saint of the town), when Bob Crandall broke th' 'Chusas' game fur six hundred dollars," and other expressions of similar tenor, which replaced the recollections of "mowing time," and "harvest," and "sheep-shearing" of older communities. (64)

Also mentioned are Charlie Brown's "Congress Hall" saloon (70, 84), and a scene in which "Charles O. Brown" is called to testify in court over a shooting he had witnessed (73). Bourke mentions the ruin of the mission of San Xavier as one extreme of Arizona's portrait: "No perfect picture of early times in Arizona and New Mexico could be delineated upon my narrow canvas; the sight was distracted by strange scenes, the ears by strange sounds, many of each horrible beyond the wildest dreams. There was the ever-dreadful Apache on the one hand to terrify and torment, and the beautiful ruin of San

Xavier on the other to bewilder and amaze" (97). McCarthy includes this ruin in *Blood Meridian* (227), but devotes relatively more time to the San Jose de Tumacacori mission (224).

Bourke's several mentions of gambling and card playing may be brought together, beginning with the importance of cards to the Apache, an observation which draws a parallel with the whites' interest in cards:

If necessary, the Apache will go without water for as long a time almost as a camel. A small stone or a twig inserted in the mouth will cause a more abundant flow of saliva and assuage his thirst. He travels with fewer "impedimenta" than any other tribe of men in the world, not even excepting the Australians, but he sometimes allows himself the luxury or comfort of a pack of cards, imitated from those of the Mexicans, and made out of horse-hide, or a set of the small painted sticks with which to play the game of "Tze-chis," or, on occasions when an unusually large number of Apaches happen to be travelling together, some one of the party will be loaded with the hoops and poles of the "mushka;" for, be it known, that the Apache like savages everywhere, and not a few civilized men, too, for that matter, is so addicted to gambling that he will play away the little he owns of clothing and all else he possesses in the world. (134–135)

Bourke writes of the Anglo's interest in gambling that "in Prescott, as in Tucson, the gambling saloons were never closed. Sunday or Monday, night or morning, the 'game' went, and the voice of the 'dealer' was heard in the land" (159).

He also writes of his perception that gambling is one of several "stumbling-blocks" for the Indian (and Anglo):

The American Indian is a slave to drink where he can get it, and he is rarely without a supply from white sources; he is a slave to the passion of gaming; and he is a slave to his superstitions, which make the "Medicine Men" the power they are in tribal affairs as well as in those relating more strictly to the clan and family. These are the three stumbling-blocks in the pathway of the Indian's advancement; how to remove them is a most serious problem. The Indian is not the only one in our country who stumbles from the same cause; we must learn to be patient with him, but merciless toward all malefactors caught selling intoxicating liquors to red men living in the tribal relation. Gambling and superstition will be eradicated in time by the same modifying influences which have wrought changes among the Caucasian nations; education will afford additional modes of killing time, and be the means of exposing the puerility of the pretensions of the prophets. (228–229)

Bourke uses the term "playas" (139), which presages elements of McCarthy's mirage-image (108) but is probably not more than an analogue to the Bartlett source given above. Bourke writes: "While we slowly marched over 'playas' of sand, without one drop of water for miles, we were tantalized by the sight of cool, pellucid lakelets from which issued water whose gurgle and ripple could almost be heard, but the illusion dissipated as we drew nearer and saw that the mirage-fiend had been mocking our thirst with spectral waters" (139).

McCarthy's gang of scalp-hunters is sympathetic to wolves (129). Bourke, writing of the Hualpais Indians of the Southwest, notes that among their "tales and myths" is the belief that "All the elements of nature are actual, visible entities . . . the stars are possessed of the same powers as man, all the chief animals have the faculty of speech, and the coyote is the one who is man's good friend and has brought him the great boon of fire" (164–165). The link the passage provides between the gift of fire and man also recalls the gang's association with fire (examined in greater detail in the essay "Tarot and Divination," Chapter 5).

Bourke includes mention of a mule bitten on the lip by a rattlesnake (187), paralleling McCarthy's horse bitten on its nose (115).

Bourke's General Crook met with the long-lived chief Pascual of the Yumas, one of the chiefs of the ferry massacre, after 1874 (233). Bourke also mentions an incident in which a "murderer [was] confined in the jail for killing a Mexican 'to see him wriggle'" (237), a "motive" reminiscent of David Brown's death in Horace Bell's account. Bourke's mention of the "self-lacerating" Mexican "*penitente*" (239) may contribute toward McCarthy's scene of the massacre of such penitents (313–315).

CHAPTER 4

Addenda

Languages

Blood Meridian's mid-nineteenth-century Southwest landscape is a crossroads for many nationalities. Spanish nouns and dialogue are included in *Blood Meridian* in what appears to be the author's impression of the appropriate language environment in which his story would have taken place. The novel also includes phrases in French and German, though these are confined to McCarthy's chapter subheadings.

SPANISH

The Spanish of *Blood Meridian* is apparently McCarthy's Spanish. Several questions concerning the irregularities of the language arise, beginning with an apparent typographical error. In one of McCarthy's chapter subheadings, *sereño* is spelled with the Spanish letter *ñ* (100). The word is not, historically, spelled with this letter.[1]

On page 301, an Indian addresses first the kid and then Tobin with what may be a question (though no question mark is present), and uses identical sentences in his remarks to each. The question that arises regarding McCarthy's Spanish in these instances concerns the use of the plural pronoun *ustedes* in both of these remarks. If the Indian had addressed both men together in the first remark, and Tobin specifically in the second (when the kid does not answer the Indian), the pronouns would have been plural and then singular. Or maybe, since "ustedes" is also used when addressing a superior, the Indian was just trying to seem respectful.

A gloss of Spanish words, of phrases in chapter subheadings, and of dialogue is provided below.

1. Describing "policemen furnished with lanterns" who "cr[y] the time of night" in smaller towns, Ober writes that their calls are "always ending up with '*Tiempo seréno*,' or, 'All serene.' From this the mischievous Mexican youth have nicknamed him the *Sereno*, although his trim appearance now, clad in neat uniform, is in great contrast to the ancient watchmen, who first acquired, and bore with serenity, this appellation" (287).

WORDS

63   *escopetas,* shotguns

70, 90 *mire,* look

83   *garraffa,* jug

96   *malabarista,* juggler

99   *pase,* come in

100   *dígame,* tell me [sir]

101   *cuánto,* how much

103   *barbaros,* barbarians

185   *Sociedad,* society

189   *bodega,* warehouse

200   *por dios,* by God; *criada,* maid [servant]

235   *Huesos,* bones [*La huesuda* is a euphemism for death.]

SUBHEADINGS

42   The ghost *manada* (pack)

74   *Los heréticos* (The heretics)

81   *Pasajeros de un país antiguo* (Travellers from an antique land)[2]

100   The *sereño* (The night watchman)

151   *Un hacendado* (A landholder) [more "aristocratic" than a rancher][3]

186   *Tierras quemadas, tierras despobladas* (Burned lands, barren lands); *Cazando las almas*
       (Hunting the souls); *Los pordioseros* (The beggars)

241   *Tierras quebradas, tierras desamparadas* (Broken lands, helpless [or unprotected]
       lands); *Un hueso de piedra* (A bone of stone)

305   *Los ahorcados* (The hanged men)

DIALOGUE

14   *Venga. Hay un caballero aquí. Venga.* (Come. There is a gentleman here. Come.)

23   *Dígame,* he said. (Tell me, sir)

       Abuelito, he said. (Grandfather)

       Qué dice el muchacho. (What is the boy saying?)

       Quiere hecharse una copa, he said. *Pero no puede pagar.* (He wants to have a drink
       . . . But he cannot pay.)

       Quiere trabajo, said the old man. *Quién sabe.* (He wants work . . . Who knows.)

2. This is almost certainly a reference to Percy Bysshe Shelley's poem "Ozymandias" (1819): "I met a
traveller from an antique land / Who said: Two vast and trunkless legs of stone / Stand in the desert."

3. Ober uses this unusual word, and defines it in context as "the *hacendado,* or proprietor of large estates" (506; see also 525).

Quieres trabajar, said one of the men at the bar. (Do you want a job)

24   *No está sucio,* said the barman. (It's not dirty)

Andale, he said. (Get going)

25   *Está borracho,* said the old man. (He is drunk)

38   *Y sus botas,* said the Texan. (And his boots)

Botas? (Boots?)

Sí. (Yes.)

64   *Qué quiere?* cried the leader. (What do you want?)

Buscan a los indios? (Looking for Indians?)

Basta, he said. (Enough)

72   *La gente dice que el coyote es un brujo. Muchas veces el brujo es un coyote.* (People say that the coyote is a sorcerer. Many times the sorcerer is a coyote.)

Y los indios también. Muchas veces llaman como los coyotes. (And the Indians also. Many times they call like the coyotes.)

Y qué es eso. (And what is that?)

Nada. (Nothing.)

Un tecolote. Nada mas. (An owl. Nothing more.)

Quizás. —Maybe.

83   *Qué pasa aquí?* (What's going on here?)

Nada, said Speyer. *Todo va bien.* (Nothing . . . Everything is okay.)

Bien? (Okay?)

Está bien, said Holden. *Negocios del Gobernador.* (It's okay . . . Business of the Governor.)

84   *Somos amigos del Señor Riddle,* said Speyer. (We are friends of Mr. Riddle)

Andale, said Glanton. (Get going)

Le presento al sargento Aguilar, he called. (Let me introduce you to sergeant Aguilar)

Mucho gusto. (It's a pleasure.)

Igualmente, said the sergeant. (Likewise)

89   *Bufones.* (Clowns.)

Sí, he said. *Sí, bufones. Todo.* He turned to the boy. Casimero! *Los perros!* (Yes . . . Yes, clowns. All of us. . . . The dogs!)

91   *Cómo?* he said. (How?)

La baraja, he said. *Para adivinar la suerte.* (The cards . . . To divine luck/to tell fortunes.)

Sí, sí. (Yes, yes.)

Todo, todo. (Everything, everything.)

Venga, he called. *Venga.* (Come . . . Come.)

92   *Bueno,* he called. *Puedes ver?* (Good . . . Can you see?)

Nada? (Nothing?)

Nada, said the woman. (Nothing)

Bueno, said the juggler. (Good)

Los caballeros, he said. (The gentlemen)

Bueno, said the juggler. *Bueno*. (Good . . . Good.)

El tonto, he called. (The fool)

El tonto, said the woman. (The fool)

Quién, quién, cried the juggler. (Who, who)

El negro, she said. (The black)

El negro, cried the juggler. (The black)

93   *Quién, quién*, he whispered. (Who, who)

94   *Cómo?* (What?)

El joven. (The young man.)

El joven, whispered the juggler. (The young man)

Una carta, una carta, he wheezed. (A card, a card)

Sí, sí, said the juggler. (Yes, yes)

Cuatro de copas, he called out. (Four of cups)

Cuatro de copas, she said. (Four of cups)

Quién, called the juggler. (Who)

El hombre . . . she said. *El hombre más joven. El muchacho.* (The man . . . The youngest man. The boy.)

El muchacho, called the juggler. (The boy)

95   *Quién, quién*, he called. (Who, who)

El jefe, said the judge. (The boss)

El jefe, hissed the judge. (The boss)

96   *La carroza, la carroza*, cried the beldam. *Invertido. Carta de Guerra, de venganza. La ví sin ruedas sobre un rio obscuro* . . . (The coach, the coach . . . Inverted. Card of war, of vengeance. I saw it without wheels on a dark river . . .)

Perdida, perdida. La carta está perdida en la noche. (Lost, lost. The card is lost in the night.)

Perdida, perdida, he whispered. (Lost, lost)

Un maleficio, cried the old woman. *Qué viento tan maleante* . . . (A curse . . . What a villainous wind . . .)

Carroza de muertos, llena de huesos. El joven qué . . . (Dead wagon, full of bones. The youngster that . . .)

97   *Una corta caridad*, he croaked to the passing horses. *Por Dios.* (A little charity . . . For God's sake.)

102   You are *sociedad de guerra. Contra los barbaros.* (. . . a company of warriors. Against the barbarians.)

Madre de Dios, he called. (Mother of God)

Que soldados tan valientes. La sangre de Gómez, sangre de la gente . . . (What brave soldiers. The blood of Gomez, the blood of the people . . .)

103 *Las diez y media, tiempo sereño.* (Ten thirty, all serene.)

120 *Amigos, somos amigos.* (Friends, we are friends.)

De dónde viene? called the strangers. (Where do you come from?)

A dónde va? called the judge. (Where are you going?)

134 *Todos muertos. Todos.* (All dead. All.)

171 *Mejor los indios.* (Better the Indians.)

181 *A dónde vas?* he said. (Where are you going?)

A casa, said the man. (Home)

197 *Por qué se esconde?* said Glanton. (Why does he hide?)

De dónde viene? (Where do you come from?)

Qué tiene allá? (What do you have there?)

Hierbas, he said. (Herbs)

Por qué me busca? called the old man after him. (Why are you looking for me?)

200 *Mozos de cuadra,* he called. *Venga. Pronto.* (Stable boys . . . Come. Quick.)

201 *Este hombre es el jefe,* he said. (This man is the boss)

Te encargo todo, entiendes? Caballos, sillas, todo. (I want you to take charge of every-thing, understand? Horses, saddles, everything.)

Sí. Entiendo. (Yes. I understand.)

Bueno. Andale. Hay caballos en la casa. (OK. Come on. There are horses in the house.)

229 *Vaya tranquillo,* he said. *Un accidente, nada más.* (Keep calm . . . Only an acci-dent.)

Mire, said the Apache. *Mire la oreja de mi caballo.* (Look . . . Look at the ear of my horse.)

Buenos días, he said. *De dónde viene?* (Good morning . . . Where do you come from?)

230 *Andale,* he said. . . . *Ellos son amigables. Un poco borracho, nada más.* (Get going . . . They are friendly. A little drunk, that's all.)

No hay whiskey, he said. (There's no)

Cómo? said Mangas. (What?)

No hay whiskey, said Glanton. (There's no)

Hay whiskey *en Tucson,* said Mangas. (There's whiskey in Tucson)

Sin duda, said the judge. *Y soldados también.* (No doubt . . . And soldiers also.)

231 *Tiene oro?* he said. (Do you have gold?)

Sí. (Yes.)

Cuánto. (How much?)

Bastante. (Enough.)

Bueno, he said. *Tres días. Aquí. Un barril de* whiskey. (Good . . . Three days. Here. A barrel of whiskey.)

Un barril? (A barrel?)

Un barril. (A barrel.)

255 *Buenas tardes*, he said. (Good afternoon)

Buenas tardes, he said. *De dónde viene?* (Good afternoon . . . Where do you come from?)

270 *Válgame Dios*, he gasped. *Qué quiere?* (Good God . . . What does he want?)

Cómo? wheezed the old man. (What?)

271 *Dígame*, gasped the alcalde. (Talk to me)

El hombre que tiene usted. Mi compañero. (The man you have. My companion.)

Búscale. (Look for him.)

In the *juzgado*. (jail)

Madre de Jesús. . . . Siete, ocho días. (Mother of Jesus. . . . Seven, eight days.)

Where is the *juzgado?* (jail)

Cómo? (What?)

El juzgado. Dónde está? (The jail. Where is it?)

Allá, she said. *Allá.* (There . . . There.)

301 *Pistola*, he said. (Pistol)

Quiero mirar su pistola, the man said. (I want to look at your pistol)

Qué pasó con ustedes? (What happened to you?)

Qué pasó con ustedes? (What happened to you?)

302 *Son muy malos*, said the speaker. (They are very bad)

Claro. (Of course.)

No tiene compañeros? (Don't you have any companions?)

Sí, said the kid. *Muchos. . . . Llegaran. Muchos compañeros.* (Yes . . . Many. . . . They will come. Many companions.

315 *Abuelita*, he said. *No puedes escúcharme?* (Grandmother . . . Can't you hear me?)

FRENCH

When McCarthy includes as one of *Blood Meridian*'s chapter subheadings the French sentence "*Et de ceo se mettent en le pays*" (74), he uses a traditional phrase from French law to describe the scene of the Glanton gang's departure from Chihuahua: "And of this they put themselves upon the country" (Black 653). This literal translation, though accounting for the scene of departure generally, can nevertheless be expanded upon by viewing Black's explanation of a similar phrase. The entry following the sentence cited above is the Latin "*Et de hoc ponit se super patriam*," translated as "And of this he puts himself upon the country." This second sentence, similar to the first but for its singular rather than plural construction, refers to "the formal conclusion of a common-law plea in bar by way of traverse." The literal sense of the French can be somewhat expanded when the reader understands that by putting himself "upon the country," a person is "thereby submitting . . . to the judgment of his peers" by facing a jury (Blackstone 3: 313; see also Black 421 [entry for "Country"], 1264 [entry for "Pais"], and Blackstone 4: 345–346).

Of further assistance toward a more complete reading is Black's note on pleas of traverse: such a plea does not involve a denial of guilt or a declaration of innocence, but rather "crosses over," or "traverses," such questions with a denial of a "material fact" in the allegations made against the defendant (1671–1672). Therefore, McCarthy's subheading refers not only to the gang travelling into a literal "country," but also to the gang's three new recruits, Toadvine, Grannyrat, and the kid, having misrepresented their credentials to Glanton in their attempt to find release from the prison in Chihuahua City. When Toadvine says, "dont let on like you aint no seasoned indiankiller cause I claimed we was three of the best" (79), he traverses the "material facts" of things while also showing his willingness to let the jury of experience, "in the country," prove or disprove their claims to Glanton's satisfaction.

GERMAN

Like the French sentence, the German sentence in *Blood Meridian* is a chapter subheading: "*Sie müssen schlafen aber Ich muss tanzen*" (316), which translates as "You must sleep [i.e., die], but I have to dance." The sentence is appropriate to the scene it heralds, the final scene of the novel, which shows the judge dancing after the death of the kid.

McCarthy's sentence is a revision of a line from the nineteenth-century poem "Hyazinthen" by Theodor Storm, which, in the original, reads: "*Ich möchte schlafen, aber du muss tanzen*" (244–247). Storm's poem is also quoted in Thomas Mann's *Tonio Kröger* (88, 130). In both the poem and the novella (132), the speakers hear music at a distance but find themselves unable to join with the dancers. McCarthy's inversion of Storm's line presumably links Holden's discourse on "the dance" with Hans Hansen in Mann's story, who can and does dance, rather than with the bourgeois Tonio Kröger, who is an artist-outsider literally looking through a window at life's dance (126–132).

Map Citations

OPENING

The kid is born in Tennessee (3); at fourteen heads west to Memphis, north in St. Louis a year later, to New Orleans downriver in forty-two days, boat to Texas (4); Galveston (3); rides north to Nacogdoches (5); out of Nacogdoches on the "road west" (14); four days out of Nacogdoches, cuts south to road west (21); into San Antonio de Bexar (21); at river (27); back to town (30).

FILIBUSTERING

Troop heading "to Sonora" (40); take "road downcountry" "through Castroville" (42); "Ten days out . . . plain of pure pumice" (45); after massacre, kid "set off south afoot": "Adrift on the Bolson de Mapimi" (55); set off "following the [Comanche] war trail" south (56); into small, destroyed town (58); "went by the southwest road" out of town (61); "crested the mountain," "immense lake lay below" (62); reach "crossroads": north-south "wagon trace" crosses kid's path (67); from north comes carreta (67); by dark, carried into a town south of crossroads (68); from town, prisoners "rode five days through desert and mountain" to Chihuahua City (71).

FIRST TRIP

Out of Chihuahua City, the gang "took the road upcountry" (80, 86); "at dusk of third day . . . [reach] Corralitos" (88); in Corralitos magicians want "passage upcountry as far as Janos" (89); reach Casas Grandes River, noon after Corralitos and one and a half days from Janos (90); to west, "ragged Carcaj"; to north, "Animas peaks" (90); at Janos (97); rode through "meatcamp" eight miles up the river from Janos (104); through gap in Animas mountains (105); on "western edge of the playa," "mountains to the east" (108); "moving north" (112); to Santa Rita del Cobre mines (113); "ascended the arroyo" "upcountry" (119); meet "ciboleros down from the north" who are "bound for the markets at Mesilla" (120–121); on the "plains of San Agustin" (138); "Anasazi" had lived in canyons (146); "Crossing the border" (151, chapter subhead); "crossed the del Norte and rode south" (152); "continued south" (153); mountains in west (153–154); Gilenos at lake (154); "riding south" (160); "through the town of Gallego" (165); "into . . . Chihuahua" (165).

SECOND TRIP

From Chihuahua to "town of Coyame eighty miles to the northeast" (171); "northeast . . . [to] Presidio on the Texas border" (172); on the "borderland for weeks" (172); to near El Paso (172–173); reach "Hueco Tanks" near El Paso (173); ride south (three days to Tiguas) (173); two more days to Carrizal (174); reach Chihuahua City (175–176).

THIRD TRIP

"West into the mountains" (176); into Nacori (177); "two days deeper into the sierras," at a town they kill soldiers (181); two nights later are three or four days above Chihuahua City (183); into Chihuahua City (185).

WESTWARD

Leave the city, and turn west (185); "nine days out of Chihuahua," "into Jesús María" (188); "out of the mountains toward the western sea" eight or nine days after encountering the *conducta* immediately west of Jesús María (197); "forded the Yaqui River" (199); "into Ures, capital of the state of Sonora" (199); "rode out north" from Ures (204); "into broad Sonoran desert" (204); "Two weeks out . . . on Nacozari River" (204); "two days later . . . [heading south] toward Ures . . . on plains west of Baviacora" (204); after skirmish, kid "trotting north on the plain" (209); kid "heading north" (210); kid "north all day" (213); kid "to the north" (217); kid had come forty miles north (218); "down long north slope" (219); "to the north" (219); "into the town of Santa Cruz," a presidio along the border (220); "following day . . . past . . . old hacienda at San Bernardino" (223); "rode on, following the course of the Santa Cruz" river (224); "passed through Tubac" (226); "through the mission of San Xavier del Bac" (227); reach "presidio of Tucson" (227); "rode west from the town" of Tucson, through saguaro forests (242); "crossed the malpais" (251); after three more days "they reached the Colorado" River at the Yuma ferry (252–253); Webster, Toadvine, and Brown head "for the town of San Diego," with five days to cross the desert (264); Webster and Toadvine return to Yuma (270); Glanton takes five men to San Diego (270); Glanton returns to Yuma alone (272); kid heads upriver after the massacre (277); heads west (278); to "wells at Alamo Mucho" (279); Carrizo Creek (277, chapter subheading); "to camp at San Felipe" (301); "entered San Diego" (303); "in June . . . in Los Angeles" (311); seven days from the coast, and then north, is dried old woman (313–315).

CLOSING

In Texas in 1878, kid crosses "Double Mountain Fork of the Brazos River" (316); crosses Arkansas River and Concho River (317); kid rides three days (317); one more day, and into Fort Griffin (324).

Tarot and Divination

Blood Meridian's odyssey, begun in a Tennessee cabin in 1833, comes to a close when the novel's unnamed protagonist, "the kid," meets death in an outhouse in Fort Griffin, Texas, in 1878 at the hands of former compatriot Judge Holden. But the murder seems to occur without intelligible motive. The kid and Holden had ridden together years before in John Glanton's gang of professional scalp hunters in Mexico and the American Southwest. Holden had earlier remarked that the kid was a traitor to Glanton's band and its principles in having shown "clemency for the heathen" (299). But McCarthy declines to share with his reader any example of this clemency, and the reader expecting logical closure may well feel puzzled about the source of Holden's charge.

Vereen Bell speculates in *The Achievement of Cormac McCarthy* that Holden "merely surmised" that the kid had not committed himself fully to the rough life of Glanton's crew (120), finding a "confirming sign" of this "breach of faith" in the kid's "inability to kill the judge" in the desert after the group was essentially wiped out by Indians. This explanation fails to satisfy on several grounds, but especially because Holden specifies "clemency for the heathen" and not clemency toward himself as the kid's failing.

This essay is an attempt to discover the thematic pattern that culminates in the kid's death, presenting two complementary motives for the judge's treatment of the kid. The first of these involves the historical accuracy of McCarthy's presentation of the kid's and the judge's dispositions toward each other, based on sources in the literature of the period. The second derives from the arcane philosophical universe in which the characters of *Blood Meridian* exist. This second presentation will raise further questions of genre, themes, and characterization.

McCarthy's source text for Judge Holden provides an insight into the relationship between the historical Holden and Sam Chamberlain, a historical analogue to the novel's kid. Though *Blood Meridian*'s John Glanton, the Brown "brothers," Sarah Borginnis, and others are found in several historical documents, Judge Holden is mentioned only in General Chamberlain's autobiographical *My Confession*, which recounts his days with the Glanton gang (259–297), when he met and rode with Holden. Of their relationship, Chamberlain writes: "I hated him at first sight, and he knew it, yet nothing could be more gentle and kind than his deportment towards me; he would often seek conversation with me." (272). Yet this "gentle" judge is also the man who stole Chamberlain's horse as they plodded across the desert after the Yuma-ferry massacre and threatened to "denounce" Chamberlain and the other survivors as robbers and murderers. "You shall hang in California!" he gloated in a "yell of triumph" (292–293). With these words, Holden finally expressed his hatred of Chamberlain in *My Confession*. McCarthy may well have based Holden's murder of the kid on his recognition of their mutual hatred in this source document.[1]

A second motive for the kid's murder is based on the premise that McCarthy provides in his novel a perfectly objectified rationale, accessible within the limits of the text, that reflects the contentions between the two men. McCarthy's clues to understanding their hostilities begin to appear quite early in the book.

Destinies in the Cards

The tarot scene in *Blood Meridian* involves the reading of several cards (91–96). The tarot deck resembles the modern poker deck in its employment of four suits (cups, wands, swords, coins) of numbered cards. Both decks use picture cards, though the tarot deck does not divide its twenty-two picture cards, the major arcana, into the four suits, maintaining each of these cards' individuality. The card the kid chooses is of special importance: the "Cuatro de copas," the four of cups (94). McCarthy writes that the kid had "not seen such cards before, yet the one he held seemed familiar to him" (94). And there is a reason the card should have seemed familiar. After the massacre of the filibustering expedition, Sproule and the kid had wandered into a Mexican town sacked by Comanches. As the kid looked for a place to sleep, he entered a house in which he found "Illustrations cut from an old journal and pasted to the wall, a small picture of a queen, a gypsy card that was the four of cups" (59). McCarthy divides mention of the four of cups into two languages, and it is clear he wants us to notice the kid's association with this card.

A study of the tarot reveals that the four of cups indicates "*blended pleasure and success, receiving pleasure but mixed with some slight discomfort and anxieties*" (Wang 82; original emphasis). The fours, of which the four of cups is but one member, indicate "*Perfection, realization, completion, making a matter settled and fixed*" (Wang 80; original emphasis). And a more inclusive grouping of the fours, and so of the four of cups as well, is designated, in kabbalistic interpretations of the tarot, by the Hebrew word "chesed," which is translated "mercy" (Wang 78). One answer to the question "Why does the judge destroy the kid?" is that McCarthy has twice associated the kid with a card whose sym-

---

1. In some ways a source for McCarthy's kid, Ruxton's character La Bonté displays a character flaw to his frontier companions with his lack of "perfect indifference to human feeling," which, I think, also operates in McCarthy's kid (*Life* 73; see also 111).

bolism suggests a divided heart and has generally associated him with the quality of mercy. As the kid's card was displayed to the men, "The judge was laughing silently" (94). Very little escapes Judge Holden's understanding. His silent laughter indicates that at the very least he understands the card's significance, or that perhaps he has in some way predetermined its selection. The presence of this card in the novel as the kid's emblem is an appropriate validation of the judge's otherwise inexplicable accusations of the kid's "clemency for the heathen." And the judge, when he can, exacts vengeance.

Two other cards emerge in the novel's tarot scene. Black John Jackson picks one before the kid's choice, and Glanton draws another. Jackson's card is "El tonto" (92). El tonto, the Fool, is "the most powerful of all the Tarot Trumps" (Nichols 23). The Fool can indicate "lost . . . wits," "divine wisdom," "Punch or Reynard the Fox or Harlequin," "Juggler," "magician," "Coyote or Raven or simply Trickster," "Dwarf," or "circus clown" (Butler 109). As Jackson turns to the judge for help in understanding the card reader's words, the judge suggests, "I think she means to say that in your fortune lie our fortunes all" (93). Holden's assertion that the "fortunes" of the various elements of the tarot Fool apply to the entire gang is accurate: it encompasses Glanton's drunkenly lost wits, the judge's intellect, the howitzer "trick" on the Yumas, the judge's "ears like a fox," the "harlequin horses," the literal juggler, the judge the magician of the coin trick, the Indian "trick" on the gang at the ferry, the dwarf whore at the saloon in Fort Griffin, and the clown-like faces of the attacking Comanches. Thus, the card's varied meanings distribute themselves and resonate through many points in the novel.

For example, Holden also tells Jackson, "I think she'd have you beware the demon rum. Prudent counsel enough, what do you think?" (93).[2] Because Jackson is the first man, of all the hungover gang, to die at the crossing, we see again that the judge possesses a remarkable, intuitive grasp of the tarot (273). Again, Holden sees into this realm with an arcane eye. Jackson's death can be taken as emblematic of the rest of the gang's deaths at the riverside and, furthermore, embodies yet another tarot card, the four of wands. McCarthy writes of Jackson's death: "a long cane arrow passed through his upper abdomen. . . . A second arrow passed him on the left and two more struck and lodged fast in his chest and in his groin. They were a full four feet in length and they lofted slightly with his movements like ceremonial wands (273–274)." Jackson is killed in a scene with four arrows, and they are likened to "wands." Wang writes that the four of wands signifies "*perfected work, settlement and rest after labor*" (81; original emphasis).[3] Jackson's death is, in-

---

2. *Blood Meridian*'s anchorite declares, "They is four things that can destroy the earth. . . . Women, whiskey, money, and niggers" (18), a list akin to Lester Ballard's assertion that "All the trouble I ever was in . . . was caused by whiskey or women or both" (*Child of God* 53).

3. Two arrows lodge in Jackson: as the two of wands, the Yumas show "Influence over another. Dominion. Boldness, courage, fierceness . . . revenge" (Wang 256).

deed, in traditional terms a "rest after labor," at once a finality and a perfection. The tarot's classification for both Jackson's "second card" and the kid's card is in chesed, "mercy." But the author's emphases appear to be on the particularity of the suits. The kid's card "blends" pleasure with discomfort, a discomfort with the life of the gang, a discomfort indicating "clemency" or mercy. Jackson's death, though, is "mercifully" quickened by the blow of the Indian's club. It may be that only the reader appreciative of McCarthy's carefully crafted prose will be reminded of the four of wands in this scene by the arrows being described as "wands." The eyewitness records state that Jackson was drowned in the river, and there are no references to arrows among the details of his death (Carr 54). Given the lack of source verification for such details, McCarthy may well have intended an allusion to this particular tarot card.

In McCarthy's sustained attention to the tarot's fours, which represent "completion" and "making a matter settled and fixed," a sense of the novel's cyclic closures may be inferred. "Hear me, man," the judge says to the book's main character: "There is room on the stage for one beast and one alone. All others are destined for a night that is eternal and without name. One by one they will step down into the darkness before the footlamps. Bears that dance, bears that dont" (331).[4] The settled and fixed matter, its time having come round, is replaced by the next matter. Thematically, the book's Anasazi, beaver-fur hats, the westward reach of the pioneers, Glanton, the kid, and the hunt of the southern buffalo herd all reach completion within the course of the novel. The fours underscore the judge's premise of "destined" cycles. In the judge's language, the name of the act by which these cycles come to completion is war.

The third card turned during the novel's tarot scene is Glanton's. But no one sees it, for it is whipped away immediately by the wind (95). A blindfolded sorceress provides an interpretation of the unseen card: "*La carroza, la carroza,* cried the beldam. *Invertido. Carta de Guerra, de venganza. La ví sin ruedas sobre un rio obscuro . . .*" (The coach, the coach . . . Inverted. Card of war, of vengeance. I saw it without wheels on a dark river . . .). Though McCarthy has helpfully provided a chapter subheading for this section, "Wheelless upon a dark river," the reader must nevertheless do some work to match the clue to the woman's words. The novel's ferry, constructed from a "pair of old wagonboxes" (253) at the Yuma crossing, is present in the woman's reading. The darkness of the river is specific to the crossing there.[5] The woman continues, saying, "*Perdida, perdida. La carta está perdida en la noche*" (Lost, lost. The card is lost in the night). And then, "*Un*

---

4. Grannyrat characterizes the Comanche attack on Captain White's filibustering expedition as a "dance" (77). John R. Kenly, interestingly, writes: "The Mexicans . . . say that their army has retired to Monterey, and that it will fight us there, *mucho fandango*," suggesting in "fandango" a dance, in addition to the word's meanings of "fuss," "trouble" (65–66; see also 94; cf. 216, and Audubon 102).

5. Bartlett describes the Colorado— McCarthy's "dark river" (81, 96)—as "dark reddish" (2: 150).

maleficio, cried the old woman. *Qué viento tan maleante . . .*" (A curse . . . What a villainous wind . . .), whereupon Glanton threatens her. "*Carroza de muertos,*" she continues, "*llena de huesos. El joven qué . . .*" (Dead wagon, full of bones. The youngster that . . .), and at the crying of her last phrase, McCarthy's judge "like a great ponderous djinn stepped through the fire and the flames delivered him up as if he were in some way native to their element" as he came to quiet Glanton in the embrace of his arms (96).[6] This "coach" is the tarot card the Chariot. In this card is a reference to Ezekiel's vision of wheels within wheels (Wang 211; see Ezekiel 1:16). For Wang, Ezekiel's wheel is, indeed, the turning wheel of fortune (196–197). There is a sphinx on the Wheel of Fortune card in some decks, a "stable element in the midst of change," and in other decks it is "the guardian of the gateway of the mysteries, holding the secret of life and death" (Wang 197). This sphinx may, therefore, be seen as an allusion to the town of Fort Griffin, Texas, in which the kid meets his end (at just the time Fort Griffin itself is dying).

The Chariot carries cyclic repetition in its turning wheels and emphasizes the cycles of dominance embodied in *Blood Meridian.*[7] Richard Cavendish provides a "divinatory meaning" of the Chariot card: "Success, triumph over difficulties, self-assertion. Travel, exploration. (*Reversed:* Tyranny. Sudden defeat, misfortune, bad news, accidents.)" (171). McCarthy's choice of this card inverted, in the gypsy reading, is an appropriate assessment of Glanton's "luck" at the Yuma ferry. The cards drawn in this pivotal reading leak their symbols and allusions into the whole of the story.[8] If there is any doubt that in the universe of *Blood Meridian* divination by cards is possible, this blindfolded, night-darkened, yet accurate reading of an absent card should dispel it.

As McCarthy unfolds the scene of the reading of the three cards, he describes the old gypsy woman as sitting "like that blind interlocutrix between Boaz and Jachin inscribed upon the one true card in the juggler's deck which they would not see come to light, true pillars and true card, false prophetess for all" (94).[9] This reference is to the evening's fourth tarot card, the High Priestess (or Female Pope). On it, the veiled Priestess is flanked by two pillars, "the two great hollow columns of bronze, named Jachin and Boaz, which stood at the threshold of the Temple in Jerusalem" (Cavendish 72).[10] "Masons," Cavendish continues, "interpret Jachin to mean 'to establish' and Boaz 'in strength,' and

6. Calming Glanton is a "historical" thing for Holden to do (Chamberlain 274).

7. When Christopher Forbis writes that *Blood Meridian* is a palindrome, a book of mirrored moments, I see him presenting an argument that the novel is circular, shaped like a wheel.

8. Even the Colorado River is suggested in the Chariot card, whose "Path Color" is "Red-Orange" and whose "Sign" is in "Cancer (Cardinal Water)." In one deck, the card represents "Odin, God of war," and a depiction of a river exists in the background of the card in another deck (Wang 210, 214, 212).

9. McCarthy also presents a sorceress in *Suttree* (423–427), who similarly embodies the power of prophecy (see also a "hanged fool . . . in motley," 5).

10. In some decks the Chariot card would show the Priestess's pillars, "*Jachim* and *Boaz*" (Wang 214).

the two together signify 'stability.'" "[T]he pillars stand for the balance of opposites of which reality is made—fire and cloud, light and darkness, positive and negative," the "pillars of Mercy and Severity—and the opposites of the other, fatal tree which grew in Eden, the tree of the knowledge of good and evil" (Cavendish 72). These opposites are in many instances represented in the world of the kid and the judge.[11] This "true" card invests a variation of McCarthy's theme of the eternal cycle of dancers: that the only claims to stability are made from strength.

Is the card of the Fool meant to be embodied by Judge Holden?[12] Bill Butler writes: "In a sense it is the spirit of The Fool which animates the entire Tarot deck. In the earliest deck known he is shown towering over midget human figures, a Giant of Folly and of super-rational sanity. It is with his madness, that of the Fool of God, that the cards are illuminated; for in any reading of the Tarot it is the Fool who asks and the Fool who answers every question" (110). Sallie Nichols writes of the Fool that he is "a wanderer, energetic, ubiquitous, and immortal. He is the most powerful of all the Tarot Trumps. Since he has no fixed number he is free to travel at will, often upsetting the established order with his pranks" (23).

In *Blood Meridian*, might this be the judge? Certainly, Chamberlain's experiences in the desert with the historical Holden, his shock at the judge's ubiquity and near indestructibility, lend weight to this supposition. Glanton's gang, out of powder and near death in the desert, had initially stumbled upon Holden sitting on a rock, Tobin says, "smilin as we rode up. Like he'd been expectin us" (125). He appears to have awaited their arrival with the same certain patience that he, elsewhere in the novel, attributes to war itself when he says: "War endures. As well ask men what they think of stone. War was always here. Before man was, war waited for him" (248). In a conversation regarding war and the "sanctity of blood" to "the dance" that is war, Holden probably, though enigmatically, refers to himself when he proposes to the kid (who is now "the man," twenty-eight years after the massacre) that, even in a world of "false dancers. . . . there will be one there always who is a true dancer and can you guess who that might be?" (331).[13] The only survivor of the Yuma-ferry massacre is, finally, the judge.

McCarthy's layers of representation, of literal object and thematic allusion, all echo in the "true" Priestess card.

11. McCarthy's epigraph taken from Jacob Boehme's *Six Theosophic Points* (92) occurs in a section of Boehme's exposition (sixth point, section 13) that also includes references to the devil, Lucifer (99), and to the thought that "gentleness is the enmity of the wrath-power [Lucifer], and each is against the other" (94–95).

12. In the Ozarks, H. L. Mencken relates, "*Judge* or *jedge* is used to mean a fool or a clown, and there is even an adjective, *jedgy*" (120).

13. The epigraph to *Blood Meridian* taken from Paul Valéry is found in the essay "The Yalu," in his *His-*

"[B]eing a creature of perpetual motion," Nichols writes, the Tarot Fool "dances through the cards each day, connecting the end with the beginning—endlessly" (27).[14] "He dances in light and in shadow and he is a great favorite. He never sleeps, the judge. He is dancing, dancing. He says that he will never die," McCarthy writes (335). The judge moves on the book's final page in the manner of the novel's true dancing bear—a beast, deadly beyond McCarthy's burlesque bear in crinoline—the judge representative, for the moment, of an endless cycle of triumphant dancers. Former scalp hunter James Box writes of a "plank" dance, accompanied by the tune of a fiddler, that he saw while in Durango: he was "astonished at the ease with which the judge controlled the motley throng and kept the peace" (147). Box is not writing of Holden; yet his observation, using the word "judge" to imply one who controls dancing (in addition to the gambling and drinking that were also present), is an analogue to the Holden of McCarthy's final page.

As the Fool is associated with eternal dancing, dancing that connects the end with the beginning, both in the tarot and the novel, Judge Holden is defined by this card, the animating force of the tarot. When the kid sees a caged idiot with a cat (312), he sees an emblem of the Fool implying the judge's presence (see also 92). Holden is both judge of the dance that was the scalp hunters' war, and a personification of those universal energies, both superrational and madly foolish, that are war itself.[15] *Blood Meridian* needs to be read not simply as a historical novel, but as a historical romance, in which characters move in intertextual regions between fiction and myth (Frye 33, 306).

---

tory and Politics, "written during the first Sino-Japanese war." The words of the epigraph are spoken to a European Valéry persona by a Chinese companion regarding differences between Eastern and Western concepts of order and disorder. A sense of the range of ideas included in the statement of the Eastern (Chinese) perception of the West, ideas that McCarthy explores in his novel, may be suggested in the following passages excerpted from the long paragraph concluded by the epigraph: "In your land, power can do nothing. Your politics consists in changes of heart; it leads to general revolution, and then to reaction against revolution, which is another revolution." "For you, intelligence is not one thing among many. You neither prepare nor provide for it, nor protect nor repress nor direct it; you worship it as if it were an omnipotent beast. Every day it devours everything. It would like to put an end to a new state of society every evening. A man intoxicated on it believes his own thoughts are legal decisions." "You are in love with intelligence, until it frightens you. For your ideas are terrifying and your hearts are faint. Your acts of pity and cruelty are absurd, committed with no calm, as if they were irresistible. Finally, you fear blood more and more. Blood and time" (373).

14. Nichols writes, in words that echo the judge's whirling dance and animating fiddle of the novel's final page: "To see [the Fool] dance is to plumb the mystery of all creation, for his essence is all-inclusive and his paradoxes many. He strides forward yet he looks backward, thus connecting the wisdom of the future with the innocence of childhood. His energy is unconscious and undirected, yet it seems to have a purpose of its own. He moves outside space and time. The winds of prophecy and poesy inhabit his spirit. Although he wanders with no fixed abode, he endures intact throughout the ages" (26).

15. Frederick Ober, citing Bernal Díaz writing of Montezuma's Mexico, notes that Huitzilopochtli, the Aztec's "war-god," was a "very fat" man in Aztec sculptures (306).

Other cards of the major arcana appear in the novel, though less centrally. The judge may stand for the Devil, as he is characterized by Reverend Green (7). The anchorite the kid meets early in the book, who speaks of God to him, represents the Monk (19; see also 107). Bathcat's butchered body is described as a "torso," suggesting the card the Hanged Man, in which the body is held aloft by a rope from an ankle (88, 226–227; see also 128, 263). The Juggler is present as the juggler whose family accompanies the gang to Janos (90). A "temperate old man" suggests Temperance (103). A "solitary lobo . . . hung like a marionette from the moon" suggests one depiction of the card the Moon (117; see also 293). The Tower is present in the scene of the Germans at the church, in which one is shot down from above (224–225; see also 335 for the judge "Towering"). A "pale green meteor" (227), the Leonids of the novel's first page, and an abundance of other star references within the novel suggest the Star (see also 256). The Wheel of Fortune is in both the pugmill turning (231) and the earth "silently milling" (247). The judge's lifting of the anvil, among other feats, echoes the card Strength (240), while the judge with his coin tricks brings to mind the Magician (245–246). And Death, if the reader of *Blood Meridian* needs assistance in locating suggestions of this card, may be found in a "carved wooden skeleton" (314) and in the judge's words "I know him well," which probably refer to death (328): "Death, the Devil's first cousin, if not his *alter ego*," dances to the Devil's "merry tune" in the Dance of Death (Rudwin 257). In sum, most of the major arcana can be found among myriad allusions in the novel.

Masons, Zoroastrians, and Fire

The tarot symbolism is appropriate on yet another level to a historical novel of scalp-hunting cutthroats in mid-nineteenth-century Mexico. The tarot shares a common heritage, out of the philosophy of the Kabbalah, with the flourishing nineteenth-century brotherhood of Freemasonry. The columns Jachin and Boaz have significance for both Masons and the students of the tarot.[16] The hexagram, assessed below, is also a symbol held in common. Historically, "Free-Masonry was introduced into Mexico" by 1820 and "derived from the Scotch branch of that order." "[P]ersons of all conditions, from the opulent magnates down to the humblest artisans" "ran to initiate themselves into the mysteries of Free-Masonry" (Wilson 68, 69).

Judge Holden first appears in *Blood Meridian* during scenes at Nacogdoches in the spring of 1849, twelve years after the Masons' Milam Lodge had been chartered in that

---

16. Eliphas Levi counsels the Masonic reader of his volume on the Kabbalah to "Get hold of a Tarot" deck in order to explore the relationships between the cards and the numerologically significant letters of the Hebrew alphabet (*Book* 130–131).

town (Vest 325). Ranger Captain Ben McCulloch, with whom Glanton and Tobin and Doc Irving had ridden during the Mexican War (Chamberlain 101, *Blood Meridian* 95), was in fact the Mason of Seguin, Texas, Lodge No. 109, for whom Lodge No. 273 (Mason, Texas) was later named (Vest 314, 349).[17] *Blood Meridian*'s mythico-magical environment seems less than simply whimsical in its grafting of arcane kabbalistic symbols onto the story if Masonic influences (and by association the kabbalistic tarot) are knit into the historical U.S. and Mexican Southwest, and (through McCulloch) into the Glanton legend itself.[18]

The Masonic heritage asserts the continuation of truths bequeathed from Persian and Egyptian antiquity (Vest 26–28). Two of the novel's scenes appear to depend on this eclectic aspect of the Masons' synthesis of beliefs: one in which St. Elmo's fire attaches itself to the gang, and another involving gestures made by the kid's companion Toadvine in the desert after the massacre. The reader may make an intuitive connection between the presence of St. Elmo's fire in *Blood Meridian* (186; see also 47) and in *Moby-Dick*, in which it clung to the mastheads and harpoons (Melville 415–417). There are similarities between the books beyond this shared event. Captain Ahab and Stubb, the second mate, on "agency" (144; see also 461), for instance, echoes through *Blood Meridian* (243, 249, 329). But, the reader who assumes only a direct allusion to *Moby-Dick* in *Blood Meridian*'s scene of St. Elmo's fire will be interested in the historical verification that Wislizenus provides when he writes that "during a sultry evening electrical flames were seen on the points of bayonets among the sentinels stationed in the mountains" at the battle of Buena Vista, during the Mexican War (55).

In the larger view, the gang members in *Blood Meridian* appear to have a particularly close relationship to fire generally. At several points the men seem protected from the fire as they reach into it for live coals (86, 126). Holden, as mentioned above, walks through fire (96). McCarthy includes a paragraph in which he writes that "each fire is all fires" and "does contain within it something of men themselves" (244). The gang undresses in a "shroud of palest fire" (222).[19] Even 1833, the year of the kid's birth, is glossed as denoting "the year it rained fire"—because of a spectacular Leonids display—in Ruxton (*Life* 8).

17. The book by scalp-hunting Captain James Box is, in fact, dedicated to "Col. Benj. McCullough, The Gallant Soldier and Ranger."

18. Inquiries to the Masonic Grand Lodges of Texas, Tennessee, and South Carolina, and to selected local lodges in Tennessee and Texas, have not produced any indication that John Glanton was himself a Freemason. At the same time, only a few of these records, given the many intervening years (and in some cases floods, and in one case Sherman's march to the sea), extend into the decade of the 1840s, though Freemasonry's presence in those states generally, at that time, is uncontested. Ralph Smith answered my question on the subject with word that he had "never heard or read that Glanton was a Mason" (letter, March 12, 1990).

19. To restate, the gang's undressing is presumably related to Wislizenus's remark that "Some persons, entitled to confidence, informed me that by changing their woolen under-dress in the night, they had at

Masonic symbolism explicates the scalp hunters' close relationship to fire as being, also, Zoroastrian. Albert Pike, in his book on Scottish Freemasonry, ties such fire events to Masonic concerns by including Ahura-Mazda and Arhiman, the Parsees' gods of light and darkness, within the canon of Masonic philosophical relationships (601, 612–613; see also Vest 27–28). *Moby-Dick*'s Fedallah the "Parsee" (462), the "fire worshipper" (362) who follows his captain to his death, stands as an analogue to Glanton's men in their arcane universe. When Holden refers to the kid as "Young Blasarius" (94), his words may be taken both as remembering the kid's participation in the burning of the hotel at Nacogdoches in Chapter 1—the kid being "an incendiary" (Black 216, "Blasarius"; 903, "Incendiary")—and as foreshadowing Holden's later charges that the kid had withheld himself from full commitment to the gang (307; see also 173), since the kid, as an incendiary, is also one who "excites factions, quarrels, or sedition" (*Webster's* 608, "incendiary"). McCarthy's choice of this "Blasarius" reference, I believe, also strengthens a reading of the novel in which the gang is associated with fire. The kid, as he joins Toadvine in the burning of the hotel, merits Holden's smiling notice as he rides out of town (14). This early association of the kid with fire may well be one basis for the judge's remark to the kid that "Our animosities were formed and waiting before ever we two met. Yet even so you could have changed it all" (307).

In a second "Masonic" scene, Toadvine, travelling west through the desert with the survivors of the massacre, talks with the others of his having "run plumb out of country" (285). In a gesture accompanying his words, he makes a tripod of three fingers and twice lowers the fingertips into the sand, making "a star or a hexagon." He then brushes the mark away. In Masonic symbolism, the hexagram, or star based on a hexagon, is, in one instance, representative of the extent of the sky, and in another instance, a sign of the reaches of the world (Churchward 190, 313–314). In the tarot, this is a sign of the macrocosm (Levi, *Magical* 20). The gesture McCarthy attaches to Toadvine's words is a representation of his spoken thought.

Other items in the novel may be taken as allusive of Masonic concerns. When McCarthy's judge asks the kid, "Is not blood the tempering agent in the mortar which bonds?" (329), he may well be referring to the blooded "puzzoalana" mortar of the Roman Empire, the durability of which the Masons take note (Vest 42). When McCarthy writes that "who builds in stone seeks to alter the structure of the universe and so it was with [the Anasazi] masons however primitive their works may seem to us," he links his theme of eternal succession with man's desire for order and stability in a metaphor involving "masons" (146).

---

first been repeatedly frightened by seeing themselves suddenly enveloped in a mass of electrical fire" (55). McCarthy has altered the source to demonstrate, in his scene, the mare and foal frightened of the fire, but does not show a frightened gang.

The Mason views the world as a moral place, and he strives to uphold that which is moral (Pike 241–245).[20] In the literature on the tarot, no such appreciation of the world as "moral" is evident. The Wheel of Fortune and the caprice of the Fool rule the tarot. The judge's remarks on war as a nonmoral contest (250) are easily derived from the heritage of the tarot, no matter its obviously shared similarities with Freemasonry. As noted above, McCarthy has the judge assert that "War is god," but also that "war is the truest form of divination" (249). Discovering fate, divining it, is important and possible in the world of the historical romance that is *Blood Meridian*. The premise for the tarot reading is, after all, Glanton's solicitation of the gypsy juggler "*Para adivinar la suerte*" (to divine luck/to tell fortunes; 91).

In the book's final chapter, the judge speaks to the kid (as the "man") of "gods of vengeance and of compassion [who] alike lie sleeping in their crypt" (330). When taken with his earlier statement that "war is the truest form of divination," his thought is remarkably Native American in its fundamentals. In Colonel Richard Irving Dodge's words: "Believing that no line of conduct of his own can avail him for good or evil . . . the Indian's first and most important concern is to find some sure means by which he can discover which of the gods has the ascendancy for him at any particular time. For this he resorts to divination" (103). The functions of the "Good and Bad Gods," to whom Dodge refers above, are:

restricted entirely to benefits or injuries in this life, and the Indian's condition after death does not in any way depend either on his own good conduct while living, or on the will of either of the gods.
    All peccadilloes and crimes bring, or do not bring, their punishment in this world, and whatever their character in life, whatever the actual "deeds done in the flesh," the souls of all Indians reach, after some days' journey, a paradise called by them the "Happy Hunting Grounds," unless debarred by accident. (101)

This thought echoes the judge's words: "Any man who could discover his own fate and elect therefore some opposite course could only come at last to that selfsame reckoning at the same appointed time, for each man's destiny is as large as the world he inhabits and contains within it all opposites as well" (330). The judge defines a world of inflexible outcomes. The exercise of will cannot supersede predestined ends. The "accidents," scalping and strangulation, to which Dodge refers are the warriors' great risks of war. "Divinations" probe the present disposition of the gods toward these risks and can hint at the future.

---

20. Madison C. Peters asserts that as many as fifty of the fifty-six signers of the Declaration of Independence were Masons (27). It is known that thirty-five of the ninety-six Supreme Court justices, through 1968, were Masons (Roberts 223). And of interest to the reader of *Blood Meridian* as a southern (and particularly Tennesseean) novel, all three United States presidents elected from Tennessee, Jackson, Polk, and Andrew Johnson, were Masons (Roberts 403).

An extension of the aboriginal desire to probe the gods, which invests *Blood Merid-ian* as a minor theme, is that deception, cheating acknowledged as a practical test of the gods' favor, is also a kind of divination, pitting one man against another in a gamble of immediate risk against immediate answer. John C. Cremony writes of the Apaches: "De-ceit is regarded among them with the same admiration we bestow upon one of the fine arts" (86). "Cheating," Dodge writes, is a "recognized part of all games among all Indi-ans," and in the case of card games, "Luck in holding, and skill in playing are both made subservient to skill in manipulation. The man who can deal himself the best hand is rec-ognized as the best player, provided he is not caught at it. If detected he loses, and this being the only penalty, the game goes on" (328).[21]

There are a remarkable number of deceptions in *Blood Meridian*, including the judge's charges against Reverend Green, the Comanches' hiding offside their horses, the short barrel of whiskey for Mangas, and the "agreed upon" attack against the ferry company that left twelve Yumas dead. Glanton's and Holden's shots into the volcano crater to de-ceive the advancing Indians into thinking the trapped gang members had committed suicide, a common enough response by men facing torture if captured, and Holden's false cry "All dead save me" to the Indians below (134), after he has rearmed the gang with gunpowder, also lethally illustrate this minor theme, McCarthy's exploration of advan-tages gained by deception. These deceptions all fit morally within the Indian, and the Holden, philosophy of winning as paramount. Glanton's "calculations concerning the enemy [which] included every duplicity" are part of this concern (148), though the reader observes that Glanton is himself fooled in the end in yet another of the novel's "dances."

McCarthy may have used the tarot system of allusions and references in *Blood Merid-ian* in part because of similarities between the tarot deck and regular playing cards. In ana-logue with the ordinary gambler's possible hands, ranging from no combination to a royal straight flush, tarot cards immediately provide the seeker with a divination of the present moment and possibly the future, of what the mix of good and bad fortune might be. The judge tells the gang a parable of "two men at cards with nothing to wager save their lives" (249). What is thought, the judge asks, of the fact that one of the men at cards will die?: "[I]t is a dull man indeed who could reckon so profound a decision with-out agency or significance either one." "War is the ultimate game," the judge continues, "because war is at last a forcing of the unity of existence. War is god" (249). Though Mc-Carthy's novel contains several scenes of card playing (see especially 101–103, 332), the scalpers do not play at cards. Their concern with their "luck" is a "ritual" that "includes

---

21. Wislizenus defines the card game "monte" as a "(hazard game)" (27). This game is the "Monte" of a chapter subheading in *Blood Meridian* (100) and is illustrative of the hazards of all the novel's "divina-tions."

the letting of blood" (329).[22] Dodge wonders at the Indians' gambling: "The stakes are high for a poor people" (328). Stakes of life and death in the divination that is war would be, and are for McCarthy, higher. Signs in dreams and on the trail can be accessible to interpretation for Dodge's Indian. But the manipulation of one's environment is a yet more sophisticated test of the gods' favor for Dodge's Indian and, as well, for McCarthy in *Blood Meridian.*

Blood Meridian contains intricate syntheses of layered allusions radiating from McCarthy's metaphor of the historical "dance" of warring peoples. Judge Holden becomes an emblem of the energy that powers the dance. McCarthy here confronts critics who found his earlier books excessively grotesque with a well-researched—yet no less grotesque—historical novel.[23] He also confronts those critics who have noted his novels' lack of theme, plot, and ethical position.[24] His organizational pattern in *Blood Meridian,* though arcanely based on kabbalistic relationships present in Freemasonry and tarot-card symbolism, is a philosophical approach to life entirely consistent with both his theme and the historical record. Only when the influence of this controlling pattern of organization is recognized can the elements of romance in *Blood Meridian* be appreciated.

22. A few pages before the tarot-card-reading scene, Bathcat asks Toadvine whether he is a "gaming man," and Toadvine answers, "Depends on the game" (87). During Chamberlain's first view of Glanton, Glanton is playing cards (39–40). An analogue to the knifing of the bartender's son during a game of cards in the bar at Janos—whose mortal wound is generally ignored—might be found in Ruxton's *Adventures* (43–44).

23. Both Walter Sullivan (343) and Thomas Daniel Young (100) suggest McCarthy consult Faulkner as a means of controlling the excesses of his gothic grotesque.

24. Vereen Bell opens his article "The Ambiguous Nihilism of Cormac McCarthy" with a general remark: "Cormac McCarthy's novels are as innocent of theme and of ethical reference as they are of plot" (31). McCarthy's *Suttree* has prompted John Lewis Longley, Jr., to remark, "It is all texture and very little structure" (81), while Sullivan responds to the book thus: "The shape of the novel is amorphous, even for McCarthy, whose long suit has never been dramatic structure" (341). As mentioned in note 7, above, Christopher Forbis argues that the shape of *Blood Meridian* is a palindrome.

CHAPTER 6

Judge Holden's Gunpowder

The gang's first meeting with Holden, as told by ex-priest turned scalper Ben Tobin, is fascinating (125–135). Tobin opens with Glanton's decimated gang out of black powder for their guns and in flight from several score Apaches. The Apaches trail them "ridin four and six abreast and there was no short supply of them and they were in no hurry" (126). "Every man jack of us knew that in that godforsook land somewhere was a draw or a culdesac or perhaps just a pile of rocks and there we'd be driven to a stand with those empty guns" (125). On a solitary rock jutting from the desert floor sat Holden, "smilin as we rode up. Like he'd been expectin us" (125).[1] Glanton leads the Indians briefly away from Holden, giving him time to gather gunpowder ingredients (saltpeter, charcoal, sulfur), which Holden then processes and mixes for use in the scalpers' guns. He thereby saves the gang from certain death.[2]

In Tobin's story, McCarthy apparently incorporates information derived from folk sources gathered in "Powder, Flint, and Balls," an article in *Foxfire 5*. Of the nine pages Carl Darden contributes to this article, the segment presented below would seem to establish Darden as McCarthy's primary source:

Then the ingredients can be mixed with a small amount of water so the mixture comes out with biscuit-dough consistency. Usually when I mix the ingredients, I add just enough stale urine to make the batch bunch about like biscuit dough. The urine, substituted for water, gives the powder more oxygen and higher performance.

Flowers of sulfur is ideal for gun powder, and it can be bought in most drug stores in four-ounce bottles or pound cans.

It can also be found in pure deposits around volcanoes, and in early times, because it was found where molten lava issued from the earth, the sulfur condensed around the rims of the volcanoes was called brimstone. (246)

1. Stephen Vincent Benét's devil "Scratch" declares to Daniel Webster that he is as old in America as the earliest of adventurers (39).

2. Even Samuel Chamberlain, who knew the man "'Judge' Holden of Texas" on whom so much of McCarthy's character is based, was perplexed by his Holden, declaring, "Who or what he was no one knew" (271).

These paragraphs anticipate the judge's call for the gang to "piss for your very souls" (131–132),[3] McCarthy's phrase "pure flowers of sulphur" (131), his "brimstone" (131, 134), and, in Darden's repeated "biscuit dough" simile, Tobin's characterization of the judge as a "bloody dark pastryman" mixing the wetted gunpowder into "a foul black dough, a devil's batter" (132).[4]

Another point linking McCarthy and the *Foxfire* article is the judge's choice of "alder charcoal" for his gunpowder. Both Darden (247) and Jim Moran (253), another *Foxfire 5* contributor, mention willow as a standard charcoal source. And McCarthy's charcoal is burned at a stream where willow trees are present (128). But McCarthy's choice of alder firmly links him to Darden: "By the way, just yesterday I took time out and made a batch of powder, and this time, when I mixed the ingredients, I added homemade alder charcoal instead of redwood and improved the powder's performance 100 per cent" (248).[5]

To make his saltpeter, the judge "leached out the guano with creekwater and woodash" (128) within two days. Carol A. Hill, a third contributor to "Powder, Flint, and Balls," describes a process for refining saltpeter that resembles Holden's and takes an unspecified but apparently relatively brief time (253–256).[6] Her contribution mentions "woodashes," and a white "precipitate" (254), and the term "nitre" (256), items that occur in the novel (127–128, 131). Her account also notes that the liquid matter in the leaching process is at one stage called "'Mother liquor'" or "'beer'" (254), terms perhaps related to McCarthy's mention of the judge and Delaware Indians appearing to be drunk (perhaps on fumes) after the leaching process, "but on what none could surmise" (128). Hill's account, then, was apparently used directly by McCarthy, who for obvious exigencies of time in this episode omits Hill's observation that "The nitrate crystals thus obtained had to be further refined and purified" before the substance was suitable for mixing into gunpowder (256).

---

3. J. R. Partington describes the use of urine when refining saltpeter for black powder (319). The judge's mixing of the three components wetted in urine does not match his process.

4. Darden's contribution to *Foxfire 5* elsewhere likens one technique for refining saltpeter to the activity of yeast in "bread dough" (247), and likens the state of the ground charcoal for gunpowder to that of a "flourlike fineness" (248).

5. McCarthy departs from Darden's gunpowder recipe, though. Darden writes of "seventy-five parts saltpeter finely ground, fifteen parts charcoal, and ten parts sulfur" (246). Reducing these numbers by five, the resulting proportions are 15:3:2. Yet, McCarthy's amounts are "about eight pounds of pure crystal saltpetre," "about three pounds of fine alder charcoal" (128), and "about two pounds" of "pure flowers of sulfur" (131). His proportions are 8:3:2, or a mixture with about half the amount of saltpeter Darden recommends.

6. The process that Darden describes for refining manure into saltpeter involves water and ashes (through which the leached liquid drains off), and drying that liquid by "evaporation in the sun" (247). This process resembles Holden's, except that the judge spent two days at his task, and Darden's process takes ten months to "let it sit" before the liquid is ready to be drained off.

McCarthy may well have added the detail of Holden's, and Glanton's, shooting into the volcano out of his reading in Frederick Ober's nineteenth-century account of ascending the Mexican volcano Popocatepetl. Ober writes that when he had reached its rim, he "rose exultingly" and:

discharged the six chambers of my revolver into the air, creating such a concussion in the crater that great stones rattled down its perpendicular sides, and the reverberation nearly deafened us. From "crag to crag" leaped the volumes of sound, like peals of thunder, and finally died away in receding murmurs, as though retreating farther and farther into the entrails of old Tlaloc, the god of storms, whose brow I now stood upon, at a height of nearly eighteen thousand feet above the sea. (390)

Faust, Satan, and Holden

Holden's gift of gunpowder has overtones of Mephistopheles's gifts to Faust and incorporates an entire series of arcane, theological, and historical issues. Of their leaders' first meeting on the desert, Tobin says to the kid, "They've a secret commerce. Some terrible covenant. You mind. You'll see I'm right" (126). Glanton, then, as Holden provides him with new powder, may be joined to his benefactor in the equivalent of a satanic pact. Too, gunpowder is one of the devil's more significant gifts to man (Rudwin 251). As McCarthy adds this detail to Tobin's story, a reading of the leaders' "covenant" as, indeed, a devil compact is affirmed.

The conjoined narrative elements of gunpowder made in the midst of conflict, and Indians hesitating at sounds associated with volcanoes, direct McCarthy's reader to yet another analogous historical tale. Several hundred years before Glanton's time, Hernán Cortés's expedition in the New World, a small force confronting the whole of Aztec Mexico, ran out of powder in the middle of the challenge (Díaz 327). Bat dung for saltpeter is easy enough to find, given mountains and caves. Charcoal takes little technological sophistication to make. But the sulfur that Cortés found upon a volcano, and that went into his gunpowder, is credited as the first such discovery and manufacture in the New World (*Diccionario Porrua* 1389). Cortés's men descended by rope into a rumbling crater (coincidentally, that of the volcano Popocatepetl, which Ober would later climb) to retrieve it. Cortés describes in a letter the dangers of the descents for sulfur, "which is deposited by the smoke," "a most evil thing" (279, 325; Wilson 110). In an account contemporary with these exploits, Cervantes de Salazar remarks that the Aztecs thought the rumblings of the volcano to be the spirits of the Indians' evil kings, in a kind of Christian-like sulfurous hell reserved only for those wicked few (260–261). References to the judge as a "sootysouled rascal" and "the devil" in this scene (124, 125) aptly describe one who can control the rumblings of such a place as the Indians' volcano hell. The Indians marvelled at the intrepidity of the Spaniards (Prescott 285). The conquistadors' energy, which the Indians "envied" in Cervantes de Salazar's account of Cortés's men, is akin to that of the judge in Tobin's account. He is able, with his powder, to direct the volcano to rumble.

Gazing into his night's fire, Glanton has access to portents (243). Yet Glanton, in his pride, McCarthy tells us, holds himself to be sufficient and complete, with a clarity and intention earlier ascribed to the gang as a whole (119).[7] Yet he has also been willing to promise his soul for more powder, a contradiction that appears to call the divinatory authority of the narrative voice into question.

Satan's intellect and cunning distinguish him in both folklore and Christian thought. In recounting his gunpowder story, Tobin muses, "what do you reckon it was in them mountains that we set out for? And how did he come to know of it? How to find it? How to put it to use?" (126). Holden's astonishing intellect marks him here as elsewhere in the book. Holden can give an "extemporary lecture in geology" (116), a "short disquisition on the history and architecture" of an old Spanish mission (224), go over "points of law" and "latin terms of jurisprudence," citing "cases civil and martial," quoting "Coke and Blackstone, Anaximander, Thales" (239; see also 127, 173, 198, 251). His breadth of knowledge would be beyond credulity, except that Chamberlain's historical Judge Holden is himself "another Admirable Crichton" (271–272) whose erudition McCarthy does not appear to overstate.[8]

Holden's coldness and his pride are, in fact, also flaws in the otherwise magnificent creation that is Satan. Out of such pride, Holden sketches for his own records a "footpiece from a suit of armor hammered out in a shop in Toledo three centuries before, a small steel tapadero frail and shelled with rot," and once his interest in the piece was satisfied, he "crushed it into a ball of foil and pitched it into the fire" (140). Holden cannot pack all he inventories of the past in his travels.[9] He may discard the footpiece as a practical matter; but, then, the gang finds it a practical "mercy" to kill its own wounded who cannot travel (205–209). Such aloofness is always at the fore, though its intellectualization is the judge's special venue.

Though Satan is traditionally represented as lean, Holden may be literally as evil as he is fat.[10] Judge Holden, as legal counsel to the gang (237), practices one of the devil's

7. In *Luste* (one of Valéry's two Faust plays, along with *The Only One*), a student character remarks, "It's all too clear that every cause is a lost cause, that defeat in the end is no more immaterial or less glorious than victory" (123).

8. According to *The Oxford Companion to English Literature* (6th ed.), James "The Admirable" Crichton (1560–1582) was a "Scots adventurer, scholar, linguist, and poet, who served in the French army, travelled in Italy, and died in a brawl in Mantua."

9. "Scratch" is Mephistopheles with a collecting box (Benét 25–26, 36), not far removed from Holden.

10. Patrick Cullen makes distinctions, relevant to a fat Holden, out of the "Flesh-World-Devil" "in-

favorite professions (Rudwin 52). Reverend Green instinctively recognizes Holden: "This is him. The devil. Here he stands" (7).

The mummified woman the kid finds kneeling in the rocks above the scene of a massacre of Mexican penitentes (315) resembles a variation on the Virgin Mary. The "stars and quartermoons" of her costume, in some distinction to the "halfmoons" of the gypsies' costumes (89), resemble elements associated with Mary in Revelation 12:1 and in the painted depiction of Mary's appearance as Our Lady of Guadalupe. The "provenance" of the "stars and quartermoons" the old woman wears is said to be unknown to the kid. In this connection, it is noteworthy that the kid at this time carried a Bible with him, "no word of which could he read" (312).

In pre-Reformation Faust tales, a last-minute plea to the Virgin for her intercession in the breaking of a devil compact is successful (Rudwin 178–179). With the rise of Protestant thought, Mary's status was redefined so that her intercession was not available to overthrow such bonds. In *Blood Meridian*, McCarthy underscores divine unresponsiveness to human pleas (60, 146, 330). The massacre of devouts in the presence of her husk may well relate to the historical withdrawal of Mexico from the profound influence of Catholicism. This episode underscores the complexity of McCarthy's development of a Faust analogue within the context of this historical setting.

Holden's association with the tarot card the Fool recalls that the animal associated with the Fool in many decks is a cat, which is in turn a traditional familiar of, and even shape of, Satan (Rudwin 41):

The demons of hell tempt men of all classes and callings. They do not distinguish between prince and pauper, philosopher and fool. "It must not be thought," assures us Charles Baudelaire, "that the Devil tempts only men of genius. He doubtless scorns imbeciles, but he does not disdain their assistance. Quite the contrary, he founds great hopes on them." (Rudwin 139)

Tobin's remark that the judge has "ears like a fox" (135) also alludes to the traditionally pointed ears of the devil (Pfaff 21; Valéry, Luste 23). Indeed, the wolves that are also frequently mentioned in McCarthy's novel are fabled animal shapes of the archfiend (Rudwin 42). Judge Holden embodies other characteristics that mark the modern conception of Satan:

---

fernal triad" of sins (xvii). On Holden's soul are the following transgressions: succumbing to temptations of the flesh, as evidenced by his corpulence (signifying intemperance, in analogue to Falstaff in *Henry V*), and his suspected murder of innocent children (116–118, 164, 275, 333); succumbing to temptations of the world, shown by his carrying a bag of gold coins into the desert after the massacre (282–283, see also 125); and succumbing to temptations of the devil, apparent in his wild "suzerain" pride (198) as he declares, indicating the earth as a whole, "This is my claim. . . . In order for it to be mine nothing must be permitted to occur upon it save by my dispensation" (199).

In our own days, the Devil has turned human, all too human for most of us. He no longer appears in the gala attire of tail, horns and cloven foot, with which he used to grace the revels on the Blocksberg. "You fancied I was different, did you not, Johannes?" Satan asks the little Dutch boy in Frederik van Eeden's novel *De kleine Johannes* (1887). "That I had horns and a tail? That idea is out of date. No one believes it now." The Devil now moves among men in their own likeness, but "the kernel of the brute is in him still." His diabolical traits appear no longer in his body, but in his face; you can see them there, though he does not mean you should. (Rudwin 49)

The Devil manifests himself to us now as a well-bred, cultivated man of the world. In appearing among us, he generally borrows a tall handsome figure, surmounted by delicate features, dresses well, is fastidious about his rings and linen, travels post and stops at the best hotels. As he can boast of abundant means and a handsome wardrobe, it is no wonder that he should everywhere be politely received. In fact, as Voltaire has already said, he gets into very agreeable society. His brilliant powers of conversation, his adroit flattery, courteous gallantry, and elegant, though wayward, flights of imagination, soon render him the delight of the company in every salon. (Rudwin 52)

Though Holden is often underdressed or naked, McCarthy also pays more attention to the judge's wardrobe than to any other character's. When Holden must rush from his room at the ferry during the massacre, he at once provides himself with a hat and a parasol devised from available materials (282, 297–298), and is as interested in finding clothing in the desert as in acquiring a gun (282–283). Holden seems always as finely dressed as his bloody mission with the gang will allow.

The novel's closing paragraphs show the judge as leader of a dance, fiddling, he claims, for eternity (334–35): "While the Devil plays all instruments equally well, he seems to prefer the violin. He was said in the Middle Ages to own a violin with which he could set whole cities, grandparents and grandchildren, men and women, girls and boys, to dancing, dancing until they fell dead from sheer exhaustion" (Rudwin 256).[11] In compacts, the devil traditionally trades the satisfaction of desires for an abbreviated lifespan and a forfeited soul. Glanton's "calculations concerning . . . every duplicity" (148), then, are limited, humanly derived calculations. If the Faust analogue were neat and precise, Glanton would die by Holden's hand, torn asunder for his soul at an appointed time. But Glanton dies of a Yuma's savage axe blow. McCarthy accedes to history by depicting Glanton's end as it actually occurred. But the price the kid pays for his association with Holden is rendered more directly to the judge.

Holden asserts that "Means and ends are of little moment" in a retrospective under-

---

11. Heinrich Heine casts his "Doktor Faust" as a "Dance Poem." The violinist Paganini was rumored to have derived his great skill through a pact with the devil, as was 1930s Mississippi blues guitarist Robert Johnson.

standing of events, that they are "Idle speculations" (306).[12] The testimonies of "witnesses" arriving "by a third and other path" (153) are basic, when available, to the prosecution of a case.[13] The circumstantial evidence of the kid's betrayal of the gang, his survival of their massacre, is addressed as Holden makes his technical legal point: "Men's memories are uncertain and the past that was differs little from the past that was not" (330). Holden is, in fact, as reliable a witness of the kid's behavior as can be found in the book. Holden has a valid point in the novel's version. The kid *is* responsible, beyond moral rights and wrongs, when, from the imagined perspective of those dead at the crossing, even a minor failure to share the common enterprise—the kid's simple survival of the massacre, for instance—may be a weakness sufficient to warrant such a charge. Holden survives as witness to the kid's inability to share fully in the scalpers' war (306–307), echoing the historical Holden's accusation against Sam Chamberlain (293), claiming that Sam's reserve allowed the Yumas' triumph.

But to condemn the kid, as the judge does, on these grounds still seems the act of a madman. The judge may in fact believe that as a result of Glanton's pact, the men have also been surrendered to Holden's will, since a "covenant," a carefully chosen word on McCarthy's part, is, unlike a contract, inheritable both in devil compacts (Rudwin 175) and in law (Black 437, "Covenant: Real"). The kid is bound to Holden, then, even though the covenant was Glanton's, and Toadvine, as agent, "guaranteed" the kid's performance (79). As the explication of McCarthy's French sentence can be found to demonstrate (see "Languages" in Chapter 4), a reading of the novel based on law and therefore upon a strictly abided covenant is not inappropriate, confirming Tobin's otherwise enigmatic remark to the kid that "You'll see I'm right" (126) that Glanton and Holden have a "terrible covenant."

In the kid's death, such foreshadowing is fully justified. C. W. Roback's nineteenth-century book on astrology and magic contains a Faust tale (155–159) that depicts a particularly gruesome end for Faust: "all the hall sprinkled with blood, the brains cleaving to the wall, for the devil had beaten him from one wall against another; in one corner lay his eyes, in another his teeth." In the yard "they found his body lying on the horse-dung, most monstrously torn, and fearful to behold, for his head and all his joints were dashed to pieces" (158–159). "O help us heaven, see, here are Faustus limbs, / All torne asunder by the hand of death" say Marlowe's scholars, on finding his Faust (lines 1988–1989). "Such was the end which it was believed awaited the magicians who entered into a direct compact with the evil one" (Roback 159). And "such" might well have been the kid's end in this novel of "guaranteed" performance (79) and "terrible" covenants

---

12. "You can make out of events whatever you like in words, embroider them as you fancy. All the motives are fabricated . . . out of purest gossamer" (Valéry, *Luste* 123–124).

13. For lack of such a neutral witness, Black John Jackson's murder of Owens goes unpunished (237).

(126; see also Marlowe, lines 163–170, 239–241, 551.0.4–551.0.6, 584, 599). Heine's "Doktor Faust" concludes with Faust in the "wild embraces" of "hellish monsters" (64), a gesture perhaps related to the judge, who "rose up smiling and gathered [the kid] in his arms against his immense and terrible flesh" (333).

As McCarthy couches his gunpowder-gift story as a Faust analogue, he also subtly varies the pattern. He does not bring Holden and the kid together at Fort Griffin until twenty-eight years after the massacre. Twenty-four years is the usual limit for a devil compact (Rudwin 174; Sayers title, 62, 95, etc.). Still, as McCarthy's choice of the year 1878 allows scenes in Fort Griffin (a final shipping depot at the end of the buffalo era), and his story can by virtue of this variation be found to signalize the historical closing of the Indian "menace" in Texas and the beginnings of barbed-wire fencing of rangeland into ranches, he may perhaps be forgiven this minor restructuring of the legend.

Although McCarthy's allusive expansion of Judge Holden links him to the devil, emphasizing his ubiquity and intellect, it is important to remember that though Holden claims he will dance for eternity (335), McCarthy does not present this analogy in the manner of an allegory. Holden is, rather, literally "a man intoxicated" by his own intelligence, one who "believes his own thoughts are legal decisions" (Valéry, "The Yalu" 373).

Toward the Death of the Kid

In sum, McCarthy provides at least ten "signals" in *Blood Meridian* to suggest that Holden kills the kid as the result of something aside from the mad caprice of the tarot card the Fool. McCarthy's historical source for both his Holden character and for a kid character analogue, Chamberlain's *My Confession*, displays a murderous tension between the men. McCarthy associates his kid with the four of cups, a card perceived to represent dissatisfaction or an ambivalence, and thereby supports Holden's charge that the kid had withheld himself in part from the gang. Other markers also point to a division in the kid's makeup. McCarthy's designation of the kid's family as unsuccessful deceivers, "hewers of wood and drawers of water" (3), is such a clue (Deuteronomy 29:11, Joshua 9). Elements of factionalism are associated with both the "Young Blasarius" name Holden calls the kid, and with the line McCarthy includes as an echo of Thomas Mann's *Tonio Kröger* (see "Languages" in Chapter 4). In astrological terms, the kid's birth during the Leonids of 1833 inclines the kid to violence, yet with some inherent kindness.

Leo, which contributes the generous and kind elements to the kid's character, is a sun sign, and since McCarthy identifies Holden's skull as a "lunar dome," still another signal of the novel's distinctions between the kid and the judge becomes apparent. The epigraph by Jacob Boehme marks a distinction between wrath and gentleness, which is, again, a relevant signal. McCarthy's use of Valéry marks Holden's intellect as signalling a self-assurance not necessarily defined only as madness, and so identifies an element of pride in Holden's character that may have contributed to the kid's death. *Blood Meridian's* analogues to Faust legends recast the kid's death, in Christian tradition and in law, as the completion of Glanton's "terrible covenant," imparting a sense of closure to the book.

McCarthy remains true to the historical sources of his novel while reorganizing the material, unwinding threads in its maze, into the world of historical romance. In Holden, McCarthy makes a fine distinction between historical authenticity, a mortal Holden, and the wildness, the romance, the immortality of the evil that is apparent in his fictional character. The novelist has, after all, used references to historical people and situations—Van Diemen's Land, Sloat, the Anasazi—to involve the world beyond *Blood Meridian's* temporal and geographic limits. As the Aztecs fell to the Spaniards' guns, so too the buffalo, and hence the Native Americans, fell to the white hunters' guns. One senses a powerful universality in the novel. A deepened sense of diabolical ubiquity in the magnificent yet monstrous Judge Holden could not be more appropriate.

CHAPTER 7

Knitting the Winds

Arguments, Title, and Book

McCarthy calls his book *Blood Meridian*. Imagine him reading *The Scalp-Hunters*, in whose first paragraph Mayne Reid writes "beyond many a far meridian." Consider that in 1845 the commander at Presidio del Norte used "two imaginary longitudinal lines," or meridians—for Ralph Smith, a "Bloody Corridor"—to define "the area of greatest Comanche and Kiowa activities" ("Comanche Invasion" 8). Holden says man's "spirit is exhausted at the peak of its achievement. His meridian is at once his darkening and the evening of his day" (146–147), and so meridians become metaphor.

And it is within such a metaphor that the gang finds Holden "about the meridian of that day" when they run out of gunpowder (125). Glanton and his gang are then in their morning balance. When Glanton later meets Mangas Colorado, he marks Glanton's morning: "Buenos dias, he said. De dónde viene?" (Good morning . . . Where are you from?) (229; see also 232). Inversely, Caballo en Pelo meets Glanton later in the day: "Buenas tardes, he said. De dónde viene?" (Good afternoon . . . Where are you from?) (255). Their contact is in Glanton's postmeridian turn of the wheel.

Blood is in the "barbarous" of "not again in all the world's turning will there be terrains so wild and barbarous to try whether the stuff of creation may be shaped to man's will" (4–5). Late, in Holden's words to the man (formerly the kid) in the Griffin saloon that begin "As war becomes dishonored" (331), there is a stepping back, a westward-travelling warrior world diminished: in the saloon scene, army coats on dancing whores lose military grandeur, the hurdy-gurdy dancing bear, shot without consequence, dies the cheapest death. Only Holden dances undiminished.

The Evening Redness in the West, McCarthy's title ends. The allusions here are intricate. The "red" in the subtitle can, according to the *Oxford English Dictionary*, refer to "North American Indians," or something "golden, made of gold" (which, the *OED* notes, is "now only *thieves' slang*"), or, probably best, something "having, or characterized by, the colour which appears at the lower or least refracted end of the spectrum, and is familiar in nature as that of blood, fire." McCarthy quotes Jacob Boehme on "the life of darkness," but in a mandala Boehme drew, "red leads to the region of fire and the 'abyss of darkness,' which forms [its] periphery" (Jung, *Archetypes* 313). The epigraph's blood pulse in time (from Valéry) is absolutely present in the title.

Spring festivals marking death and rebirth cycles are common. Simply, at equinox, spring and fall, the sun sets directly west: Easter, the first Sunday after the first full moon after the vernal equinox, occurs just before the gang's fall at the Yuma-ferry massacre (262), marking a momentary rise of the Yumas. As the man enters Fort Griffin and dies there in "late winter," McCarthy has marked it, too, as the close of a cycle (316). The sun, again, is setting directly west.

By the late twentieth century, talk of "the winning of the West" brought more catcalls than applause. McCarthy was a hundred years too late to be the novel's kid, but accept that McCarthy saw twentieth-century patterns in his nineteenth-century novel's development: he was twelve years old when World War II ended, in 1945, and thirty years later he saw the withdrawal of U.S. troops from Vietnam. Ten years later came *Blood Meridian*, with its sixteen-year-old kid and its twenty-eight-year interval between the Glanton gang's "meridian" of bloodiness and the judge talking at Fort Griffin of war "dishonored and its nobility called into question" (331). One of the judge's postulates is that "The *evening's progress* will not appear strange or unusual even to those who question the rightness of the events so ordered" (329; my emphasis). The day's movement into night, the westward movement of the novel—even the epilogue's "man progressing over the plain"—are all present in the opening of this sentence. And when this sentence is read as "The evening's progress will not appear strange or unusual *even to those who question the rightness* of the events so ordered" (329; my emphasis), rightness, ethics, the golden rule, none matters: "It makes no difference what men think of war, said the judge. War endures. As well ask men what they think of stone" (248). Stone "perseveres" and "in strength," as do Jachim and Boaz on the "one true" tarot card. In Holden, war is necessary and satisfying.

History

When the gang leaves a fire at which they had roasted a deer, McCarthy's scene stands as metaphor for his presentation of history in *Blood Meridian*:

and as they rode up into the mountains this fire seemed to become altered of its location, now here, now there, drawing away, or shifting unaccountably along the flank of their movement. Like some ignis fatuus belated upon the road behind them which all could see and of which none spoke. For this will to deceive that is in things luminous may manifest itself likewise in retrospect and so by sleight of some fixed part of a journey already accomplished may also post men to fraudulent destinies. (120)[1]

The fire is a true fire—sticks, sparks, flame, ash—and its "shifting" arises only from each

---

1. Remarkably, the *OED* on "false" lists together "coins," "prophetess," "fire," and in *Blood Meridian* are "false coins" (246; cf. "false moneyer," 310), "false prophetess" (94), and "false fires" (148).

new movement as the gang rides away. Davy Brown's satchel of coins on the merchant's counter, "doubloons minted in Spain . . . in Guadalajara and half doubloons . . . gold dollars . . . tiny half gold dollars . . . French coins . . . gold eagles . . . half eagles . . . ring dollars and dollars minted in North Carolina and Georgia that were twenty-two carats pure" (264), presents an inventory of the powerful in North America's past and then current cultures. Those coins seem remarkably stable against the novel's questions of "shifting" pasts.

History is in Holden's declaration that "the order in creation which you see is that which you have put there, like a string in a maze" (245), an image derived from the Cretan Minotaur maze, and one appropriate for this book, with its harness-maker story that sets straight the past: Theseus's string or thread is not used to find the Minotaur; the Minotaur has no trouble finding Theseus and Ariadne. The deepest meaning of the string is that it marks their true path into what had been their past.[2]

In Los Angeles in 1850, Marcus L. Webster signs William Carr's deposition, about the ferry massacre, but when the novel's Webster declines a portrait drawn by Holden (140–141), he steps out of one pathway: history then does not have his physical likeness. Some of him is lost. The judge does sketch into his book a tapadero (140), an old Spanish saddle footpiece: he crushes it with as little concern as—through the historical novelist Cormac McCarthy—he will later crush the adult kid.

In Chamberlain, twenty Mexicans are murdered—some, probably all, scalped—by American volunteers: "*No one was punished* for this outrage": the volunteer Arkansas cavalry responsible for the murders are reprimanded "*but nothing more*" (88). American "officers became disgusted with the many revolting acts committed by volunteers and Rangers, and *no reports* were ever made" (177). Atrocity after atrocity goes unreported: of Mexican "Yankedos" women "tortured to death . . . *no notice* was taken of it by General Lombardini, or any one else among the Mexican authorities" (238). "Revenge" by Americans and Salteadores that "gained no honor" produced "total casualties . . . greater than in many battles fought during the war—yet *no report* of them was ever printed" (218) [all my emphases]. In *Blood Meridian*, questions regarding witnesses (153, 237, 267), unguessable causes of death (111, 153), and the impermanence of most human structures (146) all become questions central interests.

McCarthy's book is, for all its ten thousand details, also truly present in Holden's

---

2. At a literal level, a maze is "a structure . . . in bewildering complexity, so that without guidance it is difficult to find one's way in it" (*OED*). But since a maze is also "a delusive fancy" and "a trick, deception," there comes a sense of a layered approach to meaning in *Blood Meridian*, of coin tricks (192, 245–246), of unexplainable deaths (111, 174), of its conscious sense of history as really a world of spinning delusion (245). The harness maker's wife is "amazed" at the traveler's words and manner (144). In yet another direction, the *OED* also gives for "maze" "a winding movement, esp. in a dance," suggesting the judge's greatest dance, which he says is war.

"Not that we have all the details" (306), as when, confoundingly, Holden says to the jailed kid, "Don't you know [Glanton would] have killed you?" (307), a remark for which all readers must be unprepared. This moment could have come from the narrator's "burning centroids of murder" in Glanton's eyes when he looks at the kid "as if he were no part of them" in the desert after the rest of the gang has been hounded for days (218). Did the kid tell them that he had not killed Shelby? Did the kid feel guilty he had not been with the gang to help? What did Glanton ask, the kid volunteer? Where is the scene? But look at Chamberlain's meeting with Holden in the desert west of the Yuma massacre: after a significant while with Tobin, Hitchcock, Webster, and Chamberlain, Holden races away from them on Chamberlain's horse and declares, "You cursed robbers and murderers, I go to denounce you in the settlements. You will hang in California" (293). What is absent here in Chamberlain is also missing in *Blood Meridian*. Scenes in which what had been said are not provided.[3]

When the four Chamberlain survivors met Holden after the massacre, they must have talked of what they had seen, of the circumstances of their escapes, something, anything: but nothing is in Chamberlain except Holden's response to what conversations had taken place. Holden calls them "robbers," perhaps of gang property, and "murderers," perhaps for not having been present for defense. Indeed, Chamberlain writes that he felt some guilt for his absence (290). But Chamberlain's storytelling has stumbled, and there is no commiseration scene.[4]

Too, look at Chamberlain's lottery of arrows: Glanton argues to the gang that "*mercy*," "our safety," and "the laws of the desert sanction" killing their mortally wounded fellows (280; original emphasis). When someone is injured and unable to flee or hide, and when the next person along cannot mend you and probably will torture you, swift death is a mercy. Chamberlain makes this point several times (87, 173–174, 238). But in *Blood Meridian*, Glanton presents no such lottery argument. He prepares the quiver with four tasseled arrows in palpable silence (205–206). What is true is that the group has at some earlier time already participated in this ritual: they know the argument.

At novel's end, Davy Brown's string of ears that the man wears is a last physical stamp of the gang's existence, and Elrod does not believe the man's story about them (321). "History" had already lost track of the kid. Was it that, in a sense, the sound of the shot that killed Elrod was heard by the judge—Holden is in the next scene, after many years away from the kid— or that Elrod's scoffing words are heard by Holden, and so become a signal that his presence in Griffin is appropriate, the man a selvage to be turned under? Yes, yes, there is a personal Faust pattern overlain, but one of *Blood Meridian*'s strong concerns is history.

---

3. Even the "unexpurgated" Goetzmann edition of *My Confession* has no such scene (329).

4. Or passages were cut from Chamberlain for the 1956 edition, but the point, that as of 1985 a scene is missing, remains.

Glanton

For as little as he says in the novel, when Glanton declares, "I can man anything that eats" (149), his words can echo Holden's "order . . . is . . . like a string in a maze" (245). Indeed, some of the novel's ordering is in a layering of allusions unexpected in prose and not much noted in McCarthy.[5]

Oddly, McCarthy uses "string" and not the usual word "thread." "String" in the *OED* is a "line, cord, thread," and seems an end in literalness. But "strings" can be "stringed instruments; now only, such as are played with a bow," perhaps touching on McCarthy's great judge fiddling (123, 335). And "string" is also a "cord for actuating a puppet": the woman card reader is a "mannequin raised awake by a string" (94); a wolf is "hung like a marionette from the moon" (117); Cloyce Bell holds the imbecile James Robert Bell on a "braided horsehair rope" (252), and Holden has him on a "leather lead" (297). "String" is also a "cord for binding or attaching anything," and is allusively present when Captain White's command, "Tethered to the polestar . . . rode the Dipper round" (46). But more importantly, "binding or attaching" is central to Glanton's "man anything."

Still, the next likely item, "harnessmaker"—another of McCarthy's nonce contributions—doesn't go anywhere in the *OED*. So, trying "harness": the first definition is, generally, "tackle, gear, furniture, armament," "the mechanism by which a large bell is rung"; other than Holden with James Robert Bell on a leash, this seems a cold trail. But the second *OED* definition, "the defensive body armor of a man-at-arms or foot-soldier, all the defensive equipment of an armed horseman, for both man and horse; military equipment or accoutrement," is on point for *Blood Meridian*, which is full of armed horsemen and leather equipment (78, 159, 232).

Holden's harnessmaker story (142–145) seems a twist on *The Orchard Keeper's* John Wesley Rattner, who never knew the truth of his father's meanness but doesn't reflect much on its central character's "harnessmaker" vocation. Somewhere between this harnessmaker story and Glanton's "man anything" scene is psychologist Erich Neumann's thought that "Anything situated lower down than the heart belongs to the realm of instinct. The liver and the kidneys are visceral centers of great importance for psychic life. 'God trieth the heart and reins' [Psalms 7:9] of the man whose conscious and unconscious are to be searched" (26). Roback's illustration of the human body, noted in Chapter 3 as linking the kid to "secrets," also has a zodiacal constellation pointing to the kidneys as

5. McCarthy's "like strings . . . through the eye of a ring" (84) can echo the initial confrontation between Toadvine and the kid on a narrow walk in Nacogdoches (9), and also the intersection of the lives of the gang members: "although each man . . . was discrete . . . conjoined they made a thing that had not been before" (152). Too, "string" can be "a chain or cord for carrying a watch," perhaps in some relation to the judge who checks his time (309) when visiting the kid, jailed in San Diego. Something may even be done with the rarely used "string" as "the 'thread', sequence (of a narrative)." And what of the *OED* on "string" as "a line of fencing," which could occur toward the novel's epilogue?

"reins." And the *OED* gives "reins" as "kidneys" and "the seat of affections." At this point allusions become absorbing. Now the harnessmaking father can be the focus of the son's affections, affections so strong they can lead the son over into the father's world as a "killer of men" (*Blood Meridian* 145).

"Hunger and food are the prime movers of mankind," writes Neumann (27). Glanton not only wins over the vicious Indian dog in his "man anything" scene (149), but also, to the scoffs of those lost at Santa Rita, has made a "pet" of his horse (117). Additionally, in an echo of Glanton's "man anything," one *OED* definition of "man" as a noun is "manna," the foodstuff, and as a verb, "to be the master of; manage, rule." For Glanton to "man" a man means to "invest [that one] with manly qualities or aspect; to make man-like," which echoes Holden's words on war as the greatest of man's dances. Too, the suggestive "to provide (a person) with followers or attendants" as a meaning of the verb "man" can mark that Glanton brings men, as discussed below, to Holden's truer lead. Still, "wickedness" is an *OED* aspect of this same allusion, and Boehme's epigraph has it in the "life of darkness." Glanton survives in the Southwest because he keeps his gang fed with scalps and gold, has their affections—their "reins"—and so their commitment.

For a moment, consider that in McCarthy's earlier *Outer Dark* a householder can "let fall the reins," physical reins, getting his horse to "Come up" and go (66, cf. 40). In his later *The Crossing*, Billy Parham handles literal reins (31, 49, 136). Chamberlain writes he dropped his horse Lucifer's reins and fired at attacking Mexicans over his horse's head. His companion's horse shied, but Sam's "stood like a rock" (207). Glanton would "fire between the actual ears of his horse" (156) without it shying. But given the astrological elements in *Blood Meridian*, "reins" as "affections" can color "The Delaware let drop the reins" as he went to club his fellows dead (206), the allusion here marking a moment's remove of affections. John Glanton is depicted in such a scene, dismounting his horse to coldly kill an old Indian woman. Perhaps he gets off a horse that might shy at a gunshot. Walking, he "crossed in front of his horse, passing the reins behind his back" (98). McCarthy, who tracks these things, does not have Glanton's horse shy. After the murder, Glanton "took up the trailing reins" (99), possibly a subtle marker of his return to humanity. Indeed, in *Blood Meridian* there are "trailing reins" to Grannyrat's horse (112) and "trailing straps" to the diligence (112), signalling literally to the gang—allusively to the reader—the deaths of these horses' human masters.

Do other items in the novel fit this scheme? What of both Glanton's dog and Lincoln's dog being tied to their corpses—by strings, ropes, "thongs," tethers, it hardly matters which—and tossed as man-dog pairs onto the Yumas' crematory fire in "suttee" (275)?[6]

---

6. Late in the book: "The arc of circling bodies is determined by the length of their tether, said the judge. Moons, coins, men" (245–246). The *OED* on "tether" gives the literal "a rope or cord that ties an animal to a fixed spot," but given the novel's "string" and "reins," this definition of "tether" becomes resonant, and may well increase its resonance, since a tether is also "a rope for hanging malefactors," a def-

What of Green's tent as it settles, "trailing . . . ratty guyropes over the ground" (7)? Aren't these ratty ropes broken strings, broken affections, his congregation's "trailing reins"?

Glanton is a harness maker, has the reins, controls the affections. Look at when Chamberlain first sees Glanton: his "costume was that of a Mexican herdman, made of leather" (39). Glanton's "man anything that eats," like Chamberlain's "herdman" shepherding the gang, is a dark thought indeed. This is the tether, "Moons, coins, men" (246), that the judge describes. Factor in the otherwise throwaway scene in which Tobin remarks to the kid, "you've the knack," on the kid's dexterity "mending a strap" (122), and such familiarity may well, in this whirlwind of meanings, allude to a recognition leading the judge to declare to the kid, "I'd have loved you as a son" (306; cf. 327). Now the kid is part of the reader's juggling of scenes. And most remarkably, Chamberlain, after riding with the gang, after voting against a massacre of the Pimas, and after the Yuma atrocities, yet wrote in his years-later pen-to-paper *My Confession* of that first night in San Antonio, when he saw Glanton murder a Ranger, "somehow I felt a sort of admiration" for him (40).

Kid

The kid keeps his mouth shut in the novel. Maybe he is young and just keeps quiet. Still, he provokes the first slayings of Mexicans (178–180). Maybe he is a gang member, and the book reflects his participation over his individuation: "conjoined [the men of the gang] made a thing that had not been before" (152). Despite his original "taste for mindless violence," outside Fort Griffin the man asks the boys, "You all like meanness?" and they say that they don't (319). Elrod scoffs at the man's plain story of the string of Indian ears Brown had worn. "The man looked up [at Elrod] wearily" (321) and told the other youths to keep Elrod at a distance: "I see him back here I'll kill him" (322). Killing Elrod ought to have, in *Blood Meridian*, charged the man with surplus energy (54, 157), yet the whore says, "You cant lay there" (332). Where is his regeneration? In the end, the judge "scappled" him away (173), having judged his man-possibility ended.[7] His name had become lost, his face certainly no face for a coin.

---

inition in great harmony with the "string" of "string-up," and certainly suggestive, since the verb "string" can mean "to hang, kill by hanging. Usually with *up*:" "the hanged-men at their rope-ends," McCarthy writes of Toadvine and Davy Brown (311). The parricide (5) is strung up, hanged, though this image's stronger sense, as "the man's friends run forward and pull his legs," is as a foreshadowing of Glanton and his gang members mercifully shortening their friends' sufferings in the arows-lottery.

7. The kid's desertion in "the spring of his twenty-eighth year" from the wagon train headed east would have headed him away from the Civil War (313). Perhaps the kid's Tennessee origin would have claimed him as Confederate, and yet his gang association with black John Jackson could have made the South's slightly veiled desire to retain black slaveholding disagreeable to him. True, the kid might simply have desired life in the West over that of the East. But here he is "no partisan" (299) of war, and this single fact can reduce the man in the judge's eyes.

Holden kills an Apache boy with whom the gang had played, and Toadvine doesn't shoot him (164). Holden later declares, "The straight and the winding way are one" (330): Toadvine recognizes the boy was always early-doomed.[8] Similarly, the man says to the dead Elrod, "You wouldn't have lived anyway" (322). Running counter to this fatalistic argument, the kid is noticeably helpful, beginning probably with his work at the "diptheria pesthouse" (5), certainly by removing the arrow from David Brown's leg (162), then when pulling the condemned Shelby under a bush as he had asked (208), and even when holding a horse that Holden will kill for food (219). Otherwise, at most "someone" from the gang "hazed forward the last spare horse" after Miller's was killed by a bull (224), and Holden and two Delawares go back to Jesús María for Black John Jackson after a gun battle and escape (196).

In the record, when Sam Chamberlain and a fellow soldier are attacked by Mexicans and the other cannot flee—and the fellow says, "Save yourself"—Sam stays and helps him survive (207). Chamberlain's quick thinking and expert marksmanship save them both. Three times in *Blood Meridian* the kid puts himself at risk to help men in danger— Sproule (63), Tate (210), Tobin (295), who say "Go on"—in essence, "Save yourself." But the kid stays on, doing what he can. Only Toadvine, the kid's longest-standing acquaintance in the book, displays such helpfulness, when he will not "go on" and leave the wounded kid in the desert west of the massacre (278).[9]

What opens the kid and the novel up, though, is in what Chamberlain writes after he kills an Indian on his way to join Glanton's gang. He had already killed many Mexicans in battle and for revenge, but always with claims of righteousness; here he is different: "We moved on in silence for somehow my agency in the death of the warrior affected me greatly; I felt as if I had committed a murder. Conscience said, You were safe, he never harmed you, and he was on his own soil, yet you killed him" (264). What of Chamberlain's guilt is represented in McCarthy's novel? In a historical novel in the strictest sense, what is interior in Sam Chamberlain is out of bounds for McCarthy. Chamberlain's comment that "the dying Indian troubled me in my dreams" (265) becomes Holden troubling the kid in dreams (309) and becomes exterior as the kid's "helpfulness."

Holden wants to "denounce" Chamberlain after the massacre, since Sam had been all but riding west to quit the gang the morning of the Yuma massacre. Indeed, Sam felt survivor's guilt: "We rode [away] somehow feeling sad and blaming ourselves for deserting in the hour of danger and death" (290). Conjecturally, Sam's presence might have made a difference, and perhaps this is what his Holden addresses. But in *Blood Meridian*, the kid is not literally a deserter from the Yumas' attack.

---

8. McCarthy returns to this thought in *No Country for Old Men* when Carson Wells says to Chigurh—since their path cannot then divide—"Just do it" (177).

9. A "hardlooking" "tavernkeeper's wife" tends the kid in New Orleans after he has been shot twice, and he does not pay her (4).

As previously discussed, a Faustian commitment in *Blood Meridian* makes sense: the legal term "Et de ceo se mettent en le pays" (74), which includes Toadvine, Grannyrat, and the kid in Toadvine's "guaranteed hand" assertion (79), and the judge's "spoke for your group" to Toadvine (104), can give Holden jurisdiction, the right, to judge all three. But a legal discussion on "guarantee" and "agency" turns away from this link of Toadvine's words to the man's death. In Chamberlain, enlisted men and officers all seem to swear the ordinary "By God," "Go to h——l" and the like. Still, Chamberlain writes that he "firmly pledged" he would protect wounded men after having witnessed Glanton's historical lottery of arrows (282). Chamberlain further writes that Glanton "swore he would assault" a Pima village (285). But when Chamberlain writes that he "would have sworn" he saw enemy eyes peering back as he was on night guard duty, since his replacement had been knifed and killed (181) under these circumstances, his "would have sworn" has the gravity of a hand-to-book deposition. And without reserve, when Chamberlain writes, "All believed in the legend [of El Dorado, "city of gold"], and all swore to follow Glanton to the death," Chamberlain's "all swore" is a most solemn commitment by voice vote of faith in Glanton's desire, determination, leadership (274–275).

So posit the lawyer's son Cormac McCarthy reading Chamberlain: *Blood Meridian*'s judge Holden could well be the principal behind Chamberlain's "agency," which is technically the claim that Sam had acted to further another's—for the narrator, Holden's—interests. But *Blood Meridian* presents no such commitment scene at the Chihuahua prison. What McCarthy has are questions rising out of Grannyrat's death, the man's death. Indeed, what quid pro quo "guarantee" could these only-the-clothes-on-their-backs prisoners have made? They pledged their lives. When Toadvine later says Grannyrat (Chambers) "appears to of spoke for hisself" in answer to Holden's "it was my understanding that you spoke for your group," their conversation balances these questions of agency, freedom, and commitment (104). In this exchange, Toadvine's guarantee is not contended, but agency is. Grannyrat reneged on his commitment, on the guarantee, and so the "outfit" (79) Glanton provided him comes back to the gang (112; see also 286: "Where's your outfits?"). Is Grannyrat dead? Probably, but no reader really knows. Charlie Brown leaves the gang at Tucson (242) and has no trouble from the others. Apparently, his commitment had been satisfactory. Too, when Holden talks to Toadvine, the kid, and Tobin in the desert west of the massacre, and Tobin declares, among other things, "The lad is a free agent," Holden says, "Quite so" (284): the judge does not contend the remark. Toadvine's "guarantee" seems ended, a Faustian contractual overlay resolved.

Holden

To Glanton, Holden was no superman. Glanton alone did not piss into the gunpowder batter (132), told Holden to get a horse "if you aim to ride with us" (160), would not wager Holden could lift above his head and carry Pacheco's meteorite ten feet (240).

Only in a perfection of one aspect of humanity—judgment—does Holden's character transform the novel into a historical romance.

Judgment on the "heathen" had been rendered. Words like "mercy" or "compassion" are not the judge's challenge to the kid: the legal term for overturning a judgment, "clemency," is used (299), and this clemency was an affront to Judge Holden as a "principal" in this romance, to the kid's agency, to Glanton's "claimed agency" (243). The kid becomes an everyman, the judge an emblem of the ultimately winnowing power of judgments.

As Chamberlain writes of fights with other soldiers, "science" and "judgement" seem tied in his mind. Chamberlain had watched Glanton slit the throat of a "reckless" Ranger (39), and within a few pages, Chamberlain cuts his friend Scotty with a nine-inch Bowie knife "for his want of judgement" (41). He writes of army-camp bully Crane as having "some science" (147) when commenting on Crane's hand-to-hand fighting skills. In fact, Chamberlain kills Crane. Chamberlain fights and injures but does not kill fellow soldier Gorman, who has a "want of judgement" (152). Holden sees in the Yuma chiefs that "things are seldom what they seem" (255) and acts as a counterpoint to Glanton's "party," who were "hard put to keep their composure" (254). How appropriate that Glanton dies in bed—violently, but in bed—as if asleep too long, and Holden confronts the Yuma attackers with an overwhelmingly ready cannon (274–275).

Recognize that Holden's ledgers, notebooks, and insatiable desire to know all, to control all—even to killing in the name of collecting (198)—all this leather-bound writing—makes him a double of any number of nineteenth-century explorers. John James Audubon, for example, shot, killed, and stuffed the birds he painted for his famous book. Holden is also kin to the historical novelist McCarthy: what he doesn't include doesn't survive: "nothing . . . permitted to occur . . . save by my dispensation" (199). Indeed, this novel is a portrait of Holden as an artist working in the wildest mixed medium of all—the world—working with a nudge here, a pistol shot there.

Where stand the coldforger and his faces on trial? Does everyone have a coin image, and from this world of possibilities does the judge decide? Where stands the world? Consider that when the judge takes on Bell the imbecile as his follower, from parallels of Reverend Green and his followers, McCarthy creates a saddening, chilling double of the idiotic world mass following leaders they can not possibly comprehend. So does the fool lead and Holden follow, or does Holden lead, in the desert after the massacre? The answer may structurally stand in relation to the coldforger scene: the fool before is masses leading, the judge choosing "faces" from their tide; with the fool after, and Holden leads has more power. In fact, the idiot struggles to keep the judge's pace (282) and is later on a lead line ahead of the judge (297): here, nothing is fixed.

Holden calls, "All dead save me" (134) in Tobin's gunpowder story. By book's end it has come true. All the gang is dead. The novel is a tragedy. Holden survives. To the novel's narrative voice—and probably here, honestly, it is McCarthy's—Holden is a "vast abhorrence" (243): "vast" out of the Latin "*vastus* void, of immense size, extent," but as a verb, meaning "to lay waste, destroy"; an "abhorrence" is "a horror to cause trembling" (*OED*). In war, "there will be one there always," Holden says of himself, "who is a true dancer" (331), and war is his immense horror and waste. The narrative voice says, "he is a great favorite," twice affirms, "He never sleeps" (335), and yet this voice twice retreats to Holden's assertion, "He says that he will never die" (335).

CHAPTER 8

Why Believe the Judge?

In the Fort Griffin saloon, Holden completes a thought he'd begun nearly thirty years earlier, "Before man was, war waited for him" (248), when he says, "And yet there will be one there always who is a true dancer and can you guess who that might be?" The man doesn't answer the riddle, doesn't believe in Holden, says to him, "You aint nothin" (331). In the most powerful reading of their last confrontation, the judge tore every bone from the man's fleshly body and broke them all, broke them small, made a gory heap of that human being on an outhouse floor. "He never sleeps. He says that he will never die" (335): in lunatic madness an egotistical murderer, this is the judge.

West of the Yuma massacre, the novel's Irish ex-priest Tobin can hear Holden—the novelist's most worldly and most gifted character—orating unseen, and says to the kid, "Stop your ears" to his words (293). "He aint nothing," the kid says, "made of the dust of the earth" (297). Yet at once Tobin falls back to the more freighted and more frightening "Face him down then," shoot him, kill him, "face him down if he is so." The moment passes, and the kid's fate is sealed.

Holden's been with McCarthy forever. *The Orchard Keeper*'s adjectives "fat and bald and sinister," describing the government tank, begin it (93). Legwater's threat to John Wesley Rattner, "[when we] got the rest of the evidence" (160), has an echo in Holden's "Not that we have all the details," spoken to the jailed kid (306). *Outer Dark*'s storeowner Clark, immense in a white suit and styled as "the law," is an ancestor (139–141), and when Rinthy judges the tinker who judges Rinthy (192), and when Culla judges himself guilty of trespass (202), and while being told, "I'll be the judge of that" by the leader of the small killer gang (234), there are thematic echoes.

Close it. Put it back on the shelf. It's a book. It is entertainment of a fairly high order, but it's just a book. Read a different one. What is this Holden that the genius in Cormac McCarthy respects as "the vast abhorrence of the judge" (243)? Is Holden to be believed? I side with Tobin. Kill him if you can, if he can be killed.

Holden's claims, flatly, are true. He was waiting with his demand for judgment even before there was man, and he will outlive us. Holden comes out of the archetypes. Treated as if sources, Erich Neumann's *Origins and History of Consciousness*, a brief look at the works of his mentor and fellow archetypist and depth psychologist Carl Jung, and one book by Gaston Bachelard open the reader's appreciation of the novel far beyond what comes from historical sources, tarot-card items, the Faust legend. For all the academic distancing in those works, a sense of *Blood Meridian* is not distant when Jung writes: "Life is a battleground. It always has been, and always will be; and if it were not so, existence would come to an end" ("Approaching" 75). The novel is close at hand when Neumann writes: "The womb of the earth clamors for fertilization, and blood sacrifices and corpses are the food she likes best" (54). "Consensus" was the standard used above for assessing tarot items, and is used here for these writers' arguments, which are, finally, that we as human mammals all share a few first responses to the world.

The Archetypes Speak

In the archetypes, at the beginning there is no distinction among things, only a roundness, "the egg, the philosophical World Egg," in which "there is no before and no after, no time; and there is no above and no below, no space" (Neumann 8). Such is the oneness that the "World Parents" are one: "The round is the calabash containing the World Parents. In Egypt as in New Zealand, in Greece as in Africa and India, the World Parents, heaven and earth, lie one on top of the other in the round, spacelessly and timelessly united, for as yet nothing has come between them to create duality out of the original unity" (Neumann 9). In some way forced apart, the world father on his hands and feet overarches the world mother, he the sky and she the earth. Distinctions of time, space, and color arrive "with the coming of light, of consciousness" arising out of this division of, this first distinction between the world parents (Neumann 8). With this separation also comes division into dualities: attributes of the parents begin to arise: for the mother, the earth, darkness, fertility, unconsciousness; for the father, the heavens, light, judgment, consciousness. Judge Holden's size and strength, his lightness in dancing, and his whiteness, as glimpsed at the Chihuahua baths, are here. In fact, one of Holden's most striking strengths is not far from the World Father's masculine elements; Neumann writes of the "male collective [as] the source of all the taboos, laws, and institutions" standing in opposition to the Great Mother (147): Holden is crushingly powerful at law.

Neumann attends to questions of masculine consciousness in an item as if written after a reading of *Blood Meridian*:

The correlation of consciousness with masculinity culminates in the development of science, as an attempt by the masculine spirit to emancipate itself from the power of the unconscious. Wherever science appears it breaks up the original character of the world, which was filled with unconscious projections. Thus, stripped of projection, the world becomes objective, a scientific construction of the mind. (341)

Jung writes of "our fondly believed-in world [as] a phantasmagoria of shifting scenes" (*Al-*

chemical 238). The novel's Holden is very tough: "the order in creation which you see is that which you have put there:"

The truth about the world, he said, is that anything is possible. Had you not seen it all from birth and thereby bled it of its strangeness it would appear to you for what it is, a hat trick in a medicine show, a fevered dream, a trance bepopulate with chimeras having neither analogue nor precedent, an itinerant carnival, a migratory tentshow whose ultimate destination after many a pitch in many a mudded field is unspeakable and calamitous beyond reckoning. (245)

Reverend Green's tent show collapsing in a muddy field (7) is in these sentences, as are the novel's coin tricks (245–246), the itinerant gypsy carnival with Jackson on the bill (99), and James Robert Bell as a sideshow idiot (233). The judge's scientific consciousness abhors projections. McCarthy writes of Green's tent as a "medusa" as it drops: an invertebrate sea creature literally billowing, yes, but also the old Medusa who transfixes to stone: the revival audience members are anchorites whom Holden disabuses of their folly with a lie they act on. Is this scientific violence that destroys faith and mystery the "vast abhorrence" of the judge?

The archetypal Great Father's characteristics can be found in the novel, and the Great Mother is without doubt the great whore dancing in the Fort Griffin saloon. In her immense size she is akin to Holden; in the whore's association with the dancing bear, she is the Great Mother whose constellation, Ursa Major, can be the great bear (Neumann 56–57); and since she is associated with the lion in other cultures, and the lion is the foundation animal for the griffin, she is at home in Fort Griffin (56). The calm of the Great Mother's unconsciousness is matched by the equal and terrible violence described by Neumann: "The earth must drink blood if she is to be fertile, and therefore libations of blood are offered up to increase her power. But the mistress of the blood zone is woman. She has the blood magic that makes life grow. Hence the same goddess is very often the mistress of fertility, of war, and of hunting" (55). Out of the Great Mother come "the instincts and archetypes that speak through the collective unconscious [that] represent the 'wisdom of the species' and its will" (284). "The fascination of sex and the drunken orgy culminating in unconsciousness and death are inextricably combined" in this great whore dancing among men and women randomly half clothed in army uniform parts (60).

Moving again to Judge Holden: Mephistopheles was a tongue-tied fool next to the brilliant Holden. Faust was the focus, the active one, there. McCarthy's Holden is out of yet another ancient lineage, that of alchemy:

Since alchemy actually originated in Egypt, it is not improbable that esoteric interpretations of the Osiris myth are among the foundations of the art. Osiris is one of the symbols for lead, and the transmutation of this into the solar gold of Ra is the principal object of the "great work." (Neumann 255–256)

Alchemy, particularly the psychology of alchemy, was one of Carl Jung's lifelong fascinations. In his work are explorations of the alchemical figure Mercurius. To define him, Jung writes: "In alchemical writings the word 'Mercurius' is used with a very wide range of meaning, to denote not only the chemical element mercury or quicksilver, Mercury (Hermes) the god, and Mercury the planet, but also—and primarily—the secret 'transforming substance' which is at the same time the 'spirit' indwelling in all living creatures" ("Introduction" 276). Jung notes in *Alchemical Studies* that the "alchemical Mercurius" can be of "cosmic size" and is known as "a youth of dazzling whiteness" (132).

Jung later notes that "Mercurius has the circular nature of the uroboros," the tail-eating snake that can represent the World Egg before the separation of the World Parents (233). Neumann, too, writes that "the uroboros reigns on as the great whirling wheel of life" (16), existing before any history, akin to the tarot's Wheel of Fortune card, alike with the Great Mother and the Father. Neumann provides another link to alchemy, again in an image of roundness: "This primordial image of the autarchic uroboros underlies the homunculus of alchemy, who is begotten in the round—the retort—by rotation of the elements, and it even underlies the *perpetuum mobile* of physics" (33–34). This is not the Christian devil Mephistopheles. Jung is absolute on Mercurius as other:

> To the Christian mentality, the dark antagonist is always the devil. As I have shown, Mercurius escapes this prejudice by only a hair's breadth. But he escapes it, thanks to the fact that he scorns to carry on opposition at all costs. The magic of his name enables him, in spite of his ambiguity and duplicity, to keep outside the split [between Christ and the devil], for as an ancient pagan god he possesses a natural undividedness which is impervious to logical and moral contradictions. (*Alchemical* 245; cf. 247–248)

And it is out of his alchemical relationship with the gold-dissolving element mercury, a silvery liquid metal, that Holden as Mercurius transcends his immense World Father "consciousness" relationship with the sun and becomes aligned with the moon: "Mercurius is an adumbration of the primordial light-bringer, who is never himself the light, but [one] who brings the light of nature, the light of the moon and the stars which fades before the new morning light" (248; cf. 136, 231). Still, this Mercurius is "found in the dung heaps" (232 and "in sewers" (220): Faust's end, the kid's end, echo here.

Holden was from nowhere, was sitting on the single rock in a desert flatness when Glanton's gang first laid eyes on him, on a rock now perhaps to be seen as an analogue of the alchemist's *lapis philosophorum*—the philosopher's stone—the gang out of gunpowder and desperate. Do they absolutely need Mephistopheles, since Mercurius's alchemical lead bullets can get gold coin? Neumann provides a resonance: "Originally, consciousness did not possess enough free libido to perform any activity—plowing, harvesting, hunting, waging war, etc.—of its own 'free will,' and was obliged to invoke the help of the god who 'understood' these things" (326). Holden "understood" and could "help" Glanton's gang when it was out of gunpowder. This Mercurius is in one sense a god, this Holden (Jung, *Alchemical* 245); yet he is in the novel the Judge Holden whose apparent affection—whose touch—makes men dead. He kills children he has befriended. His lunar mutability is central to the reader's hatred. Is this the argument for the judge's "vast abhorrence"?

What could the archetypists contribute toward Holden on war? Neumann writes: "Always the 'old system' hangs on until the opposing forces are strong enough to overcome it. Here, too, 'war is the father of all things'" (305), and yet this old phrase becomes a new thing in context of the Great Father's consciousness in Holden. Jung writes in *Alchemical Studies*:

In point of emotional intensity, which is a factor of decisive importance for the primitive consciousness, the most heterogeneous things—rain, storm, fire, the strength of the bull, and the passionate game of dice—can be identical. In emotional intensity, game and gambler coincide" (268).

In Holden's war metaphor of two men wagering their lives on the turn of a card (249), Jung's "game and gambler coincide," and McCarthy later works life-and-death coin flips into *No Country for Old Men* (55–58, 258–259).

But where is *Blood Meridian*'s scalping metaphor in this alchemy? Jung writes:

The head plays a considerable role in alchemy, and has done so since ancient times.
[T]he head had the meaning of the "omega element" or "round element," . . . a synonym for the arcane or transformative substance. (Alchemical 72)

Jung in his *Alchemical Studies* translates "The Vision of Zosimos," an old alchemical text, which reads: "And he drew off the skin of my head with the sword, which he wielded with strength, and mingled the bones with the pieces of flesh, and caused them to be burned upon the fire of the art, till I perceived by the transformation of the body that I had become spirit" (60; cf. 71). Here are the gang's scalping and their end on a funeral pyre. McCarthy's introductory quote from the *Yuma Daily Sun*, of evidence of scalping at a remove of 300,000 years, might also serve.

Conscious and Unconscious

The kid was born to his dying mother on the night of the great Leonid meteor shower of 1833. The archetypes contribute: "Since the stars have fallen from heaven and our highest symbols have paled, a secret life holds sway in the unconscious" (Jung, *Archetypes* 23). An infant is deep in the unconscious. In the kid's case, this unconsciousness is maintained, as McCarthy writes, in the youthful kid's "taste for mindless violence." Still, it is difficult to fathom the kid's early years, so little is told: an older sister, a father entirely self-absorbed. The kid who left home had none of Neumann's "sixteen years" of ordinary "learning and training," and "cultural education, consisting in the adoption of collective values" (398).

Here, in practical terms, an absent father, perhaps the kid's violence in Nacogdoches, and his search for a father figure all go to spark Holden's notice as the kid and Toadvine ride out of town. Another way of describing the kid's fruitless search for his father and mother is out of the psychology of archetypes: that not only are there a "personal" mother and father for a child, but also an archetypal "suprapersonal" mother and father: "Thus both the parental figures are there twice over for the hero, personally and transpersonally. Their confusion with one another, and particularly the projection of the transpersonal image of the personal parents, is an abiding source of problems in childhood" (Neumann 137). Without nurture from his biological mother and father, the kid was predisposed toward his archetypal Mother and Father: Holden says toward the end of the book, "Don't you know that I'd have loved you like a son?" (306). In fact, the psychology of this thought informs Holden's harnessmaker story, in which a son changes his life and becomes a killer after he learns that his father had secretly been a killer.

Only when the kid joins the gang does he enter a form of society, small and tough as it is. Neumann again writes a thought appearing to inform *Blood Meridian*:

The grotesque fact that murderers, brigands, gangsters, thieves, forgers, tyrants, and swindlers, in a guise that deceives nobody, have seized control of collective life is characteristic of our time. Their unscrupulousness and double-dealing are recognized—and admired. Their ruthless energy they obtain at best from some stray archetypal content that has got them in its power. The dynamism of a possessed personality is accordingly very great, because, in its one-track primitivity, it suffers from none of the differentiations that make men human. (391)

The gang's group dynamic submerges what little identity the kid brought to the moment:

This development becomes logically unavoidable the moment the individual combines with the mass and thus renders himself obsolete. Apart from the agglomeration of huge masses in which the individual disappears anyway, one of the chief factors responsible for psychological mass-mindedness is scientific rationalism, which robs the individual of his foundations and his dignity, (Jung, "Undiscovered" 355–356)

After the massacre of the gang, the kid in jail meets again with Holden, and dreams dreams with the judge as judge: "Many crises in our lives have a long unconscious history. We move toward them step by step, unaware of the dangers that are accumulating. But what we consciously fail to see is frequently perceived by our unconscious, which can pass the information on through dreams" (Jung, "Approaching" 36).

Only as years pass does the kid, now a man, seem again the work-for-wages person (sawmill, diphtheria pesthouse, riverboat) that he was before he fell in with the gang.

He now carries a Bible. He gives Elrod warning, does not kill him without cause, does not get satisfaction from it. The kid's birth in November links him, in Roback's illustration, to the lower portions of his body:

For primitive man and the child, with his overemphasized unconscious, the main accent falls on the visceral region and its dead weight of vegetative life. The "heart" is for him the highest center, representing what the thinking head means for us. For the Greeks, the midriff was the seat of consciousness, for the Indians and Hebrews, the heart. In both cases thinking is emotional, bound up with affects and passions. (Neumann 26)

Holden ends the man, and who really knows why? "There's a flawed place in the fabric of your heart," Holden says, among the many things he says; Holden's assertion is that the kid had in his "soul some corner of clemency for the heathen" (299). According to Roback, the kid's birth in November under Sagittarius does have the quality of "secrets."

But, then, Holden is a "consciousness" person, and the kid, and perhaps especially as the man who carries a Bible he cannot read, is of the unconscious type. What Holden may have seen as "mindless violence" in the kid might have been only "a taste," and a taste the kid outgrew: "It is still the case today that discrimination and differentiation mean more to the rationalistic intellect than wholeness through the union of opposites. That is why it is the unconscious which produces the symbols of wholeness" (Jung, *Alchemical* 336). If we dislike Holden for his consciousness judgments, perhaps the kid's unconscious "wholeness" makes him attractive: anyone embracing the New Testament thought "Judge not lest you be judged" can only find Holden abhorrent.

Much of the book's argument is laid in the early scene of the kid and the hermit (16–20): a man is "at odds to know his mind" and "he don't want to know" his heart (19). Jung writes in a strikingly apt passage: "[M]an must continue to resemble a hermit who knows . . . he has affinities with the anthropoids but . . . is extraordinarily different . . . in respect of his psyche. It is just in this most important characteristic of his species that he cannot know himself and therefore remains a mystery to himself" ("Undiscovered" 369). And these relationships of psyche to mind are expressed many times in Jung's work:

It is no use thinking we can ever get beyond the psyche by means of the "mind," even though the mind asserts that it is not dependent on the psyche. How could it prove that? We can say, if we like, that one statement comes from the psyche, is psychic and nothing but psychic, and that another comes from the mind, is 'spiritual' and therefore superior to the psychic one. Both are mere assertions based on the postulates of belief. (*Archetypes* 269)

In "Approaching the Unconscious," Jung writes: "Our intellect has created a new world that dominates nature, and has populated it with monstrous machines" (90), and "In spite of our proud domination of nature, we are still her victims, for we have not even learned to control our own nature" (91). The hermit's conversation with the kid is kindred to Neumann's assertion: "Only if a thought is a passion that grips the heart can it reach ego consciousness and be perceived; consciousness is only affected by the proximity of the idea to the archetype. But the heart is also the seat of ethical decision; it symbolizes the center of the personality, and, in the Egyptian Judgment of the Dead, it was weighed" (26).

What is finally central to the kid and the judge as antagonists is the human psychology of differing perceptions of the world. Jung's fundamental categories of type, extravert and introvert, fit Holden and the kid. But only Jung's further categories, including, among others, thinking, feeling, judging, the intuitive, rational, and irrational, suggest that Holden and the kid literally cannot see each other. Holden is a judging type—how can there be any question?—in this human psychology, and in Jung's framework, Holden's judgments can be both rational and irrational. What Holden does not allow is what is central to the hermit's words to the kid: that we are both mind and heart, are both conscious and unconscious. To deny unconsciousness and feeling is not to erase them, but to overlook them, to have them feed the irrational. It is Holden's irrationality that the other characters in the novel respond to with disgust. In fact, even Holden's rational judgments become colored with this disgust, and readers close the book. Holden must be human for us to care, and for all his relation to archetypes and to metaphors of a lunar dome and to mercurial and lunar mutability, he is psychologically as human as any character in the novel.

Presented here at some length, again with the disclaimer "as if it were a source," is Jung:

Since the unconscious, in spite of its separation from the conscious subject, is always appearing on the scene, we notice in the actual life of the irrational types striking judgments and acts of choice, but they take the form of apparent sophistries, cold-hearted criticisms, and a seemingly calculating choice of persons and situations. These traits have a rather infantile and even primitive character; both types can on occasion be astonishingly naïve, as well as ruthless, brusque, and violent. To the rational types the real character of these people might well appear rationalistic and calculating in the worst sense. But this judgment would be valid only for their unconscious, and therefore quite incorrect for their conscious psychology, which is entirely oriented by perception, and because of its irrational nature is quite unintelligible to any rational judgment. To the rational mind it might even seem that such a hodge-podge of accidentals hardly deserves the name 'psychology' at all. The irrational type ripostes with an equally contemptuous opinion of his opposite number: he sees him as something only half alive, whose sole aim is to fasten the fetters of reason on everything living and strangle it with judgments. These are crass extremes, but they nevertheless occur. (*Psychological* 371)

Positioned as is McCarthy's hermit scene, positioned literally underground, the hermit's words on mind and heart indeed lay out the novel's psychological core.

Religion, Fire, and Blood

Neumann and Jung lead into other thoughts relevant to an understanding of *Blood Meridian*. To begin, the novel achieves one layer of interest as a result of McCarthy's having found in the southwestern border of the United States a set of conflicts he may well first have encountered growing up Catholic in Knoxville, Tennessee. Psychological aspects of Catholic and Protestant worldviews are present both on *Blood Meridian*'s southwestern border and in Jung's work:

Naturally, a certain degree of rationalism is better suited to Protestantism than it is to the Catholic outlook. The latter gives the archetypal symbolisms the necessary freedom and space in which to develop over the centuries while at the same time insisting on their original form, unperturbed by intellectual difficulties and the objections of rationalists. In this way the Catholic Church demonstrates her maternal character, because she allows the tree growing out of her matrix to develop according to its own laws. Protestantism, in contrast, is committed to the paternal spirit. ("Answer" 326)

Holden's position here, since he is aligned with the Great Father and consciousness, is rationalist in this citation rather than necessarily Protestant; the Mexican worldview is marked Catholic.

Jung, in *Archetypes and the Collective Unconscious*, continues with other Catholic and Protestant comparisons, always with a sense of "reason" in Protestantism:

Dogma takes the place of the collective unconscious by formulating its contents on a grand scale. The Catholic way of life is completely unaware of psychological problems in this sense. Almost the entire life of the collective unconscious has been channelled into the dogmatic archetypal ideas and flows along like a well-controlled stream in the symbolism of creed and ritual.

The iconoclasm of the Reformation, however, quite literally made a breach in the protective wall of sacred images, and since then one image after another has crumbled away. They became dubious, for they conflicted with awakening reason. (12)

Mexico and the United States, Catholicism and Protestantism, the unconscious and the conscious, the irrational and the rational, the kid and Holden, all quite real, all quite human, are layer upon layer in this book.

As additional insight into the novel, color plays a role in Jung as he describes a Jacob Böhme mandala divided into quadrants with a circular outer boundary:

That the *lapis*, or in our case the floating sphere, has a double meaning is clear from the circumstance that it is characterized by two symbolical colours: red means blood and affectivity, the physiological reaction that joins spirit to body, and blue means the spiritual process (mind or *nous*).

For Böhme a "high deep blue" mixed with green signifies "Liberty," that is, the inner

"Kingdom of Glory" of the reborn soul. Red leads to the region of fire and the "abyss of darkness," which forms the periphery of Böhme's mandala. (*Archetypes* 313)

Holden's association with the World Father who rose to become the sky, and his mind-consciousness, are in these sky lapis blues. Redness as fire, on a border to an "abyss of darkness" (perhaps as unconscious mindlessness), and the bloody concerns of this novel are here.

For *Blood Meridian*, things as small as spit have archetypal significance. Indeed, the gang's spit has energy, and such energy gets them through their ordinary days and is even akin to the bodily energy that directly saves the gang in Holden's gunpowder-creation scene:

The mana-charge originally associated with everything that belongs to the body is expressed in primitive man's fear of magical influences, due to the fact that every part of the body, from hair to excrement, can stand for the body as a whole and bewitch it. Also, the symbolism of the creation myths, where everything that comes out of the body is creative, derives from the latter's mana potency. Not only the semen, but urine and spittle, sweat, dung, and breath, words and flatus, are heavy with creation. Out of it all comes the world, and the whole "turn-out" is "birth." (Neumann 25–26; see also 31, 291)

The gang pisses the gunpowder recipe into a batter that saves their lives.

Fire is deep in archetypes, in alchemy, and so deeply in *Blood Meridian* that fire could be its theme. Toadvine and the kid bond with the hotel fire in Nacogdoches. Fire is in the gang: "each fire is all fires," "the fire which does contain within it something of men themselves" (244). The "Vision of Zosimos" contributes: "hidden in man, there exists such a heavenly and divine light which . . . cannot be placed in man from without, but must emerge from within" (Jung, *Alchemical* 107).

Jung quotes Heraclitus—gold coins are in fire:

All things are an exchange for fire, and fire for all things, like goods for gold and gold for goods.

The way up and the way down are the same. (fragments 22 and 69, quoted in *Psychological* 426)

Gold rules *Blood Meridian* in metaphor and in fact. Golden rule? Golden is nothing, because gold is identically fire: "Frequently it even happens that the alchemist will attribute a value to gold, because it is a receptacle of elementary fire: 'The quintessence of gold is all fire'" (Bachelard 72). According to Jung, "Many treatises define Mercurius simply as fire" (*Alchemical* 209). The gang's spit, as the Greek *phlegma*, "means fire" (Jung, *Psychological* 542).

The gang drinks fire; even the kid's father drinks fire: "Since brandy burns before our entranced eyes, since, from the pit of the stomach, it radiates heat to the whole person, it affords proof of the convergence of inner experience and objective experiment" (Bachelard 83).

Fire is the pyre the Yumas make of the gang:

Through fire everything changes. When we want everything to be changed we call on fire. (Bachelard 57)

[F]ire suggests the desire to change, to speed up the passage of time, to bring all of life to its conclusion. . . . The fascinated individual hears *the call of fire in the funeral pyre*. For him destruction is more than a change, it is a renewal. (Bachelard 16; original emphasis)

Holden, clever Holden with his wars, is in the literature of fire:

The stirring up of conflict is a Luciferian virtue in the true sense of the word. Conflict engenders fire, the fire of affects and emotions, and like every other fire it has two aspects, that of combustion and that of creating light. On the one hand, emotion is the alchemical fire whose warmth brings everything into existence and whose heat burns all superfluities to ashes (*omnes superfluitates comburit*). But on the other hand, emotion is the moment when steel meets flint and a spark is struck forth, for emotion is the chief source of consciousness. There is no change from darkness to light or from inertia to movement without emotion. (Jung, *Archetypes* 96)

The flint, above, the cite below: the novel's epilogue is in fire:

In short, they believe so firmly in the universal empire of fire that they arrive at this hasty dialectical conclusion: since fire is *expended* in the animal, it is therefore *stored up* within the mineral. There it is hidden, inward, substantial, and hence all powerful. (Bachelard 73–74; original emphasis.)

So are the Zoroastrian magi in the literature, as is the novel's epilogue:

And as the Magi from the East found Christ in the star by means of this sign, so is fire found in the flint. Thus are the arts found in nature, and it is easier to see the latter than it was to look for Christ. ("Labyrinthus medicorum," quoted in Jung, *Alchemical* 113)

And the future—fencing, ranching, farming—are in fire in the epilogue

But let us begin by showing the equation of the seed and the spark and let us realize that, through the interplay of inextricable reciprocals, the seed is a spark and the spark is a seed. (Bachelard 46)

McCarthy was faithful to his setting and his characters. In that Southwest, nothing was moist but blood. The gang was as bloody and yet as innocent as are the mouths of feeding wolves. It is a romance but is not make-believe. Holden is utterly right about games, projection, divination, wishes, and war. Less than thirty years ago in Southeast

Asia social reformers killed eyeglass wearers as political criminals. The world's "niggers" are everywhere.

Holden is as psychologically human as a book character can be. Paradoxically, he is compelling precisely because he does not change, whereas fictional characters should capture our interest only when they do change. The war game that is the "vast abhorrence of the judge" will waltz us through cycle after cycle. Holden, like war, kills children without a twinge. Those political leaders who now act with incredibly conscious planning, who shower us with arguments of destiny, redress, security—call it what they will—toss us the lures of wishful projection, and in the world-frame the eventualities are horrifying. That men and women are at their finest for these causes—and they are, foot by bloody foot, friend by bloody friend—is as true as it is heartbreaking. Holden is right: judgment is in us eternally.

It's a book so true I can't stand it. It's a book everyone should read. Face the judge. Find a way to stop him. Neumann had his say:

Not until the differentiation into races, nations, tribes, and groups has, by a process of integration, been resolved in a new synthesis, will the danger of recurrent invasions from the unconscious be averted. A future humanity will then realize the center, which the individual personality today experiences as his own self-center, to be one with humanity's very self, whose coming to birth will finally vanquish and cast out that old serpent, the primordial uroboric dragon. (418)

Two people, two wills, two judgments, will choose each in its own favor: blood ties will spill other bloods. What would Darwin have said of war? Said what Holden said, probably.

Pay attention. Look at him. Don't say he has no presence, he "aint nothing."

Say something else.

CHAPTER 9

Concordances

Once the reader of *Blood Meridian* becomes aware of the historical characters and references embedded in the novel, sorts out its political and physical geography, and comes to appreciate the influence of its tarot-card images, the reader may then find it of interest to look at several prominent motifs that McCarthy weaves through his story. What follow are concordances of these images and themes.[1]

Readers will find other threads of reference in the novel. It may be that some category of "Dogs" needs to be included in the "Wolves" concordance (to demonstrate some relation between the gang as "wolves" and ordinary people as "dogs"). An understanding of the imaginative substructure of *Blood Meridian* might then be enhanced.

Narrative Voice

Blood Meridian's narrator occasionally intrudes, and some of these intrusions are aphoristic: "How many youths have come home cold and dead from just such nights and just such plans." (38); "How these things end. In confusion and curses and blood." (40); "Notions of chance and fate are the preoccupation of men engaged in rash undertakings." (153). Others imply that the novel is a tale told aloud: "In the afternoon they came to a crossroads, *what else to call it.*" (67; my emphasis); "Glanton watched him, *who knows if he heard at all.*" (89; my emphasis); "These details should have stood the workers entering the cantina in better stead." (178).

The narrative voice is most clearly heard in the following instances:

---

1. Images in McCarthy's works appear, to me, to have thematic significances: variations on a particular image, say, are found in several of his books in uncannily similar contexts. For instance, "The candleflame and the image of the candleflame caught in the pierglass twisted and righted when he entered the hall and again when he shut the door," which opens *All the Pretty Horses*, shares elements with his "And he saw what had been so how the lilies leaned in the hall glass and a door closed and the candleflames trembled and righted again" (428) and "he knew that in that house some soul lay dying" (427) in *Suttree*. The artisan–cold-forger in *Blood Meridian* (310) also exists as an emblem of one "from whose act all else followed" in *All the Pretty Horses* (230–231, 241). See also connections between other novels as noted in Chapter 8.

3–5—11 paragraphs	"See the child" to "town of Nacogdoches." [Note: The kid's father speaks on page 3, "Night of your birth" to "The Dipper stove."]
15–16—4 paragraphs	"Now come days" to "like a groundsloth."
38—1 sentence	"How many youths" to "just such plans."
40—2 sentences	"How these things" to "curses and blood."
43—1 sentence	"The sergeant never" to "the bore."
46—2 sentences	"They moved on" to "the ancients."
65—1 sentence	"He was wounded" to "his soul."
67—phrase	"what else to call it"
79—1 sentence	"Or he seemed to smile."
86—1 sentence	"Perhaps he saw" to "kill which."
89—phrase	"who knows if he heard"
96—1 sentence	"As if beyond" to "other destiny."
104—1 sentence	"In the predawn" to "to come."
106—1 sentence	"They camped" to "took place."
119—1 sentence	"The dying man" to "qualities themselves."
120—1 sentence	"For this will" to "fraudulent destinies."
121—phrase	"pursuing as all" to "men's journeys."
138—1 sentence	"If much in" to "whatever beasts."
138–139—phrase	"the rocks would" to "nothing was."
152—2 sentences	"They rode like" to "conjectural winds."
153—1 sentence	"Notions of chance" to "rash undertakings."
163—phrase	"the enemy who" to "the city."
172—1 sentence	"Like beings provoked" to "was all."
173—1 paragraph	"On the eve" to "rode on."
178—1 sentence	"These details should" to "better stead."
184—1 sentence	"There was no" to "once again."
204—1 sentence	"He rode near" to "with him."
222—1 paragraph	"No one moved" to "dam's flank."
243—1½ paragraphs	"That night Glanton" to "watching the judge."
244—5 sentences	"The flames sawed" to "one too."
245—1 paragraph	"The truth about" to "among others."
246—2 sentences	"Even so some" to "riding again."
247—2 sentences	"As if the" to "of reality."
255—1 sentence	"Only the judge" to "they seem."
259—phrase	"such encounters being" to "by night"
276—phrase	"contemplating towns to" to "the coals."
303—1 sentence	"They spoke less" to "a journey."
309–310—1 sentence	"Whoever would seek" to "his commencing."
313—phrase	"men who seemed" to "the world."

Wolves

Wolves "cull themselves" (146): the gang's two Jacksons demonstrate this trait in the human sphere (106–107). Glanton kills the wounded McGill (157), and orders the deaths of other wounded at the lottery of arrows (205–209). The Yumas, after the massacre, are also described in terms of wolves (280).[2] The wolf may be emblematic of the amoral rapacity, in McCarthy's terms, necessary for a dancer to take the center stage.

3	"yet a few last wolves"
15	"little prairie wolves cry all night"
20	"Followed by packs of wolves"
42	"where coyotes had dug up the dead"
44	"prairie wolves . . . yammering"
45	"wolves" follow the filibusterers
46	"there were no wolves now"
55	"wolves . . . moving north toward the slaughter"
60	"wolves or dogs" had eaten at the dead in the church
61	"wolves slank from the doorways"
65	"When the lambs is lost. . . . Sometime [come] the wolf."
105	"deer . . . harried over the plain by wolves"
117	"the howling of a wolf"
	"a solitary lobo . . . hung like a marionette from the moon"
119	"half a dozen wolves . . . trotted behind" the gang
129	"we come upon a band of wolves"
	"I would never shoot a wolf"
146	"Wolves cull themselves, man."
152	"little desert wolves yapped in the dark"
188	"wolves . . . called to [the gang] as if they were friends to man . . . Glanton's dog trotted moaning"
215	"figures . . . between him and the light. Then again. Wolves perhaps."
216	"The tracks of wolves and coyotes had walked through the horse and boot prints"
223	"they saw where wolves had crossed the road"
227	"wolf in a melon patch"
243	"desert wolves yapped"
258	"little jackal wolves cried . . . camp dogs stirred and muttered"
271	"they drank like dogs and had howled at the booming surf"

2. Chamberlain notes the Yumas' "strange sharp war cry like the bark of a Coyote" after the ferry massacre (292).

280   Yumas "squatted on their haunches like wolves"

288   "where wolves had gone to and fro"

293   "wolves and jackals . . . cried . . . until the moon came up"

317   "wolves half crazed and wallowing in the carrion"

318   "the yammer and yap of the starving wolves"

Apes

McCarthy, early in his novel, links speech with the concept of mankind when he writes of the "grunting" communication of apes (4). The point-counterpoint of apes and men continues on in his book as, perhaps, wolves and dogs are also point and counterpoint.

4   "grunting of apes"; "mankind . . . vindicated"

65   the Mexican bandits "pummel one another like apes"

74   the prisoners "picked at themselves like apes"

90   "skulls of infants like the ossature of small apes"

148   the gang "without . . . camaraderie any more than banded apes"

153   dead men "gazing up with ape's eyes at brother sun"

200   "faces gotten up . . . gaudy as the rumps of apes"

238   Cloyce's brother as an "ape"

273   idiot dances "with loping simian steps"

280   Yumas' "stoneage tongue" (cf. 4: "grunting of apes")

284   survivors "drink . . . like rival bands of apes"

288   idiot "like some dim neolithic herdsman"

Smiles and Laughter

Judge Holden's devilish smile punctuates the novel. It may be that his smile alludes to bared predatory fangs and warm encouragement at the same time (333). Chamberlain's reference to the "mocking laughter" of his Holden (275) may contribute, but McCarthy's own pencil has boldly underscored its importance with sustained attention to this detail.

8   men laugh after Green is chased out of town

13   Toadvine "laughing" after beating Old Sidney

14   judge smiles at the kid

23   Mexicans laugh at the kid (who will sweep the bar)

24   "drinkers in silent mirth"

43   "skinners jostling and grinning"

44   sutler as a "grinning tradesman"

51	Captain White "smiled grimly"

51   Captain White "smiled grimly"

62   lizards with "thin smiles"

64   Mexican leader "grinned"

66   bat's "lips crimped in a horrible smile"

71   woman "smiled" while feeding the prisoners smuggled sweets

79   judge was "smiling," entering Chihuahua

      judge "smiled" at the kid

      "the killers on their small warponies, smiling"

81   "The white man laughed"

83   Speyer "smiled nervously"

85   judge "smiled" at Black Jackson

      "A few [of the gang] smiled."

91   juggler "smiling"

92   judge smiles three times at Jackson (during tarot scene)

94   judge laughing at tarot; of the others: "none laughing"

95   juggler "smiled a crooked smile"

116   judge "laughed at [the squatters] for fools"

117   gang "smiled among themselves" at a wolf howling

124   Tobin smiles at kid's words during gunpowder story

125   judge smiled as gang found him in desert

130   judge laughs at gang (in Tobin's story)

132   judge "laughin" and "grinnin" while mixing and spreading gunpowder

134   judge "with that smile of his"

140   Webster smiles, judge laughs (sketching)

141   judge smiles at Webster's words

143   judge smiles at his listeners

145   judge "smiled" at end of his story of the old highwayman

146   "savages wander these canyons to the sound of an ancient laughter"

161   judge smiles, chuckles to wounded David Brown

164   judge smiles at Toadvine, who has had a gun to Holden's head

167   judge "as if he were smiling"

179   judge "smiled" at man he was killing

199   judge smiles at the thought of a world-sized zoo

219   judge smiles "as if the world were pleasing even to him alone"

226   judge smiles at Glanton's talk of killing second hermit

230   judge smiles at Mangas

232   judge smiles at rabble

      "idler grinned" at thought of gold and silver in saddle bags

233   judge "smiled benignly at the wastrels"

234   judge "smiling" as Owens confronts Black Jackson

249   judge smiles at David Brown's words

254   Caballo en Pelo "with a strange priapic leer that may have at one time been a smile"

283   judge smiles in desert after escape

284   judge smiles at Tobin's words

286   judge smiles that Tobin wants him killed

301   Diegueño "grinned" at the kid

305   judge "smiling" at kid in jail

306   judge "smiled again," and again, at kid

307   judge "smiled" at kid in kid's dream

310   judge "smiled" at kid in kid's dream

327   judge smiles that kid won't study "no dance"

328   judge smiles at kid, encouraging him to drink

329   judge "smiled, his great teeth shone"

333   judge "smiling" as he embraces kid in jakes

335   "fiddlers grinning hideously"

        judge "laughs deep in his throat"

Egg and Dome

McCarthy's sustained interest in Holden's hairlessness as a "dome" and an "egg" shape seems generalized into connections with arcane, alchemical eggs and metaphors of lunar mutability.[3] As such, this concordance suggests the endless cycles of rise and fall, wax and wane, meridian and decline, upon which McCarthy builds his story.

130   "the earth as he said was round like an egg"

139   "white rocks . . . round and smooth as arcane eggs"

152   "like small lucent eggs concocted alchemically"

164   "his pistol against the great dome of the judge's head"

167   "The immense and gleaming dome of his naked skull"

310   "any ultimate atavistic egg"

327   "The great pale dome of his skull shone like an enormous phosphorescent egg"

335   "the lunar dome of his skull passes palely under the lamps"

---

3. The sun-sign characteristics of Leo, which influence the kid, further distinguish him from the judge, given Holden's "lunar dome" (335).

Fools and Crazies

The immense power of the sun, bound to the harshness of the country itself, drives men mad. Judge Holden is linked to the tarot Fool. And war requires an abundance of the willing.

3	father "lies in drink"
	kid has "a taste for mindless violence"
15	kid "looks like a raggedyman"
16	hermit "half mad"
17	"Get away, fool," the kid says to his mule.
39	"the foot-high sill . . . where fools in their hundreds have tripped"
	"an old disordered Mennonite"
49	"He's a halfwit," White says of a peon.
53	"regions . . . where the eye wanders and the lip jerks and drools"
54	"the dying groaned and gibbered"
64	"Loonies, said Sproule. They're loonies."
70	"For ever takin up with such a fool."
73	"fools and sots drooling and flailing about"
77	"Bill just flat out hung them fools"
89	"dressed in fools costumes"
102	"The old man's full he said. Or mad."
	"Craziern a runaway nigger, aint ye? he said."
110	"a calculus or madstone"
115	"ragged and half crazed"
	"Out of the mad horse's throat"
116	"he laughed at them for fools"
117	"folly in its guises and forms"
127	judge "appeared to be a lunatic and then not. Glanton I always knew was mad."
132	"We were half mad anyways."
137	"a bedlam of shouts"
142	"reckoned the old man mad"
156	"this bedlam and clamor"
	"along the shore wailing crazily"
160	"they assumed once more the color of the land through which they passed"
162	"Fool, he said. God will not love ye forever."
166	"a pair of drummers one witless"
170	"mad about the eyes"

177   "half crazed with the enormity of their own presence in that immense and bloodslaked waste"

191   Glanton's "fit" at Jesús María

200   "like transvestites in a madhouse"

210   "Come on fool," Tate says to his horse.

225   "he was an imbecile"

        "The brother . . . not altogether sane"

233   "a naked imbecile"

239   "a motley collection . . . reduced indians or tontos"

249   "You're crazy Holden. Crazy at last."

254   "clad in such fool's regalia"

255   "a crazylookin bunch of niggers"

260   "any man who trusted an indian was a fool"

268   "like a man beset with bees or madness"

272   "senseless jabber"

284   "like some . . . barrister whom the country had crazed"

286   "The priest has been too long in the sun."

288   "The fool. Shoot the fool."

290   "like some mad dowser"

291   "You'll not kill him. Dont be a fool. Shoot the horses."

307   "He never took part in your craziness."

310   "The fool was no longer there"

312   "not the judge's fool but just some other fool"

323   "His grandaddy was killed by a lunatic"

        "not so much dullwitted as insane"

330   "I dont like craziness."

331   "That's crazy."

Hallucinatory Void

"They diminished upon the plain to the west first the sound and then the shape of them dissolving in the heat rising off the sand until they were no more than a mote struggling in that hallucinatory void and then nothing at all" (113). This sentence contains the only conjoined use of the words "hallucinatory" and "void" in the novel. Still, McCarthy's landscape is in many places described as if it were a heat-induced mirage. In other places, the scale of the landscape often leads into passages in which a greater "void," beyond the earth, is the intended allusion. Since McCarthy's use of "void" often suggests macro- and microcosmic interchangeability, the concordance below conflates these references into the idea of a void.

3   "blackness, holes in the heavens"

5   "scrub pine swimming in the haze"

19   "drygulch phantom"

32   "They wasnt no name to it. It was just a wilderness."

42   "a howling wilderness"

44   "all about so changed and strange"

      "lost in the immensity of that landscape"

      "whited regions where they've gone to hide from God"

46   "through the waste like a ghost army . . . like shades of figures"

      "in that cratered void"

      "blue cordilleras stood footed . . . like reflections in a lake"

47   "a land . . . whose true geology was not stone but fear"

50   "beyond the dawn to the uttermost rebate of space"

      "auguries everywhere of the hand of man before man was or any living thing"

52   "like the shade of old work through sizing on a canvas"

53   "regions beyond right knowing where the eye wanders and the lip jerks and drools"

54   "horses of the dead came pounding out of the smoke"

61   "wolves . . . dissolved in the fog of the streets"

62   "rocks trembled and sleared in the sun, rock and no water"[4]

      "the shape of the city [and lake] dissolve"

63   "People see what they want to see."

65   "the greater void beyond seemed to swallow up his soul"

67   "guidance in that emptiness"

72   "they sought to parcel from the darkness some voice or cry from among the cries that was no right beast"

75–76 "shimmering in the heat. . . . Rough likenesses"

86   "worlds past all reckoning"

91   "peered out upon the wrathful blackness"

95   "that naked bedlam beyond the fire's light"

96   "by some maelstrom out there in the void"

100   "all was darkness and without definition"

103   "It is like a dream."

105   "a dry lake shimmering like the mare imbrium"

      "the problematical destruction of darkness"

4. These words are the "Rock and no water" of line 332 of section V of T. S. Eliot's *The Waste Land* (66).

106 "eyes stood as corridors . . . from what of it lay behind to what was yet to come"

108 "the mountains in their blue islands stood footless in the void"

109 "like burnt phantoms . . . lost in the sun and lost in the [mirage] lake" (and continuing down to) "began to crumble in the serried planes of heat and to break up silently and to vanish"

113 "hallucinatory void"

120 meat hunters arrive, like the gang's "own image," lit by lightning

124 "Brown thought [the judge] a mirage."

125 "a merestone for to mark him out of nothing at all"

130 "the earth is a globe in the void"

137 "distant beltways of matter grinding mutely to the west above them all"

138 "an escarpment that seemed to rim the known world"

147 "turning in that lonely void"

148 "incoordinate waste"

152 "whited regions on old maps"

163 "like horses called forth quivering out of the abyss"
    "some ruined army retreating across the meridians of chaos and old night"
    "secular aloes blooming like phantasmagoria in a fever land"

164 "trembling in the heat . . . like a scene viewed in a diorama"

165 "heads of the enemy through that fantasy of music and flowers"

172 "Spectre horsemen . . . anonymous in the crenellated heat"

175 "mountains bespoken blue and barren out of the void"

177 "half crazed with the enormity of their own presence in that immense and bloodslaked waste"

179 "smoke drifted through like fog"

180–181 "one of the men from inside appeared in the doorway like a bloody apparition"

181 "like supernumeraries in a dream"

182 "in that perilous mist like soldiers slaughtered in a dream"

183 "a point of light out on that desert like the reflection of a single star in a lake of utter blackness"
    "they studied the arrant blackness under them where it fell away like the sheer cloven face of the world"

184 "they could see the fire . . . reflected in the sky to the east beyond the curve of the earth"

185 "sparks fugitive as flintstrikings in the unanimous dark of the world"

195 "he pitched off down the rocks into the abyss below"

205 "the fires on the plain faded like an evil dream"

213   "chartless reckonings"

       "senseless" mirage-like "collision of armies"

215   "in the eye of that cratered waste he watched the world tend away at the
       edges to a shimmering surmise"

216   finds a horse, "rider or none"

227   "pale green meteor . . . vanished . . . in the void"

244   "any sojourners upon it remote and arguable of substance"

245   "other planets in the void"

246   dead cattle "upturned upon that shoreless void"

247   the earth "silently milling the greater void"

       "in the optical democracy of such landscapes . . . a man and a rock become
       endowed with unguessed kinships"

250   "moral right rendered void and without warrant"

251   "to sense with their fingers the temporal immensities of which the judge
       spoke"

258   "pushing with his thin arms at things in the night"

265   "Standing warily in the doorway . . . until he could make out the shape of
       things within"

279   "sand and sky . . . beginning to shimmer and swim"

       "stood warped in the quaking lens . . . in welcome or warning they had no
       way to know"

281   "like beings of a mode little more than tangential to the world at large"

282   "Like things so charged with meaning that their forms are dimmed"

295   the kid and Tobin are the "locus" of a featureless world

296   "You think he cant follow your track?" "The wind's taking it. It's gone from
       the slope yonder." "Gone?" "Ever trace."

300   men "shimmering and insubstantial"

302   "sullen shores of the void"

310   "at the shore of a void"

314   "disappeared in the coming darkness like heralds of some unspeakable
       calamity leaving only bloody footprints on the stone"

330   the "ultimately empty" desert

       "the past that was differs little from the past that was not"

331   "the darkness before the footlamps"

334   "tobacco smoke circled the lamps like an evil fog"

Celestial

"Stars were falling across the sky myriad and random, speeding along brief vectors from their origins in night to their destinies in dust and nothingness" (333). The landscape of Mc-Carthy's Southwest is composed not only of deserts and mirage effects, but also of heavenly phenomena. The novel begins and ends on nights of meteor showers. It is the sun that powers the book's hallucinatory mirages. The constellations are both clock and compass in several of the book's scenes. Some references to the rising of the sun or moon appear simply to signal a new day or night, and some of these nonallusive references have been omitted from the following list (though, too, some of the references that have been included may indeed be nonallusive in the final analysis). This list is, then, somewhat abbreviated, but it is hoped that it still errs on the side of too many references rather than too few.

3	"Leonids" of "Thirty-three"
	"holes in the heavens. The Dipper stove."
15	"stars . . . fall all night in bitter arcs"
40	"stars that had been overhead lay low in the west"
44	"under the selfsame stars"
46	"whitehot stars go rifling down the dark"
	"the face of the planet Anareta"[5]
	"stars jostled and arced"
	"Western eyes that read more geometric constructions than those names given by the ancients" (regarding "meaning" put there by the participant)
47	"shapes of soft blue [St. Elmo's] fire" on the filibusters
50	"archipelagos of cloud . . . into the shoreless void"
	"stones the lightning had clove open"
52	"shields bedight with bits of broken mirrorglass that cast a thousand unpierced suns"
55	the kid "took a reckoning by the stars"

---

5. No astronomical object named "Anareta" exists. The *OED* references the word's presence in texts on genethlialogical astrology, the "charting of nativities," horoscopes based on birth times and planetary and star charts. Fred Gettings's *Dictionary of Astrology* appears, unfortunately, to complicate rather than clarify matters. He does not define "Anareta," but refers inquiries on it to his definitions of "Anaretic" and "Anaretic Places" (12). Under "Anaretic," he notes that the term is "derived from the Greek, meaning 'destroyer,' and [is] applied to the planet or degree which is for one reason or another regarded as the destroyer of life in a particular chart." The Anaretic in a natal chart, he writes, is calculated by "complex" rules on the basis of the positions of the known planets and certain fixed stars at the moment of a person's birth. "Anaretic places" are "the degrees in a horoscope figure" occupied by any of a number of planets, "should these be badly aspected by Mars or Saturn." The astrologer's "problem," Gettings writes, "besides establishing the identity of the anaretic" place, is one of "determining also not only how, but when, it will bring death."

Leo Daugherty comments interestingly on both *Blood Meridian*'s "planet Anareta" reference and on the book's epilogue.

61   "the rind of a moon"

      "Pleiades straight overhead"

      "the Great Bear walking"

67   "Does that sound like thunder to you? said Sproule."

68   "Starlight in a mud street"

76   "a low rumbling he took for thunder"

78   "Itinerant degenerates bleeding westward like some heliotropic plague."

81   "the shape he stood the sun from on that rocky ground bore something of the man himself"

86   sunset and moonrise point to "worlds past all reckoning"

88   "the cotton eye of the moon . . . at its midnight meridian"

105   "sun to the west lay in a holocaust"

      mention of "the mare imbrium" ("sea of showers," a region on the moon)

108   "the mountains in their blue islands stood footless in the void like floating temples"

117   the wolf "hung like a marionette from the moon"

120   "and there were no stars"

129   the "moon was about three quarters full and waxing"

139   "The moon rose full over the canyon"

148   "reckoning . . . that incoordinate waste by palest starlight"

151   "Under a gibbous moon"

152   "the western sky was the color of blood"

      "the dawnstar burned pale in the east"

153   "brother sun"

      "moved like migrants under a drifting star"

154   "the starsprent reaches of the galaxies"

      "the angle of the Dipper . . . set the company in motion"

159   "a small and perfect sun" in each of the dying man's eyes

163   "sourceless summer lightning" in the sky

      "meridians of chaos and old night"

164   "bats crossed silently overhead among the stars"

165   "bleached almost transparent by the sun"

167   the judge "shone like the moon so pale"

174   "in the circuit of a few suns all trace of the destination of these people would be erased"

185   "the distant pandemonium of the sun"

186   St. Elmo's fire

      the gang "rode for days through the rain and they rode through rain and hail and rain again"

187   "the sun set and no moon rose"

        "signs and wonders in the heavens themselves"

188   "hail lay nested like tectites among the leaves"

207   "he watched the enormous sun where it sat boiling"

212   "the Great Bear . . . and the Pleiades . . . in the very roof of the vault"

213   "stars burned with a lidless fixity"[6]

        "stars lay awash at his feet . . . migratory spalls"

214   "casting about . . . for some star in the overcast"

215   "A constellation of ignited eyes . . . the stars in their sockets"

216   "a half moon . . . like a child's boat"

221   "gunstones . . . on flights of their own . . . like the paths of meteorites"

227   a "pale green meteor . . . passed overhead and vanished silently"

240   "for an anvil an enormous iron meteorite"

        "that great slag wandered for what millennia from what unreckonable corner of the universe"

243   "he'd drive the remorseless sun on to its final endarkenment"

244   conversation about the past "time there had been two moons in the sky"

245–246 "The arc of circling bodies is determined by the length of their tether, said the judge. Moons, coins, men."

247   "the endless tandem suns"

248   "like beings for whom the sun hungered"

254   "they rode singlefile in cameo detailed by the winey light with their dark sides to the river"

256   "Cancer, Virgo, Leo raced the ecliptic . . . Cassiopeia burned like a witch's signature"

258   "a fishcolored moon rose"

264   "down the dunes into the cool blue dusk"

277   "there was no place the sun would not find him"

278   "the slow wheel of stars"

        "they fell out of the sun"

281   "in the red land to the west"

286   "The priest has been too long in the sun."

290   the rifle ball "passed overhead like an asteroid"

300   Sirius, Cetus, Orion, Betelgeuse "fording the void"

303   "the stars swarmed in the bottomless night"

---

6. The final sentence of Faulkner's "Dry September" reads: "The dark world seemed to lie stricken beneath the cold moon and the lidless stars" (see also McCarthy, *Child of God* 86: "eyes . . . lidless fixity," and 133: "remote and lidless stars").

304 "cobbled starlight"

317 "The ragged sparks blew down the wind."

"the night was clear and the stars were falling"

322 "where the clustered stars were burning for eternity"

333 "Stars were falling across the sky myriad and random"

the man "looked again at the silent tracks of the stars where they died"

335 the "lunar dome" of the judge's head

Marine

Several characters in *Blood Meridian* reach the shore of the Pacific Ocean. Some of the references below are simply references to that shore and are marked with asterisks. Other citations, though, are allusive and can be thought reasonably to originate in response to the fact that much of the land over which the gang travelled had once been seabed. Some of these references are also to be found in the Hallucinatory Void list as heat-induced mirages.

7 "a huge and wounded medusa"

37 "skittered and snapped like turtles"

45 "like tentacles to bind them to the darkness yet to come"

70 "the drowned and sightless eyes of his old commander"

72 "like the filaments of certain seaforms"

93 "his pleated brow not unlike a dolphin's"

97 "bells seagreen with age"

108 "the mountains in their blue islands"

"on the playa a cold sea broke and water gone these thousand years lay riffled"

109 "far out on the lake bed"

"they rode out of that vanished sea like burnt phantoms"

132 "on the topmost rim of that scalded atoll"

151 "Crossing those barren gravel reefs in the night"

154 "like the lights of a distant port"

154–157 Gilenos massacred at the shore of a lake

167 the judge "like some . . . bloated manatee"

174 "peeled skulls like polyps bluely wet"

175 "pumice . . . like the spume from sea swells"

186–187 "shimmering cities on the distant shore of that sea"

187 "rising out of nothing like the backs of seabeasts in a devonian dawn"

195 mercury cascading "deft as eels"

197   "out of the mountains toward the western sea"

202   "dragging themselves across the lot like seals or other things"

215   "coral shapes of fulgurite"

220   "iron axletrees marked the shapes of the wagons as keelsons do the bones of ships on the sea's floors"

241   "as if for a sea journey"

243   "bones of cholla . . . like burning holothurians in the phosphorous dark of the sea's deeps"

244   "a mock moon with its . . . nacre seas"

246   "dead cattle . . . lay like the ruins of primitive boats upturned upon that shoreless void"

251   "pale seabeast surfaced among the dark archipelagos"

262   *"sea"

264   *"sea" twice

265   houses like "curious dorys"

268   *"beach"

287   "the faint arc of an ancient lake shore where broken shells lay"

303   *"sea"

304   *details of the shore four times, including "the stars are drowning and whales ferry their vast souls through the black and seamless sea"

313   *"a dark and muttersome sea"

       *"the black waters of the sea where dolphins rolled through the flames, fire

in   the lake"7

324   lamps at Griffin "formed . . . a false shore of hospice"

Carnival

Horace Bell characterizes Glanton's activities as a "carnival of blood," and a "carnival of joy" (274, 277). The derivation of "carnival" from words meaning "removal of flesh" may provide some insight toward the appropriateness of the carnivals in *Blood Meridian*.[8] Many references to the concept of carnival or to the word itself are present in the book—for example, the "carnival head" of a dead Indian chief (159), a string band of musicians "in a carnival" (201), and the truth of the world "in a medicine show," an "itinerant carnival, a migratory tent show" (245). But McCarthy conflates the notion of circus with that

---

7. In Frances FitzGerald's introductory note on her title *Fire in the Lake: The Vietnamese and the Americans in Vietnam*, she writes that its opening phrase "comes from the *I Ching*, the Chinese Book of Changes, and it is the image of revolution."

8. Dodge includes in one of his chapter subheadings the phrase "Carnival of Death" (478).

of carnival. "Circus," out of the Latin word for "circle," is a particularly apt word in Mc-Carthy's novel of the eternal replacement of the center-stage dancer (331). McCarthy's "carnival" and "circus" extend from the tent of Reverend Green (5) to the dancing bear at the saloon outside which the kid is killed (324). The fool James Robert Bell is literally a "two bit" circus sideshow act to his brother (233). McCarthy's "carnival" and "circus" references form a continuous thread of allusion, both to bloody spectacle and to cyclic repetition, throughout the novel.

5	Reverend Green "play[ed] to a full house daily" in the "ratty canvas tent"
15	the kid as a "raggedyman" (comparable to the fool James Robert Bell)
53	Indians "like a company of mounted clowns"
54	"funhouse figures"
69	"a primitive circus"
89	the gypsy "family of itinerant magicians"
	"A show, said Glanton." "Bufones."
90	"he was juggling four small wooden balls"
	"the dogs were dancing"
91	the gypsy man is a "juggler"
98	"like puppets in a gallery"
99	"The circus folk"
	"his bill of entertainments"
	Black Jackson "strode about with strange posturings" in the gypsy show
104	"the fire was cold before the pitchtent"
111	horses "rolled their eyes like circus animals"
117	the wolf "hung like a marionette from the moon"
129	the gang rode "like circus riders, not a sound"
143	"in clothes of every color like a carnival clown"
152	"the sun in its circus"
159	the "carnival head" of a dead chief
165	"harlequin horses"
168	"assumed the look of tragic masks"
174	"in the circuit of few suns"
177	a "juggler" leads a funeral procession
183	"they lay in the street like dead bandsmen"
190	"alien minstrels"
191	the "parade" of the feast of Las Animas
201	"a string band of six musicians"
	"in a carnival . . . of festivity and growing ugliness"
219	"jostled along in his sleep like a mounted marionette"

233   "A rude tent . . ." "See The Wild Man Two Bits."

245   "medicine show," "itinerant carnival, a migratory tentshow" as "The truth about the world"

254   Yumas "clad in such fool's regalia"

259   "idiot" as "fool" "among its fellows" in the gang's camp

276   Yumas after the massacre as "some painted troupe of mimefolk"

278   Yumas "like baleful marionettes"

279   shot Indian "went down like a player through a trap"

298   judge as "degenerate entrepreneur fleeing from a medicine show"

324   a dancing bear

325   "motley assemblage"

328   "he was a passable thespian"

332   "musicians" at a whorehouse-saloon
       a "dark little dwarf of a whore"

Religious

This collection of allusions is by far the largest, and the most apt to include subjective distortions. "Religious," in the heading, is meant to include not only Christian references but also, to select from only the beginnings of this concordance, voodoo dolls and Moorish church domes.

3   "hewers of wood and drawers of water"[9]

4   "A shadowed agony in the garden."

5   Reverend Green's tent meeting

6   "the son of God"
      "this nomadic house of God"
      "no papers of divinity"

7   "flavor of the piety he despises"
      "Oh God"
      "his opened bible"
      "The devil."

8   "men looked like mud effigies"

13   "great clay voodoo doll"

15   "A hermit"

16   "an old anchorite"

9. Out of this biblical reference, the kid's family is established as belonging to the lowest economic class (Deuteronomy 29:11), possibly as a result of having been caught in an attempted deception (Joshua 9).

"water was salty, sulphurous"

17   "Did thieves beset ye?"

19   "God made this world"

"in the way that God has set for it"

"the devil was at his elbow"

21   "the Moorish churchdome rising"

22   "the dead themselves or spirit folk so white they were"

26   "He woke in the nave of a ruinous church"

"buzzards . . . trotted off into the sacristy"

"an array of saints . . . shot up by American troops"

27   "some wholly wretched baptismal candidate"

28   "I'm white and christian."

30   "raised me up like Lazarus"

33   Captain White swears "by God"

34   "there's no God in Mexico"

37   "Thank God for that."

39   "an old disordered Mennonite"

40   "Pray that they will."

"The wrath of God lies sleeping."

42   "flat and true as a spirit level"

43   "God's years of it"

44   "those whited regions where they've gone to hide from God"

45   "the high road to hell"

47   "prayed for rain" "Pray it up" "Amen, they said"

48   "in the evening these elect"

51   "the glass at his chest like a crucifix"

52   Indians "in costumes attic or biblical"

53   "a horde from hell"

"as if in prayer"

"the horses of war"

55   "one soul rose wondrously"

"like some reeking issue of the incarnate dam of war herself"

56   "he heard a voice calling somewhere in that vastness"

"a caution to the christians"

57   "like devouts at a shrine"

"an old reliquary"

58   "buzzards squatting" on the church's "wooden corbels"

59   "saints dressed in doll's clothes"

60   "buttresses of light"

"the great sleeping God of the Mexicans routed from his golden cup"

"a dead Christ in a glass bier"

62   "turrets stood like basalt prophets"

"little wooden crosses . . . where travelers had met with death"

63   "purgatorial waste"

66   "a howl of such outrage as to stitch a caesura in the pulsebeat of the world"

71   "God's profoundest peons"

72   vultures in "dark vestments in postures of strange benevolence"

73   "the ghosts of old martyrs and patriots"

75   "There's old pilgrims in there"

"taking the host to some soul"

76   "like a hearse from limbo"

78   "wearing scapulars . . . of . . . blackened human ears"

"like a visitation from some heathen land"

80   "the governor gave them his blessing"

81   "some ritual dormant in his dark blood"

83   "rang the bell . . . a solemn tolling"

88   "swine rose moaning . . . like oafish demons"

89   "this evil terrain"

91   "into the howling desert like supplicants at the skirts of some wild and irate goddess"

"peered out upon the wrathful blackness"

92   "The judge . . . like some great pale deity"

93   "gesture that appeared to be a benediction"

"beware the demon rum"

96   "The judge like a great ponderous djinn"

100   "Another anchorite, another dawn"

102   "poured wine into the cup and took up the jar of water and poured it sparingly after"

"and all a great stained altarstone"

103   "What I need to talk to them dolls there? I talk here."

"When even the bones is gone in the desert the dreams is talk to you, you dont wake up forever."

"The man at the wall . . . called upon his god."

106   "Here beyond men's judgements all covenants were brittle."

107   "a murdered anchorite discalced in ashes and sark"

108   "footless in the void like floating temples"

109   "augmented by planes in lurid avatars"

111   "Out of that whirlwind no voice spoke"

116 "A few would quote him scripture to confound his ordering up of eons out of the ancient chaos"

122 "There's little equity in the Lord's gifts."

123 "The gifts of the Almighty"

"The Almighty, the Almighty."

"he could out dance the devil himself" "God the man is a dancer"

"the Lord's way"

124 "the voice of the Almighty speaks most profoundly in such beings as lives in silence themselves"

"God speaks in the least of creatures"

"horses are grazing" paragraph

"that sootysouled rascal"

126 "Some terrible covenant."

127 "My hand to God."

129 "It was like a sermon"

130 "like the disciples of a new faith"

"sinners so notorious evil"

131 "sent among us for a curse"

132 "piss for your very souls"

"God in his glory knows"

133 "none to curse and none to pray"

134 "circlin past him like communicants"

137 "like some fabled storybook beast"

139 "like shapes capable of violating their covenant"

141 "every man is tabernacled"

"ignorant heathen savage"

143 "he was a loss to God"

"until he took his brother into his heart as he would take himself"

"calling for a place to be made"

"the old man repented"

144 "the old woman . . . was amazed"

145 "He is broken before a frozen god"

146 "If God meant to interfere"

147 "so like an icon . . . in his sitting"

148 "on leather wings like satanic hummingbirds"

152 "visited with a plague of hail"

155 "the dogs howling in a tableau of some hellish hunt"

162 "cursed the boy's soul"

"Fool, he said. God will not love ye forever."

163   "Like a bride to the altar"

       "secular aloes . . . in a fever land"

164   "Day found the heathen much advanced upon them."

165   "the churchspires of the city"

       "a pandemonium of teeth"

167   "Old women . . . kiss the hems . . . and hold up their . . . hands in blessing"

168   "like decorations for some barbaric celebration"

       "caved and pagan eyes"

171   "much like the sorcerer's apprentice"

172   "they were fallen upon as saints"

173   "arcane maps"

174   "that dusty pandemoniac"

       "to tell any pilgrim"

175   "descended like acolytes"

       "among catclaw and crucifixion thorn"

181   "clutching the altar . . . slain and scalped on the chancel floor"

187   "some dim sect sent forth to proselytize"

       "signs and wonders in the heavens themselves"

190   "the feast of Las Animas . . . Christ in a stained and ancient catafalque"

191   they "touched the garment the figure wore and kissed their fingertips"

       "to the church to pray"

       "when the souls of the dead were rumored to be about"

       "in spite of rain or death"

192   "in both hands . . . like a small ciborium"

193   "the sacred bandera"

194   "The priest had baptized the wounded"

195   "the animals dropping silently as martyrs"

       "some ultimate alchemic work decocted from out the secret dark of the earth's heart"

214   "a fire burned on the prairie"

215   "a lone tree burning on the desert"

       "The solitary pilgrim"

       "sandvipers like seemly gods"

       "demonic tracks of javelinas"

216   "like a burnt carcass of some ungodly beast"

220   "like fellows of some righteous initiate"

223   "A hermit"

224   the judge's "short disquisition" on "the old mission at San José de Tumacacori"

225   "to his destination in eternity"

238   "a special preacher come and pray over him"

      "like an immense and dangerous faith healer"

242   "those fluted columns [of saguaro] . . . were like ruins of vast temples"

247   "a crude wooden cross where Maricopas had crucified an Apache"

248   "The good book says"

249   "war is the truest form of divination"

      "War is god"

250   "Moral law is an invention"

      "the priest has put by the robes of his craft"

      "Journeyman priest or apprentice priest"

251   "scrabbling up out of a land accursed"

      "imponderable as the burned out floor of hell"

253   "the pilgrims on the beach"

257   "the women had started up a hymn"

      "James Robert come out of there."

258   "Imagine having this child [of God?] penned up like a wild animal."

259   "A birth scene or a baptism or some ritual"

260–261   "did he consider the pilgrims huddled on the far shore"

262   "a vulture . . . in clerical black"

      "Easter in that year"

263   "a poor Judas fashioned from straw"

      "a stink of soot and sulphur"

268   "a lazarous bodega"

269   "one eye to the judas hole"

270   "strung them onto his scapular"

271   "praying for mercy to Glanton and to God impartially"

      "Madre de Jesús."

272   "in those frail caissons the covenant itself"

273   "like some great balden archimandrite"

      "a small coin. Perhaps once lodged under the tongue of some passenger."

274   "like ceremonial wands"

      "like some wild thaumaturge out of an atavistic drama"

275   the "helve of which was carved with pagan motifs"

276   "like the prefiguration of their own ends"

280   "invocations to whatever god of war or fortune"

282   "The judge . . . like some medieval penitent"

284   "Yonder sun is like the eye of God"

285   "for the love of God"

287   "kept watch behind him on those pilgrims"

289–290   "a cross he'd fashioned . . . like some mad dowser"

293   "pilgrims were weak from their wounds"

       "whatever godless quadrant"

297   "Men are made of the dust of the earth."

300   "the fruits of their election"

306   "All in the fullness of time."

307   "If war is not holy man is nothing but antic clay."

312   "scapular of heathen ears"

       "He had a bible"

313   "just a band of pilgrims"

       "men . . . who flailed themselves with whips"

314   "a heavy wooden cross"

       "a carved wooden skeleton"

315   "it bore like a patent woven into the fabric the figures of stars and quarter moons and other insignia of a provenance unknown to him"

319   "the biggest town for sin in all Texas"

       "the aged scapular"

322   "the dark sanctuary of the prairie night"

327   "like some monster slain in the commission of unnatural acts"

       "This night thy soul may be required of thee."[10]

329   "A ritual includes the letting of blood."

330   "gods of vengeance and of compassion alike lie sleeping" sentence

334   "Good God almighty"

337   "out of the rock which God has put there"

Ritual, Music, and Dance

Some of the items in this concordance highlight McCarthy's sustained metaphor linking war to dance. Of particular interest is McCarthy's mention of some "ritual" awakened in

---

10. Holden's words are a slight revision of the biblical verse: "But God said unto him, Thou fool, this night thy soul shall be required of thee: then whose shall these things be, which thou hast provided?" (Luke 12:20). Holden's "may" distinguishes his phrase from God's omniscient "shall." The prescience McCarthy has granted Holden regarding Tate's and Shelby's fates (331) is continued in this phrase, a depth of understanding perhaps related to the biblical thought that "there is nothing covered, that shall not be revealed; neither hid, that shall not be known. Therefore whatsoever ye have spoken in darkness shall be heard in the light; and that which ye have spoken in the ear in closets shall be proclaimed upon the housetops" (Luke 12:2–3). This thought appears to inform Holden's "so shall it be made known to the least of men" (306).

Black John Jackson's "dark blood" (81), which may inform his performance with the juggling troop (99), his killing of the other Jackson (107), and the "free flowing" robes he wears the day of his death (273–274).

69	"he could hear music"
77	"I'm proud I missed that dance"
81	"some ritual dormant in his dark blood"
90	"the dogs were dancing"
107	"like some instrument of ceremony"
123	"he could outdance the devil himself" "God the man is a dancer"
148–149	"a primitive onestringed fiddle that had been crushed"
154	"the hooded beasts stood rigid and ceremonial"
166	"heralded before by a pair of drummers . . . and by a trumpeter"
170	"A sort of skiffle band had struck up a lugubrious air"
177	"a fiddler and a cornetplayer leading"
178	musicians' gestures "suggested the martial style of the air they played"
183	"they lay in the street like dead bandsmen"
189	"a fiddler appeared . . . and began to saw out some Moorish folktune"
	the judge "spied the musician . . . and tossed a coin"
190	the fiddler "struck up an air that was old among the mountebanks of Spain two hundred years before"
202	"there were fires in the street and dancing"
228	"they shouldered their horses through the party in a sort of ritual movement"
240	"the judge soon had them dancing while he fiddled"
273	"freeflowing" robes Jackson and Holden wear
274	"ceremonial wands"
326	"the bear was dancing for all that his heart was worth"
	the bear, shot, "began to dance faster"
	the bear "took a few last steps, dancing, and crashed to the boards"
327	"the woman announcing the commencement of dancing"
	"Plenty of time for the dance." "I aint studyin no dance."
	"You're here for the dance"
	"What man would not be a dancer if he could, said the judge. It's a great thing, the dance."
328–329	"This is an orchestration for an event. For a dance in fact."
329	"A ritual includes the letting of blood" paragraph
333	"A fiddler . . . calling out the order of the dance . . . in the way he wished them to go"
334–335	a man "called out the dance"

335   paragraph about the judge dancing and fiddling

Chance, Fortune, and Deception

"[W]ar is the truest form of divination," Judge Holden says in *Blood Meridian* (249). This concordance relates to Holden's assertion in nonmoral, nonreligious contexts. Divination and manipulation are integral to McCarthy's presentation of his story. Card playing, betrayals, fortune, and luck in general are collected in this section's references.

6–8   Holden's charges against Reverend Green

52   "from the offside of those ponies there rose a fabled horde"

59   "Son of a bitch is dealin me misery"

80   "drank their health and their fortune"

87   "Not a gaming man?" "Depends on the game."

91   "mimed a deal of cards" "Para adivinar la suerte."

93   "in your fortune lie our fortunes all"

96   "some new drift in her divinings"

103   "They were playin cards and one of them cut him."

134   "Wagers was laid."

142   "dressing himself as an indian"

145   "The father dead has euchered the son"

147   "He loves games? Let him play for stakes."

148   "His calculations concerning the enemy included every duplicity. He spoke of ambushes. Even he in all his pride . . ."

153   whites killing as if Indians
        "Notions of chance and fate are the preoccupation of men engaged in rash undertakings."

160   "Will it pass for him?" "No."

173   massacre of the Tiguas: "No man stood to tender them a defense." "Them sons of bitches aint botherin nobody."

180   scalping Mexicans in Nacori

183–184   scalping Mexican lancers

184–185   "They trampled the spot with their horses until it looked much like the road again"

194   "Bad luck."

199   "only by such . . . he will effect a way to dictate the terms of his own fate"

204   massacre on the Nacozari River

205–206   lottery of arrows scene

240 "the judge on a wager," "on a further wager," "a third round of wagers was laid"

241–242 short barrel of whiskey for Mangas

249 "Men are born for games" paragraph

260 "the ferry fell into [Lincoln's] hands for the most part by chance"

261 "in rage at their betrayal"

268 "you can wager on it"

283 "the judge put forward the coins . . . like a croupier"

289 "his voice was in a new place"

298 "they were beyond the point where he and Tobin had turned off from the trace"

308 the kid "told the soldier of the horde of gold and silver coins hid in the mountains"

310 "a coldforger" "this false moneyer"

311 "he was taken for a male whore"

313 "piles of gold . . . wagered on the turn of a card"
"bears and lions turned loose in pits to fight wild bulls to the death"

320 "I bet he's been a scout"

329 "A solitary game, without opponent" paragraph

332 "men at cards, dim in the smoke"

"KNITTING THE WINDS" CONCORDANCES

Reins, Straps, String, Thread

5 parricide hung

15 "hobbled mule"

17 "rope of greasy leather" at well

21 knife handle of string

27 "trailing rope"

37 recruiter "touched the horse's neck lightly with the reins"

38 "close reined"
Mexican harness makers

78 gang uses "trappings . . . of human skin . . . bridles . . . from human hair"

84 "like strings . . . through the eye of a ring"

87 Bathcat's "ears" "like a string of dried black figs"
"strings of horses"

89   old magician "took the bridle of Glanton's horse," and Glanton stops that

90   "blind man on a string"

94   woman card reader like a "mannequin raised awake by a string"

99   Glanton killed old Indian woman and "took up the trailing reins"

109   horses hobbled during Indian attack "with loops of rope ready made"

112   dead Grannyrat's horse "trailing reins"

       diligence with "trailing straps"

117   wolf "hung like a marionette from the moon"

122   kid "mending a strap"

123   "greased thread"

126   cut two pack animals' straps

130   "The malpais. It was a maze."

133   judge has a leather shirt

144   harness maker's wife is "amazed"

158   an Indian rider "reached and took the reins"

159   "slices" of the dead for "belts and harness"

180   "Hair, boys, he said. The string aint run on this trade yet."

191   Glanton is "bound to his bed"

193   Glanton ties flag to mule's tail

199   "singling . . . the thread of order from the tapestry"

205   red flannel strips on arrows

206   "The Delaware let drop the reins"

210   having met Tate, the kid picks up the "trailing reins" of his horse

217   kid "cinched his belt" over his horse's muzzle, to ride it

219   kid rides "like a mounted marionette"

226   gang has "wires of vigilance"

229   "wired into a construction"

232   gang's horses decorated with "human hair and teeth and skin"

245   "a string in a maze"

       coin "fastened to some subtle lead, horsehair perhaps"

245–246 "the length of their tether"

252   idiot "tethered . . . with a braided horsehair rope that it could not chew
       through"

253   Yuma women dressed in "willowbark woven into string"

271   alcalde's wife tries to support him, hung by Glanton

272   "on a string were two small jacks"

       "keeper of the crossroads"

274   doctor's dog "bound at the muzzle"

275   Glanton's dog "tied . . . to his corpse" is burned "howling" with the body

doctor's dog tied by "thongs" to his torso goes into fire

289 "expriest" makes cross from bones and "strips of hide"

297 judge has "idiot before him on a leather lead"

297–298 judge with parasol made of bones tied together with meat strips

298 judge has "the idiot in its rawhide collar pulling at the lead"

rope holds soles of hide to idiot's feet

320 ears Brown had worn to the gallows are on a "thong"

322 man "took the hobbles off"

326 "little girl strapped into the barrel organ"

"little girl had unbuckled herself"

329 dance "contains complete within itself its own arrangement and history and finale"

334 "plucked their strings and turned the little hardwood pegs until they were satisfied"

337 Posthole digger makes the holes: if holes are for fence, then fence is wire, string, tether, decision.

"As if . . . in a Dream"

103 "there is another caballero . . . no man hides from him." "It is like a dream."

109 kid shoots "as if he'd done it all before in a dream"

280 kid is "a cool one," Tobin says as the kid shoots Yumas

281 "He's a deadeye aint he?" Tobin says of the kid

288 kid shoots at judge, misses

290 kid "tried to steady" a shot at Holden, misses

291 kid kills horses

300 judge to kid in desert: "perhaps you have seen this place in a dream. That you would die here."

The Kid Helps

5 kid "works in a diptheria pesthouse"

53 kid would reach to remove an arrow during massacre of Captain White's party

61 kid asks about Sproule's arm: "You want me to look at it?"

63 Sproule says, "Go on," to kid

109 Tate and Doc Irving go "to see about" injured horses

112 "the black" Jackson calms diligence horses

157   kid wades out of the water to approach "skewered" McGill

162   Brown has an arrow in his leg: "The kid rose. I'll try her, he said."

191   judge "cooled [Glanton's] brow with rags of water"

196   judge and two Delawares go back for Jackson

207   kid to Shelby: "If you want me just to leave you I will."

210   Tate says, "Go on," to kid

219   kid holds horse for Holden to kill for food

224   "someone hazed forward" a horse for Miller, "other than that they offered him no help"

278   twice kid says, "go on," to Toadvine

295   Tobin says, "Go on," to kid

315   kid tells kneeling old woman he will "convey" her to "some party of her countrypeople who would welcome her"

Look . . . Look Away

5   "They cage their eyes"

14   kid "didnt look back" as he rode away on his boarded mule

        judge watches kid ride out of town, turns his horse as if it too is to watch

        kid looks and judge smiles

61   kid looks at Sproule's arm: "You want me to look at it?"

65   Sproule "would look away" from the kid's glance

73   "When their eyes lost their blindness"

79   cleaning gutters, jailed kid watches newly dressed judge

115–116   Glanton and judge look at squatters, who look at floor

117   Glanton sees squatters as part of "the wonderful invention of folly in its guises and forms"

149   Glanton "watched the dog"

178   "These details should have stood" those entering "in better stead"

189   coin held to the light "as if it might not serve"

205   kid sees judge watching him, looks at Glanton, and selects a different arrow

206   Glanton has his "forehead against the ribs of his horse" as he tightens the girth

218   Glanton looks "burning centroids of murder" at kid "as if he were no part of them"

229   Apache's "dark eyes avoiding Glanton" after Apache's horse is bitten

234   Bell's "eyes shifted"

238–239   "eyes that were white in the gloom"

239   Bell was "passing up each face as if it did not quite suffice"

243   Glanton sees kid watching judge ("vast abhorrence")

244   eyes of dog, idiot, "certain other men" all "glowing red as coals"

247   "clarity," when one part "predicates the whole," leads to "optical democracy" and "unguessed kinships"

254   Yumas clad in "fools' regalia"

255   judge is "sober . . . judging as perhaps he did that things are seldom what they seem"

295   desert "devoid of feature" with "nothing to mark their progress upon it"

307   judge says to kid, "Look at me." "Listen to me. Do you think Glanton was a fool? Don't you know he'd have killed you?"

311   kid's "eyes shifting"
       he is "taken for a male whore"

322   the man said, "I'm right here" to Elrod, who misses his shot

325   judge watching man in saloon
       "in all that motley . . . [Holden] sat by them and yet alone . . . he seemed little changed or none in all these years"

329   "Don't look away." "Look at me."

330   "See him. That man hatless." "You can read it in his face, in his stance."

334   urinating man says don't go into jakes; next man looks in, says to third: don't look; third also looks

Horses Shy, Horses Steady

88   "Glanton ordered a goat killed and this was done in the corral while the horses shied"

98   Glanton shoots old woman: "Some of the horses shied"

112   Jackson calms diligence horses

115   snake-bitten horse is kicked and bitten by gang horses

156   "began to fire between the actual ears of his horse"

157   "The horse trembled and stepped back" while Glanton "was watching . . . mounted Apaches . . . grouped against the sky."

177   gang's horses not scared by firecrackers

191   judge offers "candy deathsheads" to passing children, "but they shied away like little horses"

206   Glanton has his "forehead against the ribs of his horse" as he tightens the girth

222   "The mare at the far end of the stable snorted and shied at this luminosity in beings so endarkened"

228   Glanton's horse "seized the man's horse by the ear" and drew blood
291   horses "heard the pistol cock . . . and began to walk toward" the kid
314   "By and by the horse began to toss its head and soon it would not go"
       toward the massacred penitents
322   man "caught the horse and took the hobbles off"

Agency, Commitment, Witness

3   "poets whose names are now lost"
40   "his skull broken . . . none knew by whom"
74   "Et de ceo se mettent en le pays."
79   "a guaranteed hand"
85   Aguilar is "the witness of some third party"
93   "All will be known to you at last. To you as to every man." (cf. 306: "known
       to the least of men")
104   "It was my understanding that you spoke for your group."
105   "dry weeds lashed . . . echo . . . old encounters forever unrecorded"
106   "Here beyond men's judgements all covenants were brittle."
111   "yet who can discover the engine of his ruin?"
118   squatters "elected" to join gang
120   fire on the ground shifting "unaccountably"
138   "their own hearts alien in them"
152   "although each man . . . was discrete . . . conjoined they made a thing that
       had not been before"
153   "posting of witnesses by some third and other path"
       "what could be said to occur unobserved?"
155   "partisans nineteen in number"
172   "they moved in a constant elision, ordained agents of the actual dividing out
       of the world which they encountered"
173   judge "scappled away one of the designs"
       "As if such destinies were prefigured in the very rock for those with eyes to
       read."
174   "in the circuit of a few suns all trace of the destruction of these people would
       be erased"
       "nor ghost nor scribe, to tell to any pilgrim"
184–185 saddles and trappings burned in road, moved, buried; soldiers buried in
         road

218   Glanton looks "burning centroids of murder" at kid "as if he were no part of them"

237   Owens was shot without "witnesses"

243   Glanton had "long forsworn all weighing of consequences" and "claimed agency"

246   "a common witness"
       "coins and false coins"

248   "He'd spoke [sic] of purging oneself of those things that lay claim to a man but that body receiving his remarks counted themselves well done with any claims at all."

249   cards, "games," risk, "agency"

251   judge to Tobin: "What could I ask of you that you've not already given?"

267–268   Brown bluffs the sergeant for lack of a witness

284   "The lad is a free agent."

288   kid shoots at judge, misses

290   kid's second shot misses judge

291   kid kills judge's horses

292   "I know what you've done," the judge says

293   judge "expounded" on "property rights," and "Then he spoke of other things."

299   judge "addressed the countryside about," saying kid was no "partisan," that he was "mutinous"

300   "They are alive and in possession of the fruits of their election."

307   "you were a witness against yourself. You sat in judgement on your own deeds."
       "each was called upon to empty out his heart into the common and one did not."
       Holden asks kid: "But if I was your enemy with whom would you have shared me?"

321   "He don't speak for me," Elrod says

326–327   "It's all over, [a woman in the Griffin saloon] said. It's all over." "Do you believe it's all over, son?" the judge asks the man.

327   judge addresses the man, saying, "The last of the true. The last of the true."

328   "order is not set aside because of their indifference"

329   dance "contains complete within itself its own arrangement and history and finale"
       "were he to know he might well absent himself"
       "riddles . . . are they not part of every man's jurisdiction? What is death if not an agency?"

330   "What manner of heretic could doubt agency and claimant alike?"

"Any man who could discover his own fate and elect therefore some opposite course could only come at last to that selfsame reckoning"

331   judge asks, "Did you post witnesses?"

judge says that the man "elected to defend" Chihuahua, but "Only that man who has offered up himself entire to the blood of war . . . can dance."

CHAPTER 10

Massacre Accounts

"The Indian Troubles on the Colorado"
New York Daily Tribune, July 8, 1850

We have heard a new version of the story of massacre at the Colorado, which places the matter in a favorable light as regards the Indians. It appears that Glanton, the leader of the American party, who with several of his gang were murdered, were long before outlawed both in Texas and Mexico for their crimes. At the Colorado they established a ferry, where the Indians had also established one, and forbid their ferrying over any person on pain of death. The Indians expostulated against this, but Glanton and his party insisted, and broke up the Indians' boats. The savages placed themselves several miles below the Glanton party, and commenced swimming horses and mules over without the aid of boats, and to this operation the above-named American and his party commenced an opposition.

Finally, Glanton and his men insisted that the Indians should not swim the river, even with their private packs upon their heads, but should cross their ferry with them, and pay for such crossing. The Indians very naturally and very properly became exasperated with the Company, and united together to *murder* them, in which we think they were by every sense of justice justifiable. But while massacreing these frontier outlaws, we learn from good authority that they refrained from injuring any other party, either Mexican or American.

We are very well satisfied, from the private accounts from the Colorado, Humboldt Harbor, Trinity Bay, and the Upper Sacramento mines, that the whites are the principal cause of the hostility of the Indians. They abuse and maltreat the aborigines until they resent it by revenge.

[Alta, California]

"MASSACRE OF ELEVEN AMERICANS BY THE YUMAS INDIANS—
FURTHER PARTICULARS"
New York Daily Tribune, July 9, 1850

We extract the following details of the recent massacre at the crossing of the Colorado, from the *Sacramento Transcript* of the 30th ult.:

By a dispatch from Abel Stearns, first alcalde of the district of Los Angeles, sent by extraordinary express to Governor Burnett, we learn the following facts. On the 21st of April six of the Ferry Company crossed over the Colorado to the Mexican side for the purpose of bringing over the animals of some Sonorans; the rest of the company, numbering eight, remained on the American side of the river. Three of the company left the houses, and were cutting poles in some wood near the ferry, and while thus engaged some fifteen or twenty of the Yumas Indians came to them, saying that the captain of the ferry had sent them to cut the poles. As they had never before been thus employed, their motives were mistrusted. A hatchet, however, was given to one of them, with which he commenced cutting, and he was soon observed to strike very near the head of one of the Americans. The Americans hereupon drew their pistols, and the Indians ran, circling around towards the houses belonging to the company. The three Americans started for the houses also; but before getting out of the woods they heard a yell, and as they emerged from the brush into the open country, the Indians fired upon them. There being little chance of escape, the party commenced firing back, running at the same time to gain the houses. They succeeded in gaining their houses, where they found the dead body of Glanton, the captain of the Ferry Company.

They next ran to a Mexican camp in the neighborhood, but were there refused admittance. They then fled to the river, and succeeded in getting off from the shore in one of their boats. The Indians now commenced shooting balls and arrows at them from both banks, while the party hurried down the river. After rowing 14 miles, they found they had outstripped the Indians, and they landed opposite a place called Algodones. That night they went 14 miles down the river, built a raft, and on the 24th crossed the Colorado. During the 24th the party changed their course and went up the river, and in the course of the day fell in with a party of Indians, from which they were fortunate enough to escape. Pursuing their course up the river, they travelled all night on the 24th, and at daylight on the morning of the 25th they reached the Mexican camp that was at the ferry where the Indians' attack commenced, having been without food since 12 o'clock at noon of the 23d. From the Mexicans the party learned the fate of the rest of their companions.

Glanton and Dr. A. L. Lincoln were asleep, each in one of the houses. A Mexican woman saw the Chief of the Yumas enter the house in which the Doctor lay and hit him on the head with a stone, whereupon he rose to his feet but was immediately killed with a club. Another woman related the death of Glanton in the same manner. The three others who remained at the houses were killed, the manner not known; but none of them had an opportunity of killing any of the Indians. The party also learned from the Mexicans that the six who crossed the river with the boat for the Sonorians were also killed by the Yumas. The bodies of five were brought over to the Mexican side and burned, as also were the bodies of Dr. Lincoln, Glanton, and the rest of the five murdered at the houses. Dr. Lincoln's dog and two other dogs were tied to his body and that of Glanton, and burned alive with them. A large quantity of meat was thrown into the fire at the same time. The houses were also burned down, and the bodies of the other three Americans, named A. Johnston, Wm. Pewit and John Dorsey, were consumed with them.

The names of the five others killed in the boat were Thos. Harlin, of Texas; Henderson Smith, of Mo.; John Gunn, of Mo.; Thos. Wilson, of Philadelphia; James M. Miller, N.J.; and John Jackson, a colored man. The names of the parties killed at the house have been given. Dr. Lincoln was of St. Louis, Mo.; John J. Glanton of San Antonio, Texas; John Jackson of New York; Wm. Pewit of Texas; and John Dorsey of Mo. At the time of the massacre Dr. Lincoln had in his possession $50,000 in silver, and between $20,000 and $30,000 in gold, belonging to the Ferry Company, which it appears has fallen into the hands of the Indians.

———➤●◄———

"DEPREDATIONS BY THE YUMAS"
  Declarations Taken in Relation to the Massacre of Dr. Lincoln and
  His Party on the Colorado River.—Deposition of William Carr.
From the *Annual Publication of the Historical
Society of Southern California* (1903), 52–56

On this ninth day of May, in the year of Our Lord, Eighteen Hundred and Fifty, before me, Abel Stearns, first Alcalde of the District of Los Angeles, and Judge of the first instance in the criminal law, personally appeared William Carr, who being duly sworn, deposeth and saith, that on the 23rd day of April in said year, being one of the company hereinafter named as owning the boats and other property connected with the ferry on the Colorado at the junction of said river and the Gila, he and Marcus L. Webster and Joseph A. Anderson, were engaged about midday in the woods within three hundred yards of the houses belonging to said company at said ferry, which said houses were within one hundred yards of the river and on the American side, within the jurisdiction of the state of California. Deponent and the persons above named were cutting poles, and while thus engaged, some fifteen or twenty Indians of the Yuma tribe came out, some of them saying that the captain, that is to say, John Glanton, had sent them to cut poles, and asking for a hatchet. As it was unusual, in fact, they had never before been thus employed, deponent determined to watch them; a hatchet was given to one of them, with which he commenced cutting. Deponent observed that he was cutting very near the head of one of the said Americans, and, distrusting his intentions, drew a pistol, whereupon they ran away, circling round to get to the houses. Deponent and said companions immediately determined to make for the houses, but before they got out of the woods heard a yell; they went on out of the bushes and instantly were fired upon by the Indians. Deponent thinks at least forty guns were fired. There being little chance for escape, deponent and the others commenced firing, running at the same time to gain the houses; from these they made for a Mexican camp, but were refused admittance; they then made for the river, the Indians retreating from the boat, which deponent and the others immediately entered. When deponent went to the woods as above stated, six men of the company had crossed to the other side with one of the boats, for the purpose of bringing over the animals, etc., of the Sonoranians, many of whom were crossing at this time. The rest of the company, numbering five, remaining on the American side at the houses. Deponent, on approaching the shore, was well satisfied that the individuals last named were all killed, but thought the others who had crossed were safe, seeing them, as he supposed, in the boat; he called to them, but received no answer, though the boat was crossing then. In the meantime, the fight between the deponent's party and the Indians continued, during which they received many vollies from the Indians, both of arrows and balls, and from each side of the river, deponent receiving a wound with an arrow in his leg. Deponent's party pushed off with the boat, down the river, the Indians pursuing on foot and horseback; but after going thus about fourteen miles, deponent found they had outstripped the Indians, only one being able to keep up. He and his companions landed on the side of the river nearly opposite Algodones, abandoned the boat and took to the woods, and remained there till moonrise. Going down to the river they found the Indians had taken their boat and towed it up the river. Apprehensive that the Indians were still in the neighborhood, they returned to the woods and proceeded that night down the river some fourteen miles below Algodones, where they made a raft and crossed the river, this being the 24th; unexpectedly, having taken up a creek, they came upon some twenty Indians who had evidently been watching them. On presenting a pistol at them, all ran for their animals, except a man and a boy, who followed deponent's party, saying in Spanish: "You had better get away, for we intend to kill you."

These were repeatedly defied to come near, but they never could be got within pistol shot. Deponent turned and ran after them, when all the Indians fled, and were not seen again. At this time two of deponent's party each had five shots with their six-shooters, and one of the party only a single shot. That night the party went up the river and struck the main road within a mile of Algodones, passing in the meantime several Indians' houses where they all were asleep, and could easily have been killed, but deponent's companions were unwilling to have it done, upon the ground of being without ammunition, though deponent desired it. Pursuing the main road, they reached the Mexican camp that was at the ferry when the Indian attack commenced. They reached this camp at daylight of the 25th, not having eaten anything since dinner on the 23rd. Deponent alone had seen the dead body of Glanton at the house, which they had attempted to reach as first above stated; he did not see any of the others, but the particulars of the affair were explained by the Mexicans. As usual, that day the Indians had been playing about the establishment, some on one side of the river, some on the other, though on that day they seemed to have collected in a very large number; though, neither by their arms, or other circumstance, excited any suspicion. Glanton and Dr. A. L. Lincoln were asleep at the time of the attack. A Mexican woman who was at the time sewing in Lincoln's tent told deponent that the chief of the Yumas came in and hit the doctor on the head with a stone, whereupon he sprang to his feet, but was immediately killed with a club. Another woman relates the death of Glanton as occurring in the same manner. The three others were killed, the manner not known, and none had an opportunity of killing any of the Indians. Three of the tribe were killed in the fight with deponent's party. Deponent is well convinced that the men who had crossed the river were all killed, and the Mexicans say that the bodies of five of them were brought over to this side and burned, as also were the bodies of Dr. Lincoln, Glanton, and the others killed on shore. Dr. Lincoln's dog, and two other dogs, were tied to his body and that of Glanton and burnt alive with them. A large quantity of meat was thrown into the fire at the same time. The houses were also burnt down. The bodies of John A. Johnson, Wm. Prewett and John Dorsey were burnt up with the cook's house, which had been set fire to. One of the men in the boat was a negro; his name was John Jackson; he made some resistance and in the scuffle was thrown overboard and drowned. It seems that the attack was made just as those who had crossed with the boat struck the shore, the Indians being in the habit of jumping in to help them. The Indians immediately dressed themselves in the clothes of the men, a circumstance that deceived deponent when he first reached the river as above stated, for he then supposed he saw the men on the other side and called to them to make haste over with the boat. The names of the five thus killed in the boat were Thomas Harlin, of Texas; Henderson Smith, of Missouri; John Gunn, of Missouri; Thomas Watson, of Philadelphia; James A. Miller, New Jersey; Dr. Lincoln was of St. Louis, Mo.; John Glanton, of San Antonio, Texas; John Jackson, of New York; Prewitt, of Texas, and Dorsey, of Missouri. Deponent knows that there were in the hands of Dr. Lincoln $50,000 in silver—but knows not the amount of gold; supposes it to be between $20,000 and $30,000; all this is of the proceeds of the ferry during the time said company occupied it, to-wit, from about the first of March last. The company also owns $6000 now deposited with Judge Hays, of San Diego, California, and also 22 mules and two horses and provisions, all at San Diego. No other persons were interested in said company but the above named persons (except Jackson and Miller), and another now in San Diego, to-wit., David Brown was also interested; the Mexicans say that the Indians declare that they are at war with the Americans, do not intend to suffer them at the ferry, and will kill all who come to their country; that they want to fight with the Americans. These Indians have since pursued two Americans who are now in Los Angeles, some thirty miles, and previously robbing them of everything they had.

Deponent, since he has been in Los Angeles, has heard some reports in reference to Glanton, or others of said company, robbing or otherwise mistreating Americans and Sonoranians. He has been with said company from the beginning, and positively and unequivocally denies the truth of such reports. As to the charges of ferriage, they were high, but the expenses of maintaining such a ferry, transportation of provisions from a great distance, etc., amply justify the charges. There was one man killed, an Irishman named Callahan, who had once been in the employ of said company, but discharged for incompetency, and had worked for a while with the Indians at their ferry; he soon returned, informing us that the Indians had robbed him of money and a pistol, which deponent afterwards saw in the possession of an Indian. Some days afterwards he was found dead, lying in the river near our ferry premises. His death could not be accounted for, though he seemed to have been shot. Dr. Lincoln had furnished him with supper the night before his death; he left in good humor, and went away, saying he was going to California. Deponent believes that he was killed by the Indians.

As to the Indians, they always professed great friendship for the company, were continually about the premises, ate habitually in the houses, and were always treated with kindness personally. The boat of the Indians was set adrift, being at our ferry in the night; it was a boat of hides, the only one they had to ferry people across. It belonged to a Mexican, who consented to its being set adrift. We gave them a skiff to ferry with at the lower ferry, and never destroyed any of their property. The Mexicans say that the Yumas still have the boat Gen. Anderson gave them, and also the two boats belonging to said company.

Deponent further states that he firmly believes that said Yumas intend to do harm to all Americans who may pass through their country; that many emigrants, including women and children, are now on the point of reaching the junction of the Gila and Colorado rivers, who in all probability will arrive in small parties, unapprized of danger, and unprepared to meet it, unless some immediate steps be taken by the public authorities with this view. Deponent has made affidavit substantially of the massacre on the Gila, before the Alcalde at San Diego, and applied to the commanding officer of the U.S. troops at that place for assistance, but none has been sent. There are forty U.S. soldiers, infantry, at said town of San Diego.

WILLIAM CARR.
ABEL STEARNS.

We, the undersigned, two of the persons named in the foregoing statement of William Carr, have heard statement read, and fully concur in all the facts therein stated, believing same to be true in all respects.

JOSEPH A. ANDERSON.
MARCUS L. WEBSTER.

Signed before me.
ABEL STEARNS,
1st Alcalde de Los Angeles.

Be it remembered that on the ninth day of May, A.D. 1850, before me, Abel Stearns, first Alcalde of Los Angeles, personally appeared the aforesaid William Carr, Joseph A. Anderson and Marcus L. Webster, whose declarations are above written, and subscribed and made oath to the same in manner and form as appears above. Given under my hand this 9th of May, A.D. 1850.

ABEL STEARNS.

—————➤•◀—————

"LOS ANGELES CORRESPONDENCE"
Daily Alta California, January 8, 1851

> We have received from our valued correspondent at Los Angeles, some twelve or fifteen letters by the hands of Mr. Goodman of that city, who will please accept our thanks for his kindness and attention. These letters contain a full account of the killing of Glanton and his party, with a biographical notice of him and his companion, Dr. Lincoln. They also follow up the subsequent events, Gen. Morehead's expedition to the Colorado, &c. The account of these matters are very interesting, no full particulars having before been made public.
>
> Los Angeles, December 10, 1850.

It is not surprising that the attention of numbers of people at the north should be turned at this time, with more or less vigor to the southern portion of the State. Its excellent soil and delightful climate would of themselves, render this region attractive to great numbers of those who are wishfully seeking an abiding place on the shores of the Pacific, to say nothing of occasional adventitious subjects of excitement.

With your permission, Mr. Editor, I will, as circumstances may justify, lay before the readers of the *Alta*, a full and fair account of this portion of California, so that they may, at least, be partially enabled to form an idea of its present condition and prospective advantages. I wish it understood at the outset, that I am no speculator, not even in prospective; have no interest in gold mines and none in real estate, and am simply and solely a disinterested observer. I have been in this portion of the country about two years, and conceive myself to have formed a pretty accurate idea of its capabilities and advantages. In what I have to say I shall aim neither to exaggerate nor malign, having no inducements for the first and little taste for the latter. Better writers on California topics have been quite too partial to one or the other of these modes of misrepresentation, and I have no desire to imitate their example.

There chances to be at this time with us an engrossing subject of interest, and as it has an almost equal attraction for the citizens of the State at large, and will necessarily form a prominent topic of legislative action with the Solons at San José, the coming winter. I shall devote this letter to its consideration.

You are doubtless aware that, early last winter, a company of American outlaws stationed themselves at the crossing of the Colorado, immediately at the mouth of the Gila, and established a ferry over that great thoroughfare. Its leader, John Glanton, formerly of Texas, was a man of the most desperate character, and if report does not do them injustice, his associates were not a great deal better. Glanton had killed several men before he left San Antonio, his former place of residence. Coming into Chihuahua, he engaged in the service of that government in the delectable employment of killing Apaches, at so much per head. Finding it not to pay as well as he expected, and coming in contact with some Mexicans, whose tonsil [tonsorial] appearance resembled Indians, he coolly despatched them, and brought their scalps to his Excellency the Governor, and received from him for the murder of his own countrymen, the standard *pro rata* for killing an Apache. This affair spoiled the trade of killing Indians so far as Glanton was concerned. The atmosphere of Chihuahua had become uncomfortable.

Its government finally offered a reward of $8000 for his head, an act which at least showed how much higher it estimated the head of an American than it did that of an Apache, the highest price paid for the later being but $250. Upon this Glanton and his party "sloped," and the next we hear of him is in connection with a Dr. Lincoln and his party at the river Colorado, engaged in crossing over its turbid waters the Sonoranian hordes, whose presence in the southern mines this summer has been the cause of so much excitement and bloodshed. But Dr. Lincoln's previous history is equally pertinent of remark with Capt. Glanton's, and partiality is a fault which, as a historian, I am most anxious to avoid. Dr. L. was we believe a native of Tennessee, but previous to his leaving for this country he had been residing for several years at Shreveport, on the Red River in Louisiana. On is way hither he became "flat broke," and he threw himself upon the hospitality of one who, to the knowledge of the writer, is a very intelligent and excellent man, Mr. J. P. Brodie, *administrador* of a cotton factory in the vicinity of San Miguel, in the state of Sonora. He soon succeeded in ingratiating himself into the favor of Mr. Brodie, who fitted him out with a sufficiency to enable him to establish a ferry at the mouth of the Gila, for which it was agreed that one half of the nett proceeds should accrue to his (B.'s) benefit.

Your readers have by this time, Mr. Editor, learned sufficient of Dr. Lincoln's biography. We next find him and his party at the mouth of the Gila engaged in constructing an adobe house, boats, &c., preparatory to commencing his ferry operations. While thus employed, Glanton made his appearance, and it was soon determined that the two parties should unite and divide the profits. Glanton was elected captain of the gang. The profits of the ferry thus established was most enormous. The throng of Mexicans that passed it the last season was supposed to exceed thirty thousand, and the charges imposed upon them by the ferry company was said to be extortionate. About the 1st of April last, Gen. Anderson, of Tennessee, came through with a party of Americans, and not relishing Glanton's charges, went to work and constructed a boat for himself, and then ferried over his company, much to the annoyance of the patriots at the mouth of the Gila. Not the worst of it was, that on leaving the river, he presented his boat to the Indians, who commenced the business of ferrying on their own account at the "Algodones." This was a serious matter to Glanton and his party, and they at once proceeded to put a stop to it. Glanton took a few men, and marched down to the Indian ferry, seized their boat and destroyed it, and not content with this, took an Irishman, whom the Indians had enlisted in their service, tied his hands and heels together, and threw him into the Colorado. This conduct, as a matter of course, at once aroused the hostility of the Indians, but the old chief, with a magnanimity and a forbearance which his more savage neighbors would have done well to have imitated, took occasion to visit Glanton and his party, to expostulate with them upon their conduct. His only answer was an ignominious ejection from their tent. On returning to his village he called together his braves, and it was by them determined that the Americans must die.

Before this resolution of the Indians could be carried into effect, Glanton, with a few men, left on a visit to San Diego, and the Indians determined to suspend their fell design until his return. Upon this visit Glanton took with him a considerable sum of money, and deposited with Judge Hays of that place some $8000, which still remains to his credit in the hands of that functionary. During this visit, one of his men, Brown by name, having had a few words of altercation with a soldier at San Diego, took out a revolver and deliberately shot him through. Brown was arrested and placed under guard, there being no jail at San Diego; but having been furnished with money by Glanton, he made an arrangement with the guard to be released upon the payment of $500. He and the guard were to escape together. But him of the sentry got into a worse box than ever he did before. The moment Brown got him out of the precincts of the town, he presented a revolver at his breast, and told him if he did not fork over the $500 he would serve him as he had served his comrade. Of course the $500 was forthcoming in a twinkling. Brown escaped, and went to the north, but afterwards, as he tells me, at the solicitation of Gov. Burnett, he came down as guide for Gen. Morehead. But he found on getting here that the authorities at San Diego had offered a reward of several hundred dollars for his arrest, and in disgust he concluded to decline military employment and devote his talents to a civic career.

He is now the principal deputy of the Sheriff of the County of Los Angeles. The course of events has led me a long chase away from Capt. Glanton, and I must now return with him to the Rio Colorado.

It was on the morning of the 21st of April last, that Glanton and his party reached the camp of their associates at the mouth of the Gila. The day being quite warm, he, with several others, lay down to rest, and were soon in profound slumber. The camp they occupied was covered with bushes at the top, but open at the sides. The Houmas were scattered all about, and never appeared more sociable or friendly. But the hatred of an Indian never slumbers. Their arrangements had been well taken. A chosen band of the strongest nerved warriors were in attendance with stout clubs prepared for the occasion, and at an opportune moment the signal was given. Glanton was struck while asleep, but with the ready instinct of habit, he half rose and placed his hand upon his revolver. But his hour had come. A well directed blow from the stalwart arm of *Cavallo sin Palo* (horse without hair.) "did his business." He was in the land that is never re-visited. The fate which he had so often meted out to others, it appears had been reserved for himself. Dr. Lincoln, it is said, was one of the few that detected the movement of the Indians just as they made their attack. He defended himself with desperation, but in less than three minutes every individual belonging to the ferry company, then present, had ceased to breathe. Their mangled remains were thrown into a pile of combustibles and burned; their bones can be seen there to this day. Three of Glanton's party were distant from the camp about half a mile. Several of the Indians were dispatched to kill these at the same time the massacre of their companions was to take place, but these men were too sharp for them. From the movements of the Indians their suspicions were excited, and they rushed for the river. A shower of arrows, and not a few firearms saluted them as they passed the camp, but they managed to get to a small boat and escape down the river, from whence they reached a company of Mexicans, and in this way arrived at the settlements. Thus terminated the movements of Capt. Glanton and Dr. Lincoln, but their death was the commencement of a series of measures whose end is not yet, and for the development of which I shall require more time and additional space to develop. I will only here add furthermore, that there were present as witnesses to the murder of Glanton and his party, a large company of Mexicans, who either did not dare, or did not choose to interfere. The account I have given was related by one of the chiefs engaged i[n] it. The Indians are by no means reserved upon the subject, but dwell upon their feats of strength with infinite gusto.

Adios,
Theodoro.

Bibliography

Arnold, Edwin T. "Cormac McCarthy." *Popular World Fiction, 1900–Present.* Washington, D.C.: Beacham, 1987. 1036–1043.

———. "Naming, Knowing and Nothingness: McCarthy's Moral Parables." *Southern Quarterly* 30 (Summer 1992): 31–50.

———. Review of *Blood Meridian,* by Cormac McCarthy. *Appalachian Journal* 13 (Fall 1985): 103–104.

Audubon, John Woodhouse. *Audubon's Western Journal, 1849–1850.* Cleveland: Clark, 1906. Facsimile reprint. Glorieta, N.Mex.: Rio Grande Press, 1969.

Bachelard, Gaston. *The Psychoanalysis of Fire.* Trans. Alan C. M. Ross. Boston: Beacon, 1964.

Baen, Dan R. *Semi-Civilized Savages and Semi-Civilized Civilians.* Crockett, Tex.: Publications Development, 1985.

Bancroft, Hubert Howe. *History of Arizona and New Mexico, 1530–1888.* Vol. XVII of *The Works of Hubert Howe Bancroft.* San Francisco: History Company, 1889.

———. *History of Texas and the North Mexican States: Vol. II, 1801–1889.* Vol. XVI of *The Works of Hubert Howe Bancroft.* San Francisco: History Company, 1890.

Barnes, Lavonia Jenkins. *Nineteenth Century Churches of Texas.* Waco, Tex.: Historic Waco Foundation/Texian Press, 1982.

Barsness, Larry. *Heads, Hides, and Horns: The Compleat Buffalo Book.* Fort Worth: Texas Christian Univ. Press, 1985.

Bartlett, John Russell. *Personal Narrative of Explorations and Incidents in Texas, New Mexico, California, Sonora, and Chihuahua.* 2 vols. New York: Appleton, 1856.

Bell, Horace. *Reminiscences of a Ranger; or, Early Times in Southern California.* 1881. Reprint. Santa Barbara: Wallace Heberd, 1927.

Bell, Vereen M. *The Achievement of Cormac McCarthy.* Baton Rouge: Louisiana State Univ. Press, 1988.

———. "The Ambiguous Nihilism of Cormac McCarthy." *Southern Literary Journal* 2 (1983): 31–41.

Benét, Stephen Vincent. *The Devil and Daniel Webster.* New York: Holt, Rinehart and Winston, 1937.

Black, Henry Campbell. *Black's Law Dictionary.* Rev. 4th ed. St. Paul, Minn.: West,

1968.

Blackstone. William. *Commentaries on the Laws of England*. Vols. 3 and 4. Oxford: Clarendon, 1768, 1769. Facsimile reprint. Chicago: Univ. of Chicago Press, 1979.

Böehme, Jacob. *Six Theosophic Points, and Other Writings*. Trans. John Rolleston Earle. London: Constable, 1919.

Bonwick, James. *The Last of the Tasmanians; or, The Black War of Van Diemen's Land*. London: Sampson Low, Son, & Marston, 1870. Reprint. New York: Johnson Reprint, 1970.

Bourke, John G. *On the Border with Crook*. 2nd ed. New York: Scribner's, 1896.

Box, Michael James. *Capt. James Box's Adventures and Explorations in New and Old Mexico*. New York: James Miller, 1869.

Brandes, Ray. "Don Santiago Kirker, King of the Scalp Hunters." *Smoke Signal* 6 (Fall 1962): 2–8.

Brown, Charles H. *Agents of Manifest Destiny: The Lives and Times of the Filibusters*. Chapel Hill: Univ. of North Carolina Press, 1980.

Brown, Peter Lancaster. *Comets, Meteorites, and Men*. New York: Taplinger, 1974.

Browne, J[ohn] Ross. *Adventures in the Apache Country*. New York: Harper, 1871. Facsimile Reprint. New York: Arno, 1973.

Bufkin, Dan. Map in *Arizoniana: The Journal of Arizona History* (Winter 1962): facing page 9. Reprinted in Ralph A. Smith, "The Scalp Hunter in the Borderlands, 1835–1850." *Arizona and the West: A Quarterly Journal of History* 6 (Spring 1964): 5–22.

Burnett, Peter H. *An Old California Pioneer*. Oakland, Calif.: Biobooks, 1946.

Butler, Bill. *Dictionary of the Tarot*. New York: Schocken, 1975.

Butterfield, Herbert. *The Historical Novel: An Essay*. Cambridge: Cambridge Univ. Press, 1924.

Cady, John H. *Arizona's Yesterday: Being the Narrative of John H. Cady, Pioneer*. Rewritten and revised by Basil Dillon Woon. Patagonia, Ariz., 1915.

Capps, Benjamin. *The Old West: The Indians*. New York: Time-Life, 1973.

Carr, William. "Depredations by the Yumas: Declarations Taken in Relation to the Massacre of Dr. Lincoln and His Party on the Colorado River.—Deposition of William Carr." In the *Annual Publication of the Historical Society of Southern California and the Pioneers of Los Angeles County, 1903*. 52–56.

Carroll, H. Bailey. "Texas Collection." *Southwestern Historical Quarterly* 47 (Jan. 1944): 306, and map by F. B. E. Browne (1851), facing page.

Carroll, J. M. *A History of Texas Baptists, Comprising a Detailed Account of their Activities, Their Progress, and Their Achievements*. Ed. J. B. Cranfill. Dallas: Baptist Standard, 1923.

Carson, Kit. *Kit Carson's Autobiography.* Ed. Milo Milton Quaife. Chicago: Lakeside, 1935.

Cash, Joseph H., and Gerald W. Wolff. *The Comanche People.* Phoenix: Indian Tribal Series, 1974.

Cavendish, Richard. *The Tarot.* Reprint. New York: Crescent, 1975.

Cervantes de Salazar, D. Francisco. *Crónica de la Nueva España.* 1560–1566. Madrid: Hispanic Society of America, 1914.

Chamberlain, Samuel E. "My Confession." Edited and serialized in *Life,* July 23, 1956: 68–91; July 30, 1956: 52–71; Aug. 6, 1956: 64–86.

———. *My Confession: Recollections of a Rogue.* New York: Harper, 1956.

———. *My Confession: Recollections of a Rogue.* Ed. William H. Goetzmann. Austin: Texas State Historical Association, 1996.

Churchward, Albert. *The Signs and Symbols of Primordial Man.* London: Allen & Unwin, 1913. Facsimile Reprint. Westport, Conn.: Greenwood, 1978.

Clarke, Asa Bement. *Travels in Mexico and California: Comprising a Journal of a Tour from Brazos Santiago, through Central Mexico, by Way of Monterey, Chihuahua, the Country of the Apaches, and the River Gila, to the Mining Districts of California.* Boston: Wright & Hasty, 1852. Reprint. College Station: Texas A&M Univ. Press, 1988.

Clemens, Jeremiah. *Bernard Lile: An Historical Romance, Embracing the Periods of the Texas Revolution and the Mexican War.* Philadelphia: Lippincott, 1856.

———. *Mustang Gray: A Romance.* Philadelphia: Lippincott, 1858.

Congressional Globe. June 11, 1850. 31st Cong. Washington: Blair & Rives, 1850.

Connelley, William Elsey. *Doniphan's Expedition and the Conquest of New Mexico and California.* Includes a reprint of the work of Col. John T. Hughes. Topeka: [published by the author], 1907.

Cook, John R. *The Border and the Buffalo.* 1907. Reprint ed. Milo Milton Quaife. Chicago: Lakeside, 1938.

Cooke, Philip St. George. *Cooke's Journal of the March of the Mormon Battalion, 1846–1847. Exploring Southwestern Trails, 1846–1854.* Ed. Ralph P. Bieber. Glendale, Calif.: Clark, 1938.

Cortés, Hernán. *Hernán Cortés: Letters from Mexico.* Trans. and ed. Anthony Pagden. New Haven, Conn.: Yale Univ. Press, 1986.

Couts, Cave Johnson. *From San Diego to the Colorado in 1849: The Journal and Maps of Cave J. Couts.* Ed. William McPherson. Los Angeles: A. M. Ellis, 1932. Microfilm.

———. *Hepah, California! The Journal of Cave Johnson Couts: From Monterey, Nuevo Leon, Mexico, to Los Angeles, California, during the Years 1848–1849.* Ed. Henry F. Dobyns. Tucson: Arizona Pioneers' Historical Society, 1961.

Cremony, John C. *Life among the Apaches*. San Francisco: Roman, 1868. Facsimile Reprint. Lincoln: Univ. of Nebraska Press, 1983.

Crimmins, M. L. "John Glanton of San Antonio." *Frontier Times* 17 (April 1940): 277–281.

———. In "Texas Collection." *Southwestern Historical Quarterly* 47 (Apr. 1944): 430.

Cullen, Patrick. *Infernal Triad: The Flesh, the World, and the Devil in Spenser and Milton*. Princeton, N.J.: Princeton Univ. Press, 1974.

Daily Alta California. "Our Indian Relations." Jan. 12, 1851.

Darden, Carl. "Powder, Flint, and Balls." *Foxfire 5*. Ed. Eliot Wigginton. Garden City, N.Y.: Anchor, 1979.

Daugherty, Leo. "Gravers False and True: *Blood Meridian* as Gnostic Tragedy." *Southern Quarterly* 30 (Summer 1992): 122–133.

Davis, Britton. *The Truth about Geronimo*. Ed. Milo Milton Quaife. Chicago: Lakeside, 1951.

DeShields, James Thomas. *Border Wars of Texas*. Tioga, Tex.: Herald, 1912.

Díaz de Castillo, Bernal. *The Discovery and Conquest of Mexico, 1517–1521*. 1632. Trans. A. P. Maudslay. New York: Farrar, 1956.

Diccionario Porrua: de Historia, Biografia y Geografia de Mexico. Reprint. 3rd ed. Mexico: 1971.

Disturnell, John. "Mapa de los Estados Unidos de Mejico." New York, 1847. Reprinted in *Contours of Discovery: Printed Maps Delineating the Texas and Southwestern Chapters in the Cartographic History of North America, 1513–1930*. Austin: Texas State Historical Association, 1981.

Dobie, J. Frank. *Apache Gold and Yaqui Silver*. Reprint. New York: Bramhall, 1939.

Dodge, Richard Irving. *Our Wild Indians: Thirty-Three Years' Personal Experience*. Hartford, Conn.: Worthington, 1883.

Drinnon, Richard. *Facing West: The Metaphysics of Indian-Hating and Empire-Building*. Minneapolis: Univ. of Minnesota Press, 1980.

Dunn, J. P. *Massacres of the Mountains: A History of the Indian Wars of the Far West, 1815–1875*. 1886. Facsimile reprint. New York: Archer, 1958.

Eccleston, Robert. *Overland to California on the Southwestern Trail: The Diary of Robert Eccleston*. Ed. George P. Hammond and Edward H. Howes. Berkeley and Los Angeles: Univ. of California Press, 1950.

Eifert, Virginia S. *The Story of Illinois: Indian and Pioneer*. Springfield: Illinois State Museum, 1979.

Eliot, T. S. *The Waste Land. Collected Poems, 1909–1962*. New York: Harcourt, 1963.

Emory, W. H. *Notes of a Military Reconnaissance, from Fort Leavenworth in Missouri, to San Diego in California*. U.S. House of Representatives, 30th Cong., 1st sess. Exec. Doc. 41. Washington, D.C., 1848. Facsimile reprint in *The United States*

Conquest of California. New York: Arno, 1976.

Evans, George W. B. *Mexican Gold Trail: The Journal of a Forty-Niner.* Ed. Glenn S. Dumke. San Marino, Calif.: Huntington, 1945.

Falk, Richard A., Gabriel Kolko, and Robert Jay Lifton. *Crimes of War.* New York: Random House, 1971.

Faulkner, William. "The Bear." *Go Down, Moses.* 1942. Paperback reprint. New York: Vintage, 1973.

Favour, Alephus H. *Old Bill Williams, Mountain Man.* Chapel Hill: Univ. of North Carolina Press, 1936.

FitzGerald, Frances. *Fire in the Lake: The Vietnamese and the Americans in Vietnam.* Boston: Little, Brown, 1972.

Forbes, Robert H. *Crabb's Filibustering Expedition into Sonora, 1857: An Historical Account.* [Tucson]: Arizona Silhouettes, 1952.

Forbis, Christopher Lee. "The Judge's Two Hats; or, The Palindrome in Cormac McCarthy's *Blood Meridian.*" Unpublished manuscript. Southwestern Writers Collection, Texas State University, San Marcos.

Foreman, Grant. *Marcy and the Gold Seekers: The Journal of Captain R. B. Marcy, with an Account of the Gold Rush over the Southern Route.* Norman: Univ. of Oklahoma Press, 1939.

Froebel, Julius. *Seven Years' Travel in Central America, Northern Mexico, and the Far West of the United States.* London: Bentley, 1859. Microfiche.

Frye, Northrop. *Anatomy of Criticism.* Princeton, N.J.: Princeton Univ. Press, 1957.

Gettings, Fred. *Dictionary of Astrology.* London: Routledge, 1985.

Gillett, James B. *Six Years with the Texas Rangers, 1875–1881.* Ed. Milo Milton Quaife. Chicago: Lakeside, 1943.

Goodman, Theodoro. "Los Angeles Correspondence." *Daily Alta California,* Jan. 8, 1851.

Gorn, Eliott J. "'Gouge and Bite, Pull Hair and Scratch': The Social Significance of Fighting in the Southern Backcountry." *American Historical Review* 90 (Feb. 1985): 18–43.

Greer, James Kimmins. *Colonel Jack Hays.* New York: Dutton, 1952.

Gregg, Josiah. *Commerce of the Prairies.* Ed. Max L. Moorhead. Norman: Univ. of Oklahoma Press, 1954.

———. *Diary and Letters of Josiah Gregg: Southwestern Enterprises, 1840–1847.* Ed. Maurice Garland Fulton. Norman: Univ. of Oklahoma Press, 1941.

Guinn, J. M. *A History of California and an Extended History of Its Southern Coast Counties.* Vol. 1. Los Angeles: Historic Record, 1907.

Hague, Harlan. *The Road to California: The Search for a Southern Overland Route, 1540–1848.* Glendale, Calif.: Clark, 1978.

Hall, James. *Legends of the West.* Philadelphia: H. Hall, 1832.

———. *Sketches of History, Life, and Manners, in the West.* Vol. II. Philadelphia: H. Hall, 1835. Facsimile reprint of pages cited in Herman Melville. *The Confidence-Man.* Evanston, Ill.: Northwestern Univ. Press, 1984.

Hammersly, Thomas H. S. *Complete Regular Army Register of the United States: For One Hundred Years, 1779 to 1879.* Washington, D.C.: Hammersly, 1881.

Hardy, R[obert] W[illiam] H[ale]. *Travels in the Interior of Mexico in 1825, 1826, 1827 and 1828* [map cited]. London: Colburn and Bentley, 1829. Facsimile reprint. Glorieta, N.Mex.: Rio Grande Press, 1977.

Heine, Heinrich. *Doktor Faust: A Dance Poem.* Trans. and ed. Basil Ashmore. London: Peter Nevill, 1952.

Hill, Carol A. "Powder, Flint, and Balls." *Foxfire 5.* Ed. Eliot Wigginton. Garden City, N.Y.: Anchor, 1979.

Hobbs, James. *Wild Life in the Far West: Personal Adventures of a Border Mountain Man.* Hartford, Conn.: Wiley, Waterman & Eaton, 1872.

Horgan, Paul. *Great River: The Rio Grande in North American History.* Vol. 2: *Mexico and the United States.* New York: Rinehart, 1954.

———. *The Heroic Triad: Essays in the Social Energies of Three Southwestern Cultures.* New York: Holt, 1970.

Howard, V. E. "Against the Admission of California, and the Dismemberment of Texas." *Appendix to the "Congressional Globe."* June 11, 1850. 31st Cong. Washington: Blair & Rives, 1850.

Hufford, Kenneth. "Travellers on the Gila Trail, 1824–1850." *Journal of Arizona History* 7 (1966): 1–8; 8 (1967): 30–44.

Hughes, John T. *Doniphan's Expedition: Containing an Account of the Conquest of New Mexico.* 1847. Facsimile reprint. New York: Arno, 1973.

Jung, C. G. *Alchemical Studies.* Trans. R. F. C. Hull. Princeton, N.J.: Princeton Univ. Press, 1967. Vol. 13 of Bollingen Ser. XX.

———. "Answer To Job." *The Essential Jung.* Ed. Anthony Storr. Princeton, N.J.: Princeton Univ. Press, 1983. 321–329.

———. "Approaching the Unconscious." *Man and His Symbols.* New York: Bantam, 1968. 1–94.

———. *The Archetypes and the Collective Unconscious.* Trans. R. F. C. Hull. 2nd ed. Princeton, N.J.: Princeton Univ. Press, 1959. Vol. 9, Part 1 of Bollingen Ser. XX.

———. "Introduction to the Religious and Psychological Problems of Alchemy." *The Essential Jung.* Ed. Anthony Storr. Princeton, N.J.: Princeton Univ. Press, 1983. 253–287.

———. *Psychological Types.* Trans. H. G. Baynes. Rev. trans. R. F. C. Hull. Princeton, N.J.: Princeton Univ. Press, 1971. Vol. 6 of Bollingen Ser. XX.

————. "The Undiscovered Self (Present and Future)." *The Essential Jung.* Ed. Anthony Storr. Princeton, N.J.: Princeton Univ. Press, 1983. 349–403.

Kendall, Geo. Wilkins. *Narrative of the Texan Santa Fé Expedition.* 1844. Reprint. Chicago: Lakeside, 1929.

Kenly, John R. *Memoirs of a Maryland Volunteer: War with Mexico, in the Years 1846–7–8.* Philadelphia: Lippincott, 1873.

Kenton, Warren. *The Anatomy of Fate: Kabbalistic Astrology.* London: Rider, 1978.

Lane, Walter P. *The Adventures and Recollections of General Walter P. Lane, a San Jacinto Veteran.* 1887. Marshall, Tex.: News Messenger Pub., 1928.

Lavender, David. *Bent's Fort.* New York: Doubleday, 1954.

Lermayer, Ralph M. "Blackpowder Accessories." *Outdoor Life* Sept. 2007: 87.

Levi, Eliphas. *The Book of Splendours: Containing the Judaic Sun, the Christian Glory and the Flaming Star; Studies on the Origins of the Qabalah with Research into the Mysteries of Freemasonry Followed by the Profession of Faith and Elements of the Qabalah.* Reprint. Northamptonshire, UK: Aquarian, 1973.

————. *The Magical Ritual of the Sanctum Regnum, Interpreted by the Tarot Trumps.* 1896. Facsimile reprint. New York: Weiser, 1970.

Linn, John J. *Reminiscences of Fifty Years in Texas.* New York: Sadlier, 1883.

Lister, Florence C., and Robert H. Lister. *Chihuahua: Storehouse of Storms.* Albuquerque: Univ. of New Mexico Press, 1966.

Logan, John A. *The Volunteer Soldiers of America.* New York: Peale, 1887.

Longley, John Lewis, Jr. "*Suttree* and the Metaphysics of Death." *Southern Literary Journal* 17 (Spring 1985): 79–90.

Mann, Thomas. *Tonio Kröger.* 1903. In *Death in Venice, and Seven Other Stories.* Trans. H. T. Lowe-Porter. Paperback reprint. New York: Vintage, 1936.

Manzoni, Allessandro. *On the Historical Novel.* Trans. Sandra Bermann. Lincoln: Univ. of Nebraska Press, 1984.

"Mapa Geografico de la provincia de la nueva Vizcaya." 1792. Reprinted in *Cartografia de Ultramar: Servicios Geográfico e Historico del Ejértico, Estadio Major Central.* Number 12 in Vol. 3. Madrid: Imp. de Servicio Geografico del Ejertico, 1949–.

Marlowe, Christopher. *Doctor Faustus. The Complete Works of Christopher Marlowe.* Ed. Fredson Bowers. Vol. 2. 2nd ed. Cambridge: Cambridge Univ. Press, 1981.

Martin, Douglas D. *Yuma Crossing.* Albuquerque: Univ. of New Mexico Press, 1954.

Martin, R. Montgomery. *History of Austral-Asia: Comprising New South Wales, Van Diemen's Island, Swan River, South Australia, &c.* 2nd ed. London: Whittaker, 1839.

MacCarthy, Donald F. "Chihuahua Scalp Hunters." *Frontier Times.* (September 1929): 523–525.

McCarthy, Cormac. *All the Pretty Horses.* New York: Knopf, 1992.

————. *Blood Meridian; or, The Evening Redness in the West.* New York: Random House, 1985.

————. *Child of God.* New York: Random House, 1973.

————. *The Crossing.* New York: Knopf, 1994.

————. "A Drowning Incident." *Phoenix* [literary supplement to the *Orange and White,* University of Tennessee at Knoxville student newspaper] March 1960: 3–4.

————. *No Country for Old Men.* New York: Knopf, 2005.

————. *The Orchard Keeper.* New York: Random House, 1965.

————. *Suttree.* New York: Random House, 1979.

McCutchan, Joseph D. *Mier Expedition Diary: A Texan Prisoner's Account.* Ed. Joseph Milton Nance. Austin: Univ. of Texas Press, 1978.

McGaw, William Cochran. *Savage Scene: The Life and Times of James Kirker, Frontier King.* New York: Hastings, 1972.

McHugh, Tom. *The Time of the Buffalo.* New York: Knopf, 1972.

McIntosh, Christopher. "Leo." *World Book Encyclopedia.* Vol. 12. Chicago: World Book, 1984.

————. "Scorpio." *World Book Encyclopedia.* Vol. 17. Chicago: World Book, 1984.

McWhiney, Grady, and Perry D. Jamieson. *Attack and Die: Civil War Military Tactics and the Southern Heritage.* Tuscaloosa: Univ. of Alabama Press, 1982.

Melendy, H. Brett, and Benjamin F. Gilbert. *The Governors of California: Peter H. Burnett to Edmund G. Brown.* Georgetown, Calif.: Talisman, 1965.

Melville, Herman. *The Confidence-Man.* 1857. Evanston, Ill.: Northwestern Univ. Press, 1984.

————. *Moby Dick.* 1851. New York: Norton, 1967.

Mencken, H. L. *The American Language: Supplement II.* New York: Knopf, 1948.

Mills, Jerry Leath. "Cormac McCarthy: A Great Tragic Writer." *Independent Weekly* 7.13 (June 1–7, 1989): 9–10.

Moorhead, Max L. *New Mexico's Royal Road: Trade and Travel on the Chihuahua Trail.* Norman: Univ. of Oklahoma Press, 1958.

Moran, Jim. "Powder, Flint, and Balls." *Foxfire 5.* Ed. Eliot Wigginton. Garden City, N.Y.: Anchor, 1979.

Nacogdoches Times. Issues of 1849: Jan. 13, 20, 27; Feb. 24; Mar. 10, 24, 31; Apr. 28; May 5, 19; June 2, 16, 23, 30; July 7. Microfilm.

Neumann, Erich. *The Origins and History of Consciousness.* Trans. R. F. C. Hull. Bollingen Ser. XLII. Princeton, N.J.: Princeton Univ. Press, 1973.

Nevin, David. *The Old West: The Soldiers.* Alexandria, Va.: Time-Life, 1974.

Newmark, Harris. *Sixty Years in Southern California, 1853–1913; Containing the Reminiscences of Harris Newmark.* Ed. Maurice H. Newmark, Marco R. Newmark, and

Perry Worden. 2nd ed. New York: Knickerbocker, 1916.

New York Daily Tribune. "Mexican Items." Aug. 1, 1849; "Indian Troubles on the Colorado." July 8, 1850; "Massacre of Eleven Americans by the Yumas Indians—Further Particulars." July 9, 1850.

Nichols, Sallie. *Jung and the Tarot: An Archetypal Journey.* New York: Weiser, 1980.

Ober, Frederick A. *Travels in Mexico, and Life among the Mexicans.* Boston: Estes and Lauriat, 1885.

Officer, James E. *Hispanic Arizona, 1536–1856.* Tucson: Univ. of Arizona Press, 1987.

Oxford English Dictionary. Compact ed. Oxford: Oxford Univ. Press, 1971.

Partington, J. R. *A History of Greek Fire and Gunpowder.* Cambridge: Heffer, 1960.

Peters, Madison C. *The Masons as Makers of America.* Brooklyn: Patriotic League, 1917.

Pfaff, Lucie. *The Devil in Thomas Mann's "Doktor Faustus" and Paul Valéry's "Mon Faust."* Frankfurt: Peter Lang, 1975.

Pike, Albert. *Morals and Dogma of the Ancient and Accepted Scottish Rite of Freemasonry.* 1871. Charleston, S.C.: Supreme Council for the Southern Jurisdiction, 1905.

Prescott, William H. *"History of the Conquest of Mexico" and "History of the Conquest of Peru."* 1843, 1847. New York: Modern Library, n.d.

Raleigh Register, and North-Carolina Gazette. Nov. 19, 1833: 2.

Reid, Mayne. *The Scalp-Hunters; or, Romantic Adventures in Northern Mexico.* 1851. London: Henry Lea, 185[2].

Reid, Samuel C., Jr. *The Scouting Expeditions of McCulloch's Texas Rangers; or, The Summer and Fall Campaign of the Army of the United States in Mexico, 1846.* Philadelphia: Zieber, 1847. Microfiche.

Richardson, Rupert Norval. *The Comanche Barrier to South Plains Settlement: A Century and a Half of Savage Resistance to the Advancing White Frontier.* Glendale, Calif.: Clark, 1933.

Riddells, Ben[net]. Letter to Clayton, Aug. 27, 1850: Vol. 1, item 51; letter to Crittenden, Dec. 1, 1852: Vol. 1, item 61; U.S. Department of State. "Despatches from U.S. Consuls in Chihuahua, Mexico: 1830–1906." (M 289). Roll 1: Register, 1830–1906; Despatches, Nov. 30, 1830–June 30, 1880. Microfilm.

Roback, C. W. *The Mysteries of Astrology, and the Wonders of Magic.* Boston: C. W. Roback, 1854.

Roberts, Allen E. *Freemasonry in American History.* Richmond, Va.: Macoy, 1985.

Rosengarten, Frederic, Jr. *Freebooters Must Die!* Wayne, Penn.: Haverford House, 1976.

Rudwin, Maximilian. *The Devil in Legend and Literature.* Chicago: Open Court, 1931.

Ruxton, George F. *Adventures in Mexico and the Rocky Mountains.* 1847. London: Murray, 1861.

———. *Life in the Far West.* 1849. Ed. Leroy R. Hafen. Norman: Univ. of Oklahoma Press, 1951.

Sack, John. *Lieutenant Calley: His Own Story.* New York: Viking, 1971.

Sartorius, Carl. *Mexico: Landscapes and Popular Sketches.* 1858. Facsimile reprint. Stuttgart: Brockhaus, 1961.

Sayers, Dorothy L. *The Devil to Pay: Being the Famous History of John Faustus the Conjurer of Wittenberg in Germany; How He Sold His Immortal Soul to the Enemy of Mankind, and Was Served XXIV Years by Mephistopheles, and Obtained Helen of Troy to Be His Paramour, with Many Other Marvels; and How God Dealt with Him at Last.* London: Victor Gollancz, 1939.

Sherman, Edwin A. *The Life of the Late Rear-Admiral John Drake Sloat of the United States Navy.* Oakland, Calif.: Carruth, 1902.

Smith, Ralph A. "Apache Plunder Trails Southward, 1831–1840." *New Mexico Historical Review* 37 (Jan. 1962): 20–42.

———. "The Comanche Bridge between Oklahoma and Mexico, 1843–1844." *Chronicles of Oklahoma* 39 (Spring 1961): 54–69.

———. "The Comanche Invasion of Mexico in the Fall of 1845." *West Texas Historical Association Year Book* 35 (1959): 3–28.

———. "The Comanche Sun over Mexico." *West Texas Historical Association Year Book* 46 (1970): 25–62.

———. "The Fantasy of a Treaty to End Treaties." *Great Plains Journal* 12 (Fall 1972): 26–51.

———. "Indians in American-Mexican Relations before the War of 1846." *Hispanic American Historical Review* 43 (Feb. 1963): 34–64.

———. "John Joel Glanton, Lord of the Scalp Range." *Smoke Signal* 6 (Fall 1962): 9–16.

———. "The 'King of New Mexico' and the Doniphan Expedition." *New Mexico Historical Review* 38 (Jan. 1963): 29–55.

———. Letter to the author, November [27], 1989. Held in the Southern Historical Collection of the Library of the University of North Carolina at Chapel Hill.

———. Letter to the author, March 12, 1990. Held in the Southern Historical Collection of the Library of the University of North Carolina at Chapel Hill.

———. "'Long' Webster and 'The Vile Industry of Selling Scalps.'" *West Texas Historical Association Year Book* 37 (1961): 99–120.

———. "The Mamelukes of West Texas and Mexico." *West Texas Historical Association Year Book* 39 (1963): 65–88.

———. "Mexican and Anglo-Saxon Traffic in Scalps, Slaves, and Livestock, 1835–1841." *West Texas Historical Association Year Book* 36 (1960): 98–115.

———. "Poor Mexico, So Far from God and So Close to the Tejanos." *West Texas Historical Association Year Book* 44 (1968): 78–105.

———. "The Scalp Hunter in the Borderlands, 1835–1850." *Arizona and the West* 6

(Spring 1964): 5–22.

―――. "The Scalp Hunt in Chihuahua, 1849." *New Mexico Historical Review* 40 (Apr. 1965): 116–140.

Sonnichsen, C. L. *Roy Bean: Law West of the Pecos.* 1943. Albuquerque: Univ. of New Mexico Press, 1986.

―――. *Pass of the North: Four Centuries on the Rio Grande, 1529–1917.* Vol. 1 of 2. El Paso: Texas Western, 1968.

―――. *Tucson: The Life and Times of an American City.* Norman: Univ. of Oklahoma Press, 1982.

Spurlin, Charles D. *Texas Veterans in the Mexican American War: Muster Rolls of Texas Military Units.* [Victoria, Tex.]: C. D. Spurlin, [1984].

Storm, Theodor. "Hyazinthen." *German Poetry from 1750 to 1900.* Ed. Robert M. Browning. Trans. Herman Salinger. New York: Continuum, 1984.

Stout, Joseph Allen, Jr. *The Liberators: Filibustering Expeditions into Mexico, 1848–1862, and the Last Thrust of Manifest Destiny.* Los Angeles: Westernlore, 1973.

Sullivan, Walter. "Model Citizens and Marginal Cases: Heroes of the Day." *Virginia Quarterly Review* 55 (Spring 1979): 337–344.

Sweeney, Thomas W. *Journal of Lt. Thomas W. Sweeney, 1849–1853.* Ed. Arthur Woodward. Los Angeles: Westernlore, 1956.

Thrapp, Dan L. *The Conquest of Apacheria.* Norman: Univ. of Oklahoma Press, 1967.

Trimble, Marshall. *Arizona: A Panoramic History of a Frontier State.* Garden City, N.Y.: Doubleday, 1977.

United States. Department of State. Consular Register. Page 85 of "Despatches from U.S. Consuls in Chihuahua, Mexico: 1830–1906." M 289. Roll 1: Register, 1830–1906; Despatches, Nov. 30, 1830–June 30, 1880. Microfilm.

Valéry, Paul. *Luste. Plays.* Trans. David Paul and Robert Fitzgerald. New York: Pantheon, 1960. Vol. 3 of *The Collected Valéry.* Bollingen Ser. XLV.

―――. *The Only One. Plays.* Trans. David Paul and Robert Fitzgerald. New York: Pantheon, 1960. Vol. 3 of *The Collected Valéry.* Bollingen Ser. XLV.

―――. "The Yalu." *History and Politics.* Trans. Denise Folliot and Jackson Mathews. New York: Pantheon, 1962. Vol. 10 of *The Collected Valéry.* Bollingen Ser. XLV.

Vest, Deed Lafayette. *Pursuit of a Thread.* San Antonio, Tex.: Watercress, 1983.

Wagoner, Jay J. *Early Arizona: Prehistory to Civil War.* Tucson: Univ. of Arizona Press, 1975.

Wallace, Edward S. *General William Jenkins Worth: Monterey's Forgotten Hero.* Dallas: Southern Methodist Univ. Press, 1953.

Wang, Robert. *The Qabalistic Tarot: A Textbook of Mystical Philosophy.* York Beach, Maine: Weiser, 1983.

Wasserman, Mark. *Capitalists, Caciques, and Revolution: The Native Elite and Foreign*

Enterprise in Chihuahua, Mexico, 1854–1911. Chapel Hill: Univ. of North Carolina Press, 1984.

Weber, David J. *The Mexican Frontier, 1821–1846.* Albuquerque: Univ. of New Mexico Press, 1982.

Webster's Ninth New Collegiate Dictionary. Springfield, Mass.: Merriam-Webster, 1986.

Wharton, Clarence R. *Texas under Many Flags.* Vol. 2 of 5. New York: American Historical Society, 1930.

Whipple, Amiel Weeks. *The Whipple Report.* Los Angeles: Westernlore, 1961.

White, Owen P. *Lead and Likker.* New York: Minton, Balch & Company, 1932.

Whiting, William Henry Chase. *Journal. Exploring Southwestern Trails, 1846–1854.* Ed. Ralph P. Bieber. Glendale, Calif.: Clark, 1938.

Wilbarger, J. W. *Indian Depredations in Texas.* [Austin, Tex.]: Hutchings, 1889. Facsimile reprint. Austin: Steck, 1935.

Wilson, Robert A. *Mexico and Its Religion; With Incidents of Travel in That Country during Parts of the Years 1851–52–53–54.* New York: Harper, 1855.

Winchell, Mark Royden. "Inner Dark; or, The Place of Cormac McCarthy." *Southern Review* 26 (Apr. 1990): 293–309.

Wislizenus, Frederick Adolphus. *Memoir of a Tour to Northern Mexico, Connected with Col. Doniphan's Expedition, In 1846 and 1847.* 30th Cong., 1st sess. Misc. Sen. Doc. 26. Washington: Tippin & Streeper, 1848.

Woodward, Arthur. *Feud on the Colorado.* Los Angeles: Westernlore, 1955.

———. "The Great Western: An Amazon Who Made History." *Branding Iron* 34 (June 1956): 4–8.

———. "Scalp Hunters of Chihuahua." *Pony Express Courier* Feb. 1938: 12–13; Mar. 1938: 5, 11.

———. "Side Lights on Fifty Years of Apache Warfare, 1836–1886." *Arizoniana: The Journal of Arizona History* 2.3 (1961): 3–14.

Worchester, Donald E. *The Apaches: Eagles of the Southwest.* Norman: Univ. of Oklahoma Press, 1979.

Young, Thomas Daniel. *Tennessee Writers.* Knoxville: Univ. of Tennessee Press, 1987.

Young, Thomas D., Jr. "Cormac McCarthy and the Geology of Being." Diss. Miami (Ohio) University, 1990.

Index